Policy and Governance in Sport

Policy and Governance in Sport

Issues, Organizations, and Practical Application

Edited by

Jason W. Lee

Robin Hardin

CAROLINA ACADEMIC PRESS

Durham, North Carolina

Library of Congress Cataloging-in-Publication Data

Policy and Governance in Sport : issues, organizations, and practical application
/ edited by Jason W. Lee and Robin Hardin.
  pages cm
Includes bibliographical references and index.
ISBN 978-1-59460-534-5 (alk. paper)
1. Sports administration. 2. Sports--Social aspects. I. Lee, Jason W. II.
Hardin, Robin.

GV713.P63 2015
796.06'9--dc23

2014037533

CAROLINA ACADEMIC PRESS
700 Kent Street
Durham, North Carolina 27701
Telephone (919) 489-7486
Fax (919) 493-5668
www.cap-press.com

Printed in the United States of America
2018 Printing

Contents

Policy and Governance in Sport

Chapter 1

Introduction and Defining Sport Governance

Joshua R. Pate, James Madison University

Governance is a unique term that is be defined in many ways. Oftentimes, when people think of a governing body, they think of the corrective nature of governance. Politicians argue for big government or against it. They argue for a government that provides and government that sustains. Yet governance is much more than iron-fist rule or corrective nature. Governance is the act of guidance and oversight offered by a single body or group of bodies to achieve the stated mission. Within governance is the role of management, or, simply, how guidance and oversight are executed through planning, organizing, leading, and controlling (Lussier & Kimball, 2009).

Corporate governance expert Bob Tricker (1984) wrote of governance and management, "If management is about running the business, governance is about seeing that it is run properly" (p. 7). There are numerous areas of sport management, one of which is governance. Yet governance itself impacts other areas of sport management as well. Individuals seem to have a clear idea of what governance is, yet it is extremely difficult to define.

Governance

The difficulty in defining sport governance stems from how one defines "proper," to relate back to Tricker's explanation of governance. A high school governing body in a football-rich state like Texas or Georgia, for example, may have a different perspective on how to properly oversee high school football programs in competition compared to an organization in outdoor-rich states like Montana or Wyoming. Similarly, intercollegiate athletic conferences may govern differently according to their membership or institution size, or perhaps the size of member athletic departments. No two governing bodies have the same philosophy in regards to oversight. Thus, it presents difficulty in agreeing upon the specifics of defining governance.

Merriam-Webster defines governance as "the way a city, company, etc., is controlled by the people who run it" (Merriam-Webster, n.d.). Scholars have defined governance with attention to specifics. Scott, Laws, Agrusa, and Richins (2011) explain governance in terms of "relationships between multiple stakeholders and how they interact with one another," involving the setting of objectives, exerting influence, and obtaining support for policies (p. 205). The definition relays the ideal oversight situation where one individual or group defines the framework of rules and decisions that another individual or group must work within (Kahler & Lake, 1994).

Hoye and Cuskelly (2007) offer a definition of governance as a "system by which the elements of an organization are directed, controlled, and regulated" (p. 3). Those three branches of governing—directing, controlling, and regulating—encompass the expected actions of a governing body. For example, it may be expected of the International Olympic Committee (IOC) to provide directives for national governing bodies submitting bids to host events, control the number of athletes and nations entered into competitions, and regulate the criteria by which athletes must abide for competition. In turn, those governing bodies must assure stakeholders that checks and balances are in place for proper and fair governance by that body (Hoye & Cuskelly, 2007). Interestingly enough, the IOC has had its fair share of critics with regard to offering those checks and balances in governance. Perhaps most notable is the scandal during the bidding process for the 2002 Winter Olympic Games when it was revealed that several members of the IOC accepted bribes. The IOC has since refurbished its membership and board criteria, addressing a checks-and-balances approach.

In the IOC example, addressing membership and board criteria goes directly to the top of the governing body, to the rule makers and rule enforcers. Sawyer, Bodey, and Judge (2008) state that governance is how those governing bodies are directed and controlled, pointing directly to the board or individuals in charge of oversight. The decisions made by an organization's board or individuals in charge are the act of governance.

Sport Governance

Hums and MacLean (2009) state that governance is the "exercise of authority" (p. 3) that includes policy making "to determine organizational mission, membership, eligibility, and regulatory power, within the organization's appropriate local, national, or international scope" (p. 4). Southall (2008) identifies sport governance as exercising power and authority to determine mission, membership, eligibility, and regulatory power.

Sport organizations fit well within those explanations of sport governance. On the local level, high school athletic associations and governing bodies of youth athletics (e.g., programs provided by local parks and recreation organizations) are examples of sport governance. On the national scale, professional sport leagues and intercollegiate athletic governing bodies, both at the national and conference level, are examples of sport governance. Those leagues and governing bodies enact a mission, secure membership, ensure eligibility, and exhaust power over members.

Governance of international sport such as the Olympic Games, Paralympic Games, and World Cup requires a governing body (e.g., IOC, International Paralympic Committee, or FIFA) that oversees competition. These governing bodies may oversee annual, biennial, or quadrennial events. The Professional Golfers Association (PGA) and the Ladies Professional Golf Association (LPGA) are similar in that they govern professional golf events and their annual appearance on the PGA or LPGA schedule. The primary difference between these organizations lies in the competitors and event locations. For organizations like FIFA, events are held worldwide and competitors come from every corner of the planet. However, the PGA operates the PGA Tour, which has a schedule of professional golf tournaments held in North America, most of which are in the United States. Still, the competitors have an international background. For example, 11 of the top 50 finishers (22%) in the 2013 FedEx Cup Standings were from outside of the United States (PGA Tour, n.d.).

Sport governance may stand on multiple platforms, which can result in little consensus toward one single definition of sport governance. A case example is how the NCAA has rules, but conferences and schools may have rules that are more stringent. Clearly, each sport and each league operates differently. It is impossible to say that all governing bodies offer direction or regulation in the same manner considering the intricacies of sport. Effective governance may be difficult to define but easy to identify. Sawyer et al. (2008) identified eight characteristics of good governance: (a) participatory, (b) responsive, (c) equitable and inclusive, (d) consensus oriented, (e) transparent, (f) accountable, (g) effective and efficient, and (h) follows the rule of law. The authors offered a more straightforward measure to identify effective governance: "The test of effective governance is the degree to which any organization is achieving its stated purpose" (p. 11).

It is best to define sport governance in a broad sense to maintain the flexibility previously discussed. Keohane and Nye (2000) define governance as the "processes and institutions, both formal and informal, that guide and restrain the collective activities of a group" (p. 12). The terms "guide" and "restrain" support the multi-faceted role governance plays in both providing a framework in which organizations may operate and correcting missteps when an organization goes beyond that framework. Sawyer et al. (2008) offer the example of Major League Baseball (MLB) and the dichotomy between guiding its membership as an advocate for professional baseball in the United States while also offering restraint to membership and the players who compete. MLB may see advantages of its players hitting a high number of home runs in a season, as occurred during the 1998 home run chase between Mark McGwire and Sammy Sosa or with Barry Bonds becoming the all-time leader in home runs in 2007. However, the steroid era that rocked the respective home run chases tarnished the image of the records. MLB's stance against performance-enhancing drugs and subsequent suspensions that have been levied put it at odds with the very athletes that created interest and publicity.

Sport governance, for the purposes of this text, may be defined as oversight within a designated framework of operating an organization in sport for the purpose of fulfilling its mission. The flexibility of this definition allows for application to the wide-ranging group of governing bodies that exercise authority at all levels of sport. It allows the governing body to set the parameters of defining its own sport governance, and acknowledges that sport governance may be situational.

What Sport Governance Encompasses

Sport governing bodies must provide coordination in areas of championships, media contracts, membership, and scheduling, all of which may be essential for the organization to achieve its mission. Such execution requires management to operate each division within the governance structure. Therefore, sport governance encompasses four primary functions: (a) planning, (b) organizing, (c) leading, and (d) controlling (Lussier & Kimball, 2009; Sawyer et al., 2008). These four functions with regard to management are seen at the micro level where employees carry out daily tasks and also at the macro level where employees execute strategic management. However, the functions planning, organizing, and leading also are executed with regard to governance at a macro level in that the governing body plans and organizes with regard to the areas previously mentioned: championships, media contracts, membership, and scheduling. The fourth function—controlling—outlines the oversight provided by governing bodies, most notably through rules and regulations that guide its membership.

This book addresses how sport governance is executed through planning, organizing, leading, and controlling in the multiple levels of governance (e.g., local, national, and international). The chapters examine sport governance in youth and high school sports, intercollegiate athletics, professional sport, and amateur sport. Additionally, the following chapters examine issues sport governing bodies face during oversight of their members. These issues include women in sport and disability sport, in addition to areas of concern that transcend all levels of sport governance such as globalization, commercialization, competitive balance, and human rights.

[*Note: See Appendices A–C for additional information pertaining to sport governance and international sport considerations.*]

References

Hoye, R., & Cuskelly, G. (2007). *Sport governance*. Burlington, MA: Elsevier.

Hums, M. A., & MacLean, J. C. (2009). *Governance and policy in sport organizations* (2nd ed). Scottsdale, AZ: Holcomb Hathaway Publishers.

Kahler, M., & Lake, D. A. (1994). Globalization and governance: Definition, variation and explanation. In M. Kahler, & D. Lake (Eds)., *Governance in a global economy* (pp. 1–30). Princeton, NJ: Princeton University Press.

Keohane, R. O., & Nye, J. S. (2000). Introduction. In J. S. Nye, & R. O. Keohane (Eds.), *Governance in a globalizing world* (pp. 1–44). Washington, DC: Brookings Institution Press.

Lussier, R. N., & Kimball, D. C. (2009). *Applied sport management skills*. Champaign, IL: Human Kinetics.

Merriam-Webster. (n.d.). *Governance*. Retrieved from http://www.learnersdictionary.com/search/governance.

PGA Tour. (n.d.). *2013 PGA Tour FedEx Cup Regular Season Points*. Retrieved from http://www.pgatour.com/stats/stat.02394.html.

Sawyer, T. H., Bodey, K. J., & Judge, L. W. (2008). *Sport governance and policy development: An ethical approach to managing sport in the 21st century*. Champaign, IL: Sagamore Publishing.

Scott, N., Laws, E., Agrusa, J., & Richins, H. (2011). Tourist destination governance: Some approaches and suggestions for future research. In E. Laws, H Richins, J. Agrusa, & N. Scott (Eds.), *Tourist destination governance: Practice, theory and issues* (pp. 203–212). Cambridge, MA: CAB International.

Southall, R. (2008). *Introduction to sport governance*. Presentation for Sport and Leisure Governance class, University of Memphis, Memphis, TN.

Tricker, R. I. (1984). *Corporate governance: Practices, procedures, and powers in British companies and their boards of directors*. London: Gower Publishing.

Chapter 2

Ethics and Ethical Decision Making in Sport

Susan P. Mullane, University of Miami

A discussion of ethics and ethical decision making needs to begin with a clarification of terms. Exactly what is "ethics"? According to Malloy, Ross, and Zakus (2003),

> Ethics is concerned with issues of right and wrong in human conduct. It is concerned with what is good and what is bad; what is authentic and not authentic. Ethics is also concerned with the notions of duty, obligation, and moral responsibility. As such, ethics are manifested in behavior and assessed through the application of ethical inquiry and critical moral reasoning (p. 55).

Etymologically "ethics" is derived from the Greek word "ethicke," which means the science of morals or character (Lumpkin, Stoll, & Beller, 2003). Although *ethics* and *morals* are sometimes used interchangeably, DeSensi and Rosenberg (2003) offer the distinction that while *ethics* deals with right and wrong conduct and decisions, *morality* considers society, social values and attitudes, and motives. Morality considers good and bad within the context of social customs and provides limits on behavior while ethics involves the application of moral principles in one's decision making. In fact, the word "moral" comes from the Latin "mos" and refers to an individual's actual customs or manners (Lumpkin et al., 2003). In addition, ethics can be considered "standards of conduct that indicate how one should behave based on moral duties and virtues arising from the principles about right and wrong" (Osland, Kolb, & Rubin, 2001, p. 101), and the study of ethics is a prescriptive rather that a descriptive one in that it deals with how people ought to treat each other rather that how they actually do treat one another (Morgan, 2007).

Values, on the other hand, are personal beliefs, and, according to Hitt (1990), are very closely related to ethics. Rokeach (1973) defined a value as "an enduring belief that a specific mode of conduct or end-state of existence is personally or socially preferable to an opposite or converse mode of conduct or end-state of existence" (p. 5). Given this definition, a value system, then, is a set of these values or an organization of these beliefs. In addition, values are beliefs, not facts, and they are enduring and not transient. They guide behavior, both in everyday conduct and in desired goals. Rokeach (1973) referred to these distinct types of values as "instrumental" and "terminal" values, respectively. He suggested that a relationship between terminal and instrumental values was important for internal consistency and found that all combinations are possible. Hitt (1990) notes that a unified value system is one in which the means (instrumental values) and the ends (terminal values) are consistent and mutually reinforcing. Refer to Exhibit 2.1 for examples of instrumental and terminal values as suggested by Rokeach (1973).

Exhibit 2.1: Examples of Instrumental and Terminal Values

Instrumental Values	Terminal Values
Ambitious	A Sense of Accomplishment
Capable	Equality
Forgiving	Freedom
Honest	Happiness
Independent	Mature Love
Loving	Self Respect
Responsible	Wisdom

Values are core beliefs or desires that guide or motivate attitudes and actions. Whereas the study of ethics is concerned with how a moral person should behave, values concern the various beliefs and attitudes that determine how a person actually behaves (Osland et al., 2001). It is often a good first step for people identify and articulate their values. This can be done in a number of ways including values analysis and values clarification. Values clarification exercises help to see the relative importance of one's values and, often, how two or more values are compared. Values change over time in response to changing life experiences. Recognizing these changes and understanding how they affect one's actions and behaviors is the goal of the values clarification process. Values clarification will not tell one what his or her values should be; it simply provides the means to discover what one's values are. Raths, Harmin, and Simon (1966) identified criteria that must be met if a value is to be considered a full value. They are: choosing freely, choosing from alternatives, considering consequences, prizing and cherishing, publicly affirming, and acting. These criteria can be divided into three categories: choosing, prizing and acting. To be a full value, the value must be chosen freely from a list of alternatives, only after thoughtful consideration has been given to the consequences of each alternative. The value must be cherished and made known to other people. The value must also be translated into behaviors that are consistent with the chosen value and integrated into the lifestyle (Raths et al., 1966).

A few other terms need to be defined as well. "Integrity" is often used in ethics discussions. How is integrity different than honesty? Given the Latin "integritat," meaning "complete" and the fact that an "integer" is a whole number, integrity might be considered a holistic approach to values or a "wholeness of character." What about character, then? Particularly in the school setting, one often hears about "character education." Character can be considered the moral or ethical qualities or the characteristics of a person. It is often heard that character is what we do when we think no one is looking. Effective managers and leaders must be aware of their values, morals, and system of ethics and ethical decision making. Osland et al. (2001) suggest that, "ethical mistakes are responsible for ending careers more quickly and more definitively than any other errors in judgment or accounting" (p. 102). Good character and integrity are what we look for in our leaders. In fact, in their research, Kouzes and Posner (2007) identified honestly as the number one characteristic most identified by leaders.

Rudd, Mullane, and Stoll (2010) also note that for many years, unethical decision making and scandalous behavior have marred corporate America. They cited Ford's defect in the Pinto's gas tank, false advertising by Nutri-System and Jenny Craig, fraud and illegal cash management by E. F. Hutton, Salomon Brothers' Treasury auction scandal, fraudulent accounting schemes by Enron, embezzlement practices from Tyco managers, and mutual fund abuses by Morgan Stanley. Bernard Madoff pleaded guilty to the biggest investor scheme in history, defrauding investors of billions of dollars. The sport industry has certainly not escaped scandal and faulty decision making with the endless focus on banned performance-enhancing drug use and inappropriate conduct of high visibility professional athletes.

Osland et al. (2001) indicate that employees choose their work environments based on their ethical preferences and the connection of their values and those of their workplace. There must be a connection between a sound value system and the ability of the leader to use these values in his/her decision making.

When important values come into conflict, an ethical dilemma emerges. Lumpkin et al. (2003) point out that an ethical dilemma occurs when one must choose between conflicting values, and conflicting values can occur between moral values, a moral value and a nonmoral value, or moral values against social values. Furthermore, Osland et al. (2001), distinguished between ethical and nonethical values. "Ethical values are those values that directly relate to beliefs concerning what is right and proper (as opposed to what is simply correct or effective) or that motivate a sense of moral duty" (p. 104). These might include values like responsibility, respect, compassion, and fairness. In contrast, nonethical values simply refer to things people like or find personally important such as money, pleasure, and popularity (Osland et al., 2001).

Kidder (2005) offers two classifications of ethical dilemmas. In the first type of dilemma, a *right* versus *wrong* dilemma, ethical issues emerge when a core moral value has been violated or ignored. When *honesty* is an important value to a person, and another person is found to be acting *dishonestly,* it is generally acknowledged that the action was unethical. In this case, ethics is simply the obvious difference between what is right and what is wrong. In the second type of dilemma, a *right* versus *right* dilemma, however, ethical issues emerge when two core values come into conflict with each other. When one important value raises powerful moral arguments for one course of action, while another value raises equally powerful arguments for an opposite course, we must make a choice since we can't do both. In such cases, ethics is a matter of right versus right (Kidder, 2005).

Other characteristics of ethical dilemmas include uncertainty of the outcome, the possibility of numerous stakeholders or those affected by the decision, and a need to maximize and minimize important values. Kidder (2005) identifies four paradigms of dilemmas. In the first category of truth versus loyalty, honesty or integrity is in conflict with commitment, responsibility, or promise-keeping. In the justice versus mercy dilemma, fairness, equity, and equal application of the law conflict with compassion and care. The individual versus community paradigm is geared toward us versus them, self versus others, or smaller versus larger groups. And finally, the short term versus long term dilemma deals with immediate needs versus future goals (Kidder, 2005).

Ethics Theories and Systems

How does a person or group make the right ethical decisions? The framework for this is grounded in philosophical models.

Utilitarianism and Teleological Approaches to Ethics

Utilitarianism suggests that decisions should be based on possible consequences or the end-result (Hitt, 1990). Made popular by English philosophers Jeremy Bentham and John Stuart Mill in the 19th century, they believed that the "best decisions (a) generate the most benefits as compared with their disadvantages, and (b) benefit the largest number of people" (Johnson, 2001, p. 130). Leaders use this type of decision making when dealing with many constituencies or large numbers of stakeholders, those affected by the decision. Another aspect of utilitarianism is the promotion of pleasure and the absence of pain (DeSensi & Rosenberg, 2003; Hitt, 1990). DeSensi and Rosenberg state, "the only moral duty one has is to promote the greatest amount of happiness" (p. 60). Decisions must necessarily be practical and possess usefulness or "utility." This approach is used to determine bureaucratic and governmental policies such as issues related to tax and health, to name a few, where one tries to provide the greatest benefits for the greatest number of people (DeSensi & Rosenberg, 2003).

Therefore, in the decision-making process, using the utilitarian approach, one must first identify the various courses of action available to us. Second, one must ask who will be affected by each action and what benefits or harm will be derived from each action. Thirdly, one chooses the course of action that will produce the greatest benefits and least harm. Thus, the ethical action is the one that provides the greatest good for the greatest number of people (Velasquez, Andre, Shanks, & Meyer, 1996).

A utilitarian perspective was cited by Johnson (2001) identifying America's nuclear weapons program as a utilitarian decision, where Harry Truman determined that the benefits of ending the war outweighed the costs of destroying Hiroshima and Nagasaki. Of course, all theories have disadvantages when applied. Among the problems with a utilitarian viewpoint is the uncertainty of an outcome, trying to define "happiness," "pleasure," and "utility," measuring these concepts, and choosing between short term and long term happiness. In addition, what does one do if about 10% of the population is unhappy when the other 90% is fine? An example of this application is that of slavery. More recently, Lee, Whisenant, and Mullane (2008) sought to apply this theory to the age-old dilemma of using the Confederate flag in sport settings. Why be concerned with the relatively small part of the population that view it as inflammatory and even racist if most people are not offended and see it as a part of history and their heritage? When one focuses on the likely outcome or results of an action, a system of teleology has been applied. Utilitarianism is only one example of a broad range of ethical theories known as "teleology" or theories that focus on consequences, the measuring of goodness or badness of an action, rather than focusing on the act itself (Malloy et al., 2003).

Deontological Approaches to Ethics

Another prominent view of ethics is known as rule-based ethics (Hitt, 1990), principle or virtue ethics, or specifically, the Categorical Imperative, made popular by German philosopher Immanuel Kant. This approach to ethics is the best-known example of deontological ethics. Deontological ethicists argue that we ought to make choices based on our duty (*deon* is the Greek word for duty) to follow universal truths that are imprinted on our consciences (Johnson, 2001). Among the tenets of a rule-based approach are that ethics should be described as the relation between the "is" and the "ought," and that the "ought" cannot be derived from the "is" (Hitt, 1990). In making ethical decisions, one must practice virtue and principles, rather than be concerned with consequences. In addition, deontologists insist that people always be treated as ends in themselves rather than means. In other words, although others can help us reach our goals, they should never be considered solely as tools (Johnson, 2001).

> According to Kant, what is right for one is right for all. We need to ask ourselves one question: 'Would I want everyone else to make the decision I did?' If the answer is yes, the choice is justified. If the answer is no, the decision is wrong. Based on this reasoning, certain behaviors like truth telling and helping the poor are always right. Other acts, such as lying, cheating, and murder, are always wrong (Osland et al., 2001, p. 133).

Obvious problems with this theory include the fact that there are exceptions to rules and that no universal principles can be followed in every situation. What if two universal rules or principles are in conflict with one another? For example, telling your best friend the truth in a matter that might hurt her feelings might violate your value of compassion and consideration of another's feelings. However, telling a lie would violate your guiding principle of honesty. Both are equally important principles, so it would be difficult to make a choice in such a situation (Hitt, 1990).

A second type of deontological approach to ethics with its roots in the philosophy of Kant and others, focused on the individual's right to choose for himself. What makes human beings different from other things is that people have a dignity based on their ability to freely choose what they will do with their lives, and they have a right to have these choices respected. People are not objects to be manipulated; it is a violation of human dignity to use people in ways they do not freely choose (Velasquez et al., 1996). There are many other types of rights besides this basic one. These other rights can be thought of as different aspects of the basic right to be treated as we freely choose to be treated. They include the right to the truth, the right to privacy, the right not to be injured, and the right to what is agreed, or promise keeping (Velasquez et al., 1996). When using this approach, it is important to make sure that the action respects everyone's moral rights. In other words, actions are wrong if they violate a person's rights. Furthermore, the action is more wrongful as the violations get more serious (Velasquez et al., 1996).

A third deontological approach to ethics is one that focuses on the concepts of justice and fairness. It has its roots in the teachings of the Greek philosopher Aristotle. The basic moral question in this approach is how fair is an action? Does it treat everyone the same, or does it show favoritism or discrimination? Justice requires that we treat people in ways that are consistent, and not arbitrary. Basically, this means that actions are ethical only if they treat people the same, except when there are justifiable reasons for treating them differently. Since both favoritism and discrimination imply not treating people equally and fairly, both actions are wrong and unjust (Velasquez et al., 1996).

These three deontological approaches suggest that once the facts have been ascertained, there are three questions we should ask when trying to resolve a moral issue: (1) What benefits and what harms will each course of action produce, and which will produce the greatest benefits or the least harm for the public as a whole? (2) What moral rights do the affected parties have, and which course of action best respects these moral rights? (3) Which course of action treats everyone the same except where there is a justifiable reason not to? Does the course of action show favoritism or discrimination?

Velasquez et al. (1996) emphasized that this method does not provide an automatic solution to moral problems, and it is not meant to. The method merely helps to identify most of the important factors that should be considered when thinking about a moral issue, and the questions that are one should ask. In some situations, the three approaches may conflict. A decision that produces the most benefits for everyone may also violate the rights of some or not be fair to someone else. Conflicting rights could be involved. When these types of conflicts arise, one needs to look at the values identified by each of the three approaches and decide based on those values and their relative importance (Velasquez et al., 1996).

The Ethics of Social Contract

Another system of ethics, made popular by Rousseau, is referred to as the ethics of social contract. The focus is on the general will of the community, and a collective and moral body produced by the community. The people make the rules and submit to abiding by them (Hitt, 1990). A similar, but more modern type of ethics, "communitarianism," evolved in the early 1990s, and focuses on community responsibilities rather than individual rights (Johnson, 2001).

Moral Development

Moral development deals with the question of how and when people gather and decide on values and methods of making moral decisions. Lawrence Kohlberg extended Piaget's theory of moral judgment/moral development by studying the moral development of adolescence (10- to 16-year-old boys). Kohlberg used a similar methodology, posing moral dilemmas to his subjects. Subjects were asked primarily what they thought the protagonist in the story should do and why. For example, one dilemma entitled "Heinz and the Drug" involves a man named Heinz whose sick wife is dying of cancer. The only way to save her is to steal an expensive drug that he cannot afford (Kohlberg, 1984). Kohlberg's interviews suggested that adolescent aged boys advanced through six different moral stages (Kohlberg, 1984; Rest, 1979). Kohlberg later postulated that his six stages could be grouped into three major levels: pre-conventional, conventional, and post-conventional (Kohlberg, 1984). At the pre-conventional level, moral decisions are made from obedience to rules and avoidance of punishment (stage 1) or by considering the importance of what one might get in return by meeting the needs of others (stage 2). Individuals' reasoning at the conventional level has moved beyond their own self-interests and is more concerned with their membership within a group or larger society. For persons at stage 3, what is right is based on approval and meeting the expectations of others. Moral decision making at stage 4 hinges on one's obligation to uphold the law and contribute to the well-being of society. Those reasoning at the post-conventional level are not only committed to their membership of society but more importantly, believe every individual must be committed to moral principles. Stage 5 moral reasoning is based on one's sense of obligation to uphold a contract with society. At stage 6, the highest stage, what is right is based on comprehensive moral principles and judgment.

Individuals progress through stages one step at a time in an upward fashion; there is no regression or skipping of stages (Kohlberg, 1984; Rest, 1979). Kohlberg also found that stage advancement was highly related to age. Use of higher, postconventional moral reasoning does not typically occur until adult age (20s), and college students, for the most part advance to stages 3 and 4 (Kohlberg, 1984). Kohlberg's moral judgment theory has been met with criticism, however. Most notably, was Carol Gilligan's concern with male gender bias in what constitutes higher levels of moral judgment (Gilligan, 1982). Gilligan's (1992) research with women contemplating abortions led to her theory that women and men make their moral decisions differently, and that women operate from a "care voice" concerned with relationships, compassion, and concern for others, while men reason predominantly from a "justice" or fairness voice. Other important moral development theories came from Karen Kitchener (2000), who viewed moral development from a principle approach, and specifically an adherence to five basic principles: beneficence (doing good, benefiting others), nonmaleficence (not causing harm to others), autonomy (freedom of action), fidelity (keeping promises), and justice (fairness).

As an alternative, Rest (1974) developed a moral judgment measure that is evaluative rather that production based. Instead of requiring subjects to verbally explain the reasons behind their moral judgment (production oriented), Rest's Defining Issues Test (DIT), asks subjects to rate (evaluative) in written form the importance of a variety of issue statements that relate to one's moral judgments of six different moral scenarios (some of which are from Kohlberg's assessment; e.g., Heinz and the Drug). Each issue statement (different ways of considering the most important issue in the moral dilemma) is associated with one of Kohlberg's 6 stages of moral development. Subjects are also asked to rank the four most important issue statements that are believed to represent their moral judgment rationale for each moral scenario (Rest, 1974; 1979). A variety of indices have been developed based on both the ratings and rankings (Rest, 1979). The most widely reported index is the P score which is an indication of how much a person's moral reasoning is represented at stages 5 and 6 (Rest, 1979). The DIT is now being used or referenced in hundreds of studies (Rest, 1986).

Ethical Theory Applied to Sport

A number of important concepts drawn from the more general field of ethics have a particular application to sports ethics. These include: deontology, teleology (specifically, utilitarianism), rule, principle and the Categorical Imperative, situational ethics, and the ethics of social contracts.

Deontology refers to ethical decision making based on moral obligations and responsibilities or actions that are taken for reasons other than consequences, such as telling the truth and respecting others. In sport, helping an injured opponent, equal participation, and being honest with officials or referees serve as examples of deontology.

Teleology suggests that ethical behavior is based on ends, consequences or goals, often manifested in sport by the focus on winning. How one wins is not as important as the victory itself. The utilitarian view looks at the pursuit of pleasure and the avoidance of pain as a measure of the "rightness" of an action, and when more than one person is involved, what is best for the greatest number of people. In youth sports, for example, when a coach chooses to play only the best players in an effort to win, and thus ignores the notion that equal participation is important at this level, a teleological approach has been used. If happiness is achieved, especially for the greatest number of people (e.g., team, coaches, players, and parents), then the fact that a few players sat on the bench is unimportant.

Another aspect of teleology, and perhaps a more practical way of approaching ethical theory, lies with a situational approach, or "letting conscience be your guide." In this theory, an individual views each moral episode as a separate and unique event, and decisions are based on what is right in a given situation without regard to a specific set of rules, likely consequences, or moral obligations. Examples of this type of behavior might be a coach looking at another team's play book or an athlete tampering with the equipment of an opponent.

Teleological ethics maintains that right and wrong is concerned with achieving the greatest amount of good over evil. Right decisions are based on an appeal to the amount of nonmoral good (e.g., money, power, or winning) that can be obtained rather than the upholding of moral values (Frankena, 1973). In other words, achieving good consequences is prioritized over moral principles. Winning is considered a good consequence and clearly, many ethical dilemmas are born from winning being a priority over principles.

A rule or principle based perspective, based on the work of Kant, is predicated on the maxim that an action is acceptable as a universal law. The cheater in sports does not want everyone to violate the rules; otherwise, cheating would offer no rewards. This includes the virtuous aspect of sport, or what it "ought" to be, as opposed to what it is, or winning the "right way" instead of "winning at all costs."

The social contract view of ethics maintains that the community or group dictates what is ethical or not. Athletes on a team, for example, agree to the rules and parameters of their participation, and decision making takes the form of give and take. When athletes take steroids, the action violates the social contract that athletes have agreed to abide by (i.e., not have an unfair advantage over their opponents).

Lumpkin et al. (2003) applied four universal values to sport settings: justice, honesty, responsibility, and beneficence (see Exhibit 2.2). In addition, they noted that we should place our stated values into principles that give us a perspective on how to make right (or wrong) decisions. From these principles come our everyday rules. The following are examples of sport applications:

Exhibit 2.2: Four Universal Values to Sport Settings

Value	Principle	Rules
Justice	Do not be unfair	Do not violate game rules, do not use steroids
Honesty	Do not lie, cheat, or steal	Do not cheat in a game; do not lie to opponents or officials
Responsibility	Do not be irresponsible	Do not play an injured athlete; do not play an athlete who is not academically eligible
Beneficence	Do not be unkind	Do not intentionally harm or let other players harm another player

(Lumpkin et al., 2003)

Hums, Barr, and Gullion (1999) proposed managers in the "business of sport" or sport management are also faced with a variety of ethical dilemmas related to professionalism, equity, legal management, personnel issues, team ownership, responsibilities of professional team franchises, and social justice. According to Hums et al. (1999), ethical issues for sport managers are embedded in five major segments of the sport industry: professional sport, intercollegiate athletics, recreational sport, health and fitness, and facility management.

Principles of Sport

The Josephson Institute's (1999) Six Pillars of Character might easily be applied to sport and sport participation. They are:

- Trustworthiness—(honesty, integrity, reliability, loyalty, keeping promises and not deceiving others). Allegiance to one's teammates might fall into this category.
- Respect—(using the Golden Rule or treating others as you wish to be treated, in addition to being courteous, listening to others, and accept-

ing individual differences). Avoidance of name calling, and shaking hands after a sporting contest might serve as examples of this principle.
- Responsibility—(accountability, self-control, the pursuit of excellence, and considering consequences of our actions prior to making them). Attending practices and putting forth maximum effort to improve one's skills are examples of this pillar.
- Fairness—(playing by the rules, not taking advantage of others, making informed judgments without favoritism or prejudice, and not blaming others). This might include not trying to gain an unfair advantage by taking head starts or doctoring equipment.
- Caring—(kindness, compassion, and altruism, acting to minimize hardship and to help others whenever possible). Empathy for one's teammates and opponents falls into this category.
- Citizenship—(working to make one's community better, protecting the environment, making our democratic institutions work, and operating within the law). This might include keeping the grounds clean before and after a sporting event, and promoting the positive aspects of sport in the community.

In addition to Josephson's pillars, four ethical sport principles can be considered: (1) promise keeping, which refers to knowing the rules and agreeing to abide by them and indirectly agreeing not to cheat; (2) respect for persons, with particular application to Kant's Categorical Imperative as to what acts might violate the respect for another person; (3) responsibility and/or duty, which would include accountability and one's obligations when participating or coaching a sports contest; and (4) balance, or keeping sport participation in its proper perspective (Malloy et al., 2003).

Many of the ethical dilemmas in sport emanate from the various views of winning and the answer to the question, how much emphasis should be placed on winning? Since sports contests are generally designed to produce a winner and a loser at the end of the contest, the manner in which victory is attained can result in unethical behavior. Malloy et al. (2003) offer three "conceptions" of winning: *winning is the only thing, winning is about how you played the game,* and *winning is a mutual quest for excellence.* In the first view, "winning is the only thing," losing equates to nothing and therefore has no value. Conversely, winning is everything, has all the value and must be the goal no matter how it is achieved. Given the pressure to win, it is obvious that unethical behavior will result. In the second view, "how you played the game," it is the process and not the product or result that is important. The focus is on appropriate behavior and the spirit of the rules. And finally, in the view that "winning is a mutual quest for excellence," both the process and the outcome are important. Respect for the opponent as well as the challenges of the competition are inherent in this view of winning (Malloy et al., 2003). In summary, one's view and perspective on winning has everything to do with ethics in sport.

Sportsmanship versus Gamesmanship

"Sportsmanship" and "gamesmanship" are very different concepts, and an understanding of the difference is essential in a discussion of sport ethics. "Sportsmanship" includes winning the right way, being willing to lose, respect for people and rules, safety, spirit of the rules, integrity of the game, and the way sports *ought* to be played. In contrast, "gamesmanship" includes winning at any costs, it's only cheating if you get caught, rules are meant to be broken, and the way sports are played, as opposed how they ought to be played (Josephson, 2001). In the gamesmanship model, the focus is on winning, which would include achieving that goal in any way possible. As previously discussed, such a perspective on winning is an unhealthy one with little or no regard for the process, the opponent, or the rules. Unethical behavior is almost guaranteed.

Exhibit 2.3: Sportsmanship vs. Gamesmanship

Sportsmanship	Gamesmanship
Commitment to principles	No criteria for what is right or wrong
"Ought" versus "Is"	"Is" versus "Ought"
Spirit of the rules and integrity of the game	Rules are meant to be broken
Winning the right way	Winning any way you can
Love of competition and honorable pursuit of victory	It's just about the victory

(Josephson, 2002)

Analyzing Ethical Dilemmas

Ethical dilemmas surround us in our daily lives, if not personally, than certainly in the media. Previously and recently the steroids in baseball controversy is but one example of a dilemma with wide visibility and media coverage.

The first step in analyzing moral issues is an obvious one: get all the facts. Some moral issues create controversies simply because people do not bother to check out the facts. This first step of analysis, although obvious, is also the most important one and the one that is most frequently overlooked.

However, having the facts is not enough. Facts by themselves only tell us what is; they do not tell us what ought to be. In addition to getting the facts, resolving an ethical issue also requires an appeal to values. It is crucial to identify the values involved or those in conflict. Additionally, as Kidder (2005) suggested, it should be determined whether the dilemma is a right/wrong or a right/right type of dilemma. That is, in the dilemma, is a core value, such as honesty, being ignored (right/wrong dilemma), or are two core values, such as honesty and safety or success, in conflict with each other (right/right dilemma)?

Other things to consider when gathering the facts are whether there are legal implications or if there is something wrong personally, interpersonally, or socially (Velasquez et al., 1996). Also, who could be injured or damaged in this ethical conflict? Is there missing information, and if so, can this information be obtained? Who are the stakeholders (those whom might be affected by the decision) and which of those needs to be considered the most? Perhaps one has to consider those that might have special needs or those to whom one might have a special obligation.

In analyzing the ethical issues, one must consider the values involved, which ones are in conflict, and what values need to be maximized in the decision making process. This is where one's values clarification skills come in handy. It is important to fully understand the nature of the ethical dilemma in being able to properly resolve it. Malloy et al. (2003) suggests considering the time factor; that is, "the time before the incident, the time of the incident, and the consequences that resulted because of the incident" (p. 66). In other words, it is helpful to understand what led up to an incident, and the intentions and motivation behind it. As Malloy et al. (2003) point out, "At times good motives produce bad results and, conversely, evil motives produce good results" (p. 56).

Listing and evaluating alternatives comes next in the decision making process. It is prudent to evaluate alternative actions from the various ethical perspectives. Malloy et al. (2003) emphasize the need to "identify and enunciate the ethical maxim(s) to be used" (p. 64). An example might be to apply the Categorical Imperative to the use of steroids in baseball. Would steroid use be acceptable across the board, if all baseball players did it? Or, using the "greatest good for the greatest number of people" approach to utilitarianism, would cutting a men's sport in a college athletic department because of Title IX be a "good action" since it would help lead to gender equity in the program? In other words, most of the athletes, especially the women, are now happy, so why worry about the 20 or so men who lost their sport entirely?

Josephson (1999) encourages, prior to making a decision, that one clarify what exactly needs to be decided, and in the process, eliminate alternatives that are impractical, illegal, or otherwise not viable. After careful consideration of all reasonable, lawful, and ethical alternatives, and a close examination of the consequences of each, a decision must be made. Once a careful decision is made, it needs to be implemented and evaluated. The flowchart below illustrates the steps in ethical decision making.

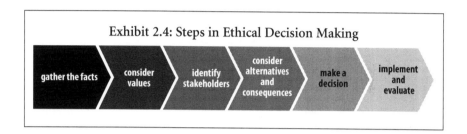

Exhibit 2.4: Steps in Ethical Decision Making

gather the facts → consider values → identify stakeholders → consider alternatives and consequences → make a decision → implement and evaluate

Kidder (2005) refers to the need for "moral courage" when making difficult moral decisions. Specifically, he defines moral courage as consisting of three intersecting circles: applying values, recognizing risks, and enduring the hardship. The last one, "enduring the hardships," is the perseverance piece of the moral courage model. Kidder's model appears below, and the "moral courage" is represented where the three circles actually intersect.

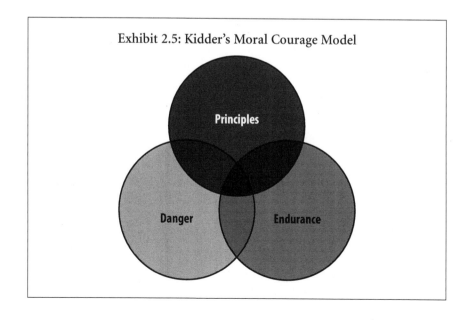

Exhibit 2.5: Kidder's Moral Courage Model

Principles

Danger   Endurance

For example, the act of "whistle blowing" is an example of moral courage. Kidder (2005) defines whistle blowing in four parts: (1) an individual acts with the intention of making information public; (2) the information is conveyed to parties outside the organization who makes it public and a part of the public record; (3) the information has to do with possible or actual nontrivial wrongdoings in an organization; and (4) the person exposing the agency is not a journalist or ordinary citizen but a member of former member of the organization. Famous cases include Enron, WorldCom, the Pentagon Papers, Deep Throat in the Watergate scandal, and the coverage of the tobacco industry depicted in the movie *The Insider*. Although examples of whistle-blowers in sports are difficult to come by, Jan Kemp, a University of Georgia professor, gained notoriety after being fired for publicly criticizing the university for allowing student-athletes to continue playing sports after failing remedial classes. As a result of her lawsuit against the University, reforms were made at the University of Georgia and nationwide to raise academic standards for college athletes (Associated Press, 2009). Perhaps baseball's steroid dilemma would not have reached its current level if there were more whistle-blowers in sports. Whistleblowers certainly must have a great deal of moral courage.

When it comes to evaluation, how does a person know if he made the "right" decision? Obviously, it is advisable to monitor short term and long term effects of any significant decision. However, there are ethics tests that are quicker and easier in some cases. One hopes to pass the "sleep test" (Can you sleep at night?), the newspaper test (Would I like to see this decision in the headlines tomorrow morning?), the "Mom/Dad [or someone else important to you] test" (Would I feel comfortable telling my mom about this?), and so on. Questions such as "would I do the same thing if I were on the other side of this dilemma," and "did I treat the other person(s) the way I would want to be treated" are important in dealing with the aftermath of an ethical dilemma.

In working through ethical dilemmas, Rest (1986) suggested these four components in sequential order:

1. The person must be able to *interpret* whether or not there is an ethical dilemma, and if so, what actions might be possible.
2. The person must be able to make a *judgment* about what course of action is ethically right.
3. The person must be able *give priority* to ethical values above other personal values such that a decision is made to intend to do what is ethically right.
4. The person must have sufficient perseverance, ego strength, and implementation skills to be able to *follow through* on his or her intention.

Solutions: A Code of Conduct

When discussing solutions to ethical dilemmas in the workplace, written guidelines in the form of a code of conduct are useful. Driscoll and Hoffman (2000) state:

> a code of conduct is intended to be a central guide and reference for users in support of day-to-day decision making. It is meant to clarify an organization's mission, values, and principles, linking them with standards of professional conduct. As a reference, it can be used to locate relevant documents, services and other resources related to ethics within the organization (p. 77).

Codes provide standards of behaviors, and are not merely lists of rules. They are based on organizational values, a philosophy of ethics, and the mission statement of the organization (Hitt, 1990). They require the commitment of the higher levels of management, and should address the needs of the various constituencies and stakeholders in the organization. For example, in a college athletic department, the athletic director and associate/assistant athletic directors would be considered, as would the coaches, student-athletes, boosters and fans, trainers, and staff.

A code is an open disclosure for the way an organization operates. It provides visible guidelines for behavior. A well-written and thoughtful code also serves as an important communication vehicle that "reflects the covenant that an organization has made to uphold its most important values, dealing with such matters as its commitment to employees, its standards for doing business and its relationship with the community" (Driscoll & Hoffman, 2000, p. 77). A code is also a tool to encourage discussions of ethics and to improve how employees/members deal with the ethical dilemmas, prejudices, and "grey areas" that are encountered in everyday work. A code is meant to complement relevant standards, policies, and rules, not to substitute for them. Codes of conduct offer an excellent opportunity for organizations to create a positive public identity for themselves, which can lead to a more supportive political and regulatory environment and an increased level of public confidence and trust among important constituencies and stakeholders (Driscoll & Hoffman, 2000).

Conflict

In trying to develop a moral solution to a dilemma, conflict is inevitable, partially due to conflicting interests of stakeholders, either between or among them. For example, in the Major League Baseball (MLB) steroid controversy, the players and their union are in conflict with the League. While the management and owners are charged with the integrity of the product, the players have a duty to perform at their best. Further complicating the situation are the advertisers and sponsors who do not want to be associated with a tainted product. While some need to consider the "virtuous" and "good" (sportsmanship) side of the dilemma, others look at the consequences and ultimate outcome of winning and success (gamesmanship). Another example of this type of conflict in sports is the case of Michael Phelps in the controversial photograph depicting marijuana usage. Some, but not all of Phelps' sponsors, canceled their endorsement with the athlete, claiming their need to sever themselves from a tarnished image. After the famous photograph became public, Kellogg (cereals) canceled his contract and long standing relationship with the company, citing the fact that his recent behavior was not consistent with the company (Huffington Post, 2009). Embedded in that controversy is the ethical dilemma of athletes as role models, and the often debated question of whether it is fair to hold athletes to higher standards.

Conflict in Sport and Conflict Management

Regarding conflict in general, Slack and Parent (2006) note that "because conflict has both positive and negative consequences, it has to be managed" (p. 225). It is also important to promote positive conflict, and create "win-win" solutions when possible. They suggest various strategies including formal authority of the senior management, confrontation, and negotiation. They point out that negotiation requires maturity and a focus on points of agreement with the example of owners and players. Sometimes, it is also necessary to use a third party if the conflict is particularly drawn out. This can be seen in labor disputes between owners of professional teams and their players in football, basketball, baseball, and hockey. Nugent (2002) suggests four steps for managers to decide the appropriate level of involvement when faced with conflict:

1. Can the protagonists be made to handle conflict themselves or must a third party be involved?
2. If an intervention is required, what is the most appropriate type of intervention—autocratic, arbitration, facilitating, bargaining, or collaborative problem solving
3. The manager must determine whether she is the best person to intervene. Is someone with more power better?

4. If the manager is the best person, does she need assistance from an independent resource person (and how will that person be used)?

Regardless of the strategy, conflict in organizations is inevitable, and sport organizations are no different. Values may be in conflict, usually involving money and success, and many stakeholders have to be considered. On a more local level conflict exists in athletic contests as well, with the emphasis on winning versus sportsmanship. It is incumbent on the successful sport manager to learn to manage and resolve conflict while keeping important values in check and pursuing a moral course of action.

Conclusion

Ethics and ethical decision making are a necessary part of any effective organization, and sport organizations are no exception. As sport managers realize the importance of utilizing appropriate values and making sound ethical decisions, the ethical dilemmas facing sport will be reduced, and the term "sport ethics" will regain its relevance. While the focus on winning, and gaining a competitive "edge" is prevalent in all areas of our society, we must continue to look for ways to win "the right way."

References

Associated Press. (2009, January 8). Kemp's suit fostered reform. Retrieved from http://sports.espn.go.com/ncaa/news/story?id=3756812.

DeSensi, J. T., & Rosenberg, D. (2003). *Ethics and morality in sport management.* Morgantown, WV: Fitness Information Technology, Inc.

Driscoll, D. M. & Hoffman, W. M. (2000). *Ethics matters: How to implement values-driven management.* Waltham, MA: Center for Business Ethics.

Frankena, W. K. (1973). *Ethics* (2nd. ed.). Englewood Cliffs, NJ: Prentice-Hall, Inc.

Hitt, W. D. (1990). *Ethics and leadership.* Columbus, OH: Batelle.

Huffington Post. (2009, February 5). Michael Phelps' sponsors sticking with him after bong photo. Retrieved from www.huffingtonpost.com/2009/02/02/michael-phelps-sponsors-s_n_163276.html.

Hums, M. A., Barr, C. A., & Gullion, L. (1999). The ethical issues confronting managers in the sport industry. *Journal of Business Ethics, 20(1),* 51–66.

Johnson, C. E. (2001). *Meeting the ethical challenges of leadership.* Thousand Oaks, CA: Sage Publishers.

Josephson Institute (2009). The six pillars of character. Retrieved from http://charactercounts.org/sixpillars.html.

Josephson, M. (2001). Pursuing victory with honor: A training program for coaches on ethics sports, and character-building in sports. Retrieved from http://charactercounts.org/sports/Olympic/olympic-report-ethicssportsman ship2.htm.

Kidder, R. M. (2005). *Moral courage.* New York: HarperCollins Publishers, Inc.

Kitchener, K. S. (2000). *Foundations of ethical practices, research, and teaching in psychology.* Mahwah, NJ: Lawrence Erlbaum Associates.

Kohlberg, L. (1984). *Essays on moral development. The psychology of moral development* (vol. 2). San Francisco: Harper & Row Publishers.

Kouzes, J. M. & Posner, B. (2007). *The Leadership Challenge.* New York: John Wiley and Sons.

Lee, J., Whisenant, W., & Mullane, S. (2008). Confederate Imagery in Sport: Heritage, Hate, or Hypocrisy. Sport and Recreation Law Association (SRLA). 21st Annual Conference on Sport, Physical Activity, Recreation and Law, Myrtle Beach, SC.

Lumpkin, A., Stoll, S. K. & Beller, J. M. (2003). *Sport ethics: Applications for fair play* (3rd ed.). New York: McGraw-Hill.

Malloy, D. C., Ross, S., & Zakus, D. H. (2003). *Sport ethics* (2nd ed.). Quebec, Canada: Thompson Educational Publishing, Inc.

Morgan, W. J. (Ed.) (2007). *Ethics in sport* (2nd ed.). Champaign, IL: Human Kinetics.

Nugent, P. S. & Broeding, L. A. (2002). Managing conflict: Third-party interventions for managers. *The Academy of Management Executive, 16*(1), 139–155.

Osland, J. S., Kolb, D. A., & Rubin, I. M. (2001). *Organizational behavior: An experimental approach.* Upper Saddle River, NJ: Prentice-Hall, Inc.

Raths, L. E., Harmin, M., & Simon, S. B. (1966). *Values and teaching.* Columbus, OH: C.E. Merrill Books.

Rest, J. (1974). *Manual for the Defining Issues Test: An objective test of moral judgment development.* Unpublished manuscript, University of Minnesota, Minneapolis.

Rest, J. R. (1979). *Development in judging moral issues.* Minneapolis, MN: University of Minnesota Press.

Rest, J. R. (1986). *Moral development: Advances in research and theory.* New York: Praeger.

Rokeach, M. (1973. *The nature of values.* New York, NY: The Free Press.

Rudd, A., Mullane, S. P., & Stoll, S. (2010). Development of an instrument to measure the moral judgment of sport managers. *Journal of Sport Management, 24*(1), 59–83.

Slack, T., & Parent, M. M. (2006). *Understanding sport organizations: The application of organizational theory.* Champaign, IL: Human Kinetics.

Velasquez, M., Andre, C., Shanks, T., & Meyer, M. J. (1996). Thinking ethically: A framework for moral decision making. *Issues in ethics, 7*(1), 1–3.

Chapter 3

Governance of Collegiate Sport

Robin Hardin & Jim Bemiller, University of Tennessee

Development of Collegiate Sport

College sport in the United States can trace its roots back to a rowing competition between Yale and Harvard in 1852 in which 1,000 spectators witnessed the event (Rader, 2008). No one could have foreseen that this one competition on Lake Winnipesaukee in New Hampshire some 160 years ago would lead to billion dollar television rights and athletic department budgets in excess of $100 million (Fulks, 2013; Rovell, 2005; Weinbach, 2007).

Athletic competitions following the rowing event included the first baseball game between Amherst College and Williams College in 1859, and, 10 years later, the first football game, where Rutgers defeated Princeton 6–4 on the Rutgers campus in New Brunswick, New Jersey (Rader, 2008). Competitions between institutions became more and more prevalent in the following decades and administrators became concerned about a perception of the unproductive nature of athletic contests (Hums & MacLean, 2009). This concern, however, did not slow the popularity of college sports and not only did the desire for competition grow, but so did the desire to win.

College sports were becoming more than a just an activity organized and played by students in late 1800s and early 1900s. Administrators began to realize that the interest and growth of college sports were going to continue to rise. Football and other sports were unifying not only for students but also for alumni. Winning teams meant proud alumni and proud alumni meant financial support for the university. Financial support not only came in the form of alumni donations but also in the form of ticket revenue. Sports news also began appearing in newspapers during the closing years of the nineteenth century, which was free publicity for the universities and served as positive public relations (McChesney, 1986; Mott, 1962). Athletic contests were becoming more than just a contest between two universities; they were becoming the talk and the interest of the sporting world (Dougherty, 1976).

University administrators knew that the positives of college sport far outweighed any negative consequences (i.e., injuries, de-emphasis of academics), so they began the process of taking control of collegiate athletics. The Southern Intercollegiate Athletic Association, which eventually became the Southeastern Conference, was formed in the Southeastern United States in 1894—and thus began the first step in governance and control of college athletics (Dougherty, 1976). The Intercollegiate Conference of Faculty Representatives held its inaugural meeting January 11, 1895, and this was the first step in organizing and legitimizing collegiate athletics in the Midwest (Davenport, 1985). This organization, which would eventually become the Big Ten Conference, established guidelines for eligibility, financial assistance, and scheduling, and also ensured standardized rules of play would be enforced. Similar organizations began to appear around the country, and the conference structure of college athletics began to take shape.

College athletics really caught the nation's eye 10 years later when President Theodore Roosevelt began to intervene in the affairs of the nation's universities and colleges because of the brutality that existed in college football. Eighteen student-athletes were killed and nearly 150 were seriously injured in 1905 while playing football (Rader, 2008). This was primarily the result of gang tackling, the "flying wedge" and other brutal football tactics at the time (McQuilkin, 2002). President Roosevelt was concerned with the high number of deaths and injuries and called two meetings between Harvard, Yale, and Princeton. These meetings were followed by another meeting, called by New York University Chancellor Henry MacCracken (Rader, 2008). Thirteen universities sent representatives to this meeting in December 1905 to discuss issues related to football—but many more issues were brought to the forefront and the eventual result was the formation of the Intercollegiate Athletic Association of the United States (IAAUS). The constitution and the bylaws of the organization were adopted March 31, 1906 (Crowley, 2006). Many colleges and universities would have dropped football if not for the formation of a governing body, and the growth of college sports would have been hindered (Dougherty, 1976).

The purpose of the organization was to strike a balance between academics and athletics and to establish rules and bylaws in which all institutions must abide. These two items are still very much a part of the ongoing mission of the organization. The organization took its current name, the National Collegiate Athletic Association (NCAA), four years later on December 29, 1910 (Crowley, 2006). The organization was comprised of faculty members from member institutions with the primary focus on developing policies related to how to govern collegiate athletics both on and off the field. The NCAA began to expand and eventually started sponsoring championships with the first being in the sport of track and field in 1921.

The organization continued to grow and evolve during the next 30 years. Membership continued to increase, and there were more than 400 institutions belonging to the NCAA by the 1950s (Crowley, 2006). Several issues also had drawn unwanted to attention to the organization during this time. The organization's initial goal was for member institutions to police themselves but winning began to outweigh ethical behavior (Hums & MacLean, 2009). The notion of amateurism in college football was being questioned as scholarships were being awarded to student-athletes, and recruiting based on athletic ability was becoming a part of the college athletics. There were rules in place to govern scholarships, recruiting and amateurism, but they were not always followed and the NCAA had little power to enforce them. Noted sportswriter Paul Gallico wrote that college football was "the leader in the field of double-dealing, deception, sham, cant and organized hypocrisy" and the amateurism in college sport only meant not watching a student-athlete take money (Gallico, 1938, p. 208).

It had become apparent that the organization needed full-time, professional leadership and Walter Byers became the first executive director of the NCAA in 1951. Byers began his tenure at the NCAA in 1947 as one of the small group of people who had been managing business operations. He believed in the potential of college sport and wanted to prove the skeptics wrong. The NCAA established an office and a full-time staff and the organization continued to bring order to college sports. Byers led the NCAA for 36 years (Byers, 1995).

Divisional Split

College sport had a governing body in place with professional leadership, a full-time staff and the ability to manage collegiate athletics. The next major moment in the NCAA came in 1973 when the decision was made to split into separate divisions. The organization has 664 active members at the time, and discussions had previously occurred in regard to splitting into separate divisions (Byers, 1995; Crowley, 2006). The reason for the divisional split was due to the disparity in the athletic budgets of members, no common mission for all the members, and the issue of ensuring a level playing field for all members. Thus, the organization decided to split into three divisions. These would simply be Division I, Division II, and Division III. Division I programs sponsored more sports, had a national fan and recruiting base, and would supposedly be financially self-sufficient. Division II would draw its student-athletes and fans from a regional base and rely on institutional funding. Division III based its philosophy on the premise that sports were for students and the campus community. There would be no financial aid awarded based on athletic ability, and no distinction between the participants and the general student population would exist (Byers, 1995; Crowley, 2006).

Current NCAA Structure

The NCAA presently has an executive director and full-time staff but the governance of the organization comes from its member institutions. The Executive Committee is at the top of the governance structure of the NCAA (see Exhibit 3.1). It consists of 20 members with four of those being ex-officio members. The committee composition is: (a) eight presidents or chancellors from the Division I Board of Directors from Football Bowl Subdivision institutions; (b) two presidents or chancellors from the Division I Board of Directors from Football Championship Subdivision institutions; (c) two presidents or chancellors from the Division I Board of Directors from institutions that do not sponsor football; (d) two Division II presidents or chancellors from the Division II Presidents Council; and (e) two Division III presidents or chancellors from the Division III Presidents Council. The other four members are ex-officio members: (a) the NCAA president, (b) chair of the Division I Leadership Council, (c) chair of Division II Management Council, and (d) chair of the Division II Management Council (NCAA National Membership Services Staff, 2013a).

Division I

The current form of the NCAA is based on the divisional split from the early 1970s but adjustments have occurred with the divisions as the organization has expanded. Division I subdivided in three divisions in 1978 with football being the criteria for division affiliation. The result was Division I-A, which is now known as the Football Bowl Subdivision (FBS), Division I-AA, known as the Football Championship Subdivision (FCS), and Division I-Non Football (sometimes referred to as Division I-AAA), which encompass universities without football. A concern among the division classifications is the perception that there are other distinguishing factors when there are only two major differences. FBS members must sponsor 16 sports whereas other Division I

Exhibit 3.1: NCAA Governance Structure

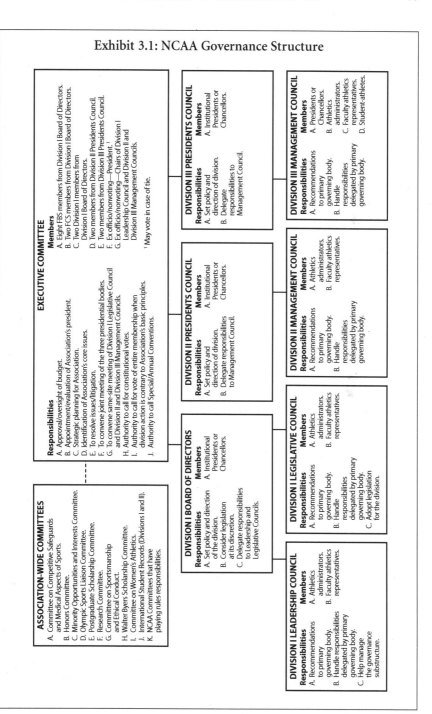

members only have to sponsor 14, and FBS members have 85 football scholarships while FCS members have 63. Members of the division compete for championships in all other sports with the same scholarship allowances. Initial and continuing eligibility requirements are the same for all members of Division I regardless of their football competition level (NCAA National Membership Services Staff, 2013a).

There is also a staggered voting pattern within the Division I Legislative Council and Leadership Council. Seven of the 32 conferences that comprise Division I have their votes count for three; four conferences have their votes count for 1.5, and 21 conferences have their votes count for 1.14. The majority of the authority and decision-making power in the NCAA lies within those conferences competing at the Football Bowl Subdivision level, and they also comprise half of the voting members on the NCAA Executive Committee (NCAA Membership Services Staff, 2013a).

Division II

Division II has a Presidents Council within the NCAA organizational structure and two members on the executive committee. The members of the Division II Presidents Council are selected based on the four geographical regions into which Division II is divided. A president or chancellor from each of the regions is on the committee per every 22 institutions in the region. There are also two at-large positions on the committee. Efforts are made not to have representatives from the same conference on the Presidents Council. There is also an effort not to have members of the Management Council from the same institution as members of the Presidents Council. The Management Council is comprised of athletic department personnel with membership consisting of at least one representative from multi-sport conferences and two at-large members. Division II also has its own governance structure that addresses issues specific to Division II, such as eligibility, student-welfare, legislative aspects and championships (NCAA National Membership Services Staff, 2008b).

Division III

The Division III Presidents Council is comprised of 15 members with at least two from each of the four geographic regions into which Division III is divided. There are also seven at-large members. Division III also has requirements as to the demographic composition of the council in terms of its members, as well as considerations of institution enrollment size and public and private designation.

The Management Council has 19 members and is comprised of presidents or chancellors, faculty athletics representatives, athletic administration personnel, and student-athletes. Division III is the only division that has student-athletes in the organizational structure of the NCAA. Similar to Division II, Division III has its own administrative structure with committees to address issues specific to Division III in terms of eligibility, infractions, and championships (NCAA National Membership Services Staff, 2013c).

Association for Intercollegiate Athletics for Women (AIAW)

The AIAW was founded in 1971 to govern collegiate athletics for women. It grew out of the Commission on Intercollegiate Athletics for Women and provided an opportunity for female student-athletes to compete for national championships. NCAA Division II and III began offering championships for women in the late 1970s, and Division I began offering championships for the 1981–82 season. The AIAW eventually disbanded because members began competing in NCAA championships only. The AIAW did not have the financial resources of the NCAA or its membership numbers, which led to it ceasing operations in 1982 (Byers, 1995). A full discussion of the AIAW is available in Chapter 6 but its importance in helping women gain acceptance in collegiate sport cannot be discounted.

Television and Antitrust

The ruling in the antitrust case *NCAA v. Board of Regents of University of Oklahoma* caused a dramatic change in college football and college sports (Byers, 1995). This 1984 court ruling helped pave the way for the hundreds of millions of dollars in television rights fees for college football games.

The decision came in 1984, but television broadcasting rights became an issue as soon as television began to spread across the American landscape. Notre Dame's president, the Rev. Ned Joyce, led the initiative to enable colleges and universities to control their own television rights negotiations and thus reap the financial rewards of such contracts. The College Football Association (CFA) was formed in the early 1950s in an attempt to do this but there was not enough support or members in the organization to wrestle away control from the NCAA. The organization was comprised of more than 60 members and was ready to battle with the NCAA by the mid 1970s.

The NCAA policy at the time was that teams could not appear on television any more than six times during a two-year period (Hiestand, 2004). Institutions were convinced millions of dollars were being kept from their coffers because of the limitations placed on them regarding television appearances. The advent of cable television in the late 1970s and early 1980s only increased the visibility of the issue.

The CFA signed a contract with NBC nonetheless. The deal with NBC eventually fell through but the CFA went to court against the NCAA on the basis of antitrust laws. The member institutions wanted the right to negotiate their own television rights deal, and the NCAA prohibited them from doing so. Oklahoma and Georgia were listed as the plaintiffs against the NCAA. The NCAA lost the first court battle, and then the appeal, but the case eventually made it to the Supreme Court. The Supreme Court ruled that the NCAA's attempt to limit "output" televised games was in violation of antitrust law. College sports were never the same following the precedent setting case. *USA Today* sports media columnist Michael Hiestand (2004) quoted Tom Duke in 2004 on the 20th anniversary of the decision: "The state of college football today is the direct result of that decision, including the arms-race mentality, conference realignments, money pressures, the dilution of rules and regulations." Duke was an original member of the NCAA staff in 1952 and was the Big Ten commissioner from 1971 to 1989.

The ruling eliminated NCAA marketed television contracts as conferences began to sell the broadcasting rights, and this has led to near 24-hour game coverage on Saturday with games sprinkled throughout the week as well. The networks are willing to ante up millions of dollars for broadcasting rights for the power conferences, whereas the smaller conferences and their members are on the outside looking in. Thus, the majority of revenue goes to the conferences and then to the universities. The NCAA determines how the more than $700 million from rights to broadcast the NCAA Men's Basketball Tournament each year is distributed with conferences receiving equal shares based on performance. However, the NCAA is not in the discussions in regard to football television money distribution.

This legal decision paved the way for the split in Division I and the split between the haves and the have nots. The decision was beneficial in many ways though. The increased revenue from television rights allowed universities to boost compliance with Title IX by adding more sports for females and the quality of experiences for all student-athletes improved. Expenditures are geared toward football but better facilities, coaches and support services are also possible for non-revenue sports. Non-revenue sports are not financially viable but the millions of dollars generated through football and men's basketball are used to subsidize those sports.

Amateurism/Student-Athlete Compensation

The NCAA and collegiate administrators have continued to vigilantly defend the amateur status of college athletes. Collegiate student-athletes may receive full or partial scholarships for being members on their school's teams. Restrictions are placed, in the form of NCAA rules, on receiving extra benefits or compensation. The debate continues to grow regarding the issue of adequate student-athlete compensation because of the expansion of men's football and basketball revenue through multi-million-dollar television contracts. The issue is multi-faceted and involves far-reaching questions. The role of athletics in higher education has to be addressed as well as the issue of compensating only athletes in revenue-producing sports.

Revenue-producing teams are often comprised of a high percentage of minority students, yet their efforts produce millions of dollars which fund the multi-million-dollar salaries of white coaches and the budgets of non-revenue producing sports made up of mostly white men and women. The issue of whether institutions would be bound by Title IX to pay men and women student-athletes equally is also of concern. There are many issues to consider regarding this, but they should be tempered by the fact that these situations only apply to a relatively small number of colleges and universities. These are primarily members of Division I—Football Bowl Subdivision, as approximately 20 institutions actually operate without any financial assistance from the university (Fulks, 2013). The majority of NCAA members would not be able to operate under such a model for lack of revenue; therefore, many believe controlling the amateur nature of collegiate sport is a necessity.

The NCAA decrees student-athletes will be amateurs and should be motivated primarily by education and by the physical, mental and social benefits of being in collegiate athletics. The Association continues to balance the historic ideal of the amateur collegiate athletic experience as part of the educational mission with life skills benefits versus the increasing competitiveness and huge entertainment and revenue aspects of elite college sport. Thus far the NCAA has withstood major challenges to its definition of amateurism. Courts have historically embraced the amateur student model. A college sports scholarship is not considered a liberty or property right rising to the level of constitutional protection. Athletes have not been considered employees of the university for workers' compensation and disability claims. NCAA rules prevent student-athletes from receiving any financial benefit associated with their participation in college sport other than scholarship aid. Student-athletes who compete at the Olympic level or in other world class competitions such as extreme skiing or biking will forfeit their NCAA eligibility if they accept funding from their national federations or corporate sponsors (e.g., Jeremy Bloom situation). Student-athletes are also not allowed to use their overall athletic ability for financial gain. So participation in events that award prize money but may not be sport specific (e.g., an all-star-type competition) is not permissible and would jeopardize a student-athlete's amateur status. Student-athletes may however receive compensation for providing lessons or coaching in their sport provided guidelines set forth by the NCAA are followed (NCAA Membership Services Staff, 2013a).

College administrators continue to closely guard the amateur status of student-athletes. Pressure from lawsuits and recent aggressive proposals from several state legislatures, including Nebraska, Texas, Colorado, Oklahoma, and California, have kept equitable compensation for student-athletes a hot topic. The proposed legislation suggests paying football players, providing extra stipends for travel, clothing and medical care, easing restrictions for transferring, and allowing representation by an agent without penalty. These state acts would be a direct challenge to the NCAA's governing authority.

The NCAA has taken positive steps on behalf of student-athletes by enacting rules allowing athletes who are projected as high professional draft picks in football and men's and women's basketball to purchase insurance related to career-ending injuries. Rule changes have also allowed student-athletes to work during the school year outside of the athletes' competitive seasons to cover the cost of attending school. These rules were implemented in part to alleviate the pressure of interference by agents enticing student-athletes with gifts and payments prior to the exhaustion of their collegiate eligibility.

Student-Athlete Misconduct

Colleges and universities are becoming increasingly exposed to sexual harassment lawsuits involving student-athletes. Male athletes are named in 23% of sexual assault cases even though they only comprise approximately 2% of a campus' population (Osborne & Duffy, 2005). These incidents are costly both monetarily and in damage to the reputation and integrity of the school and its athletic program (Osborne & Duffy, 2005). This trend of incidents has fostered a growing concern as to whether or not a university should be held legally responsible for the behavioral misconduct of its student-athletes. College athletic departments and their administrators are under increased scrutiny with regard to student-athlete behavior, specifically sexual harassment and assault.

The United States Supreme Court has held in *Davis v. Monroe County* (1999) that a private Title IX action may lie against an educational institution in cases of student-on-student harassment, where the institution, as a Title IX funding recipient, has been deliberately indifferent to sexual harassment, despite actual knowledge of such harassment.

One of the most notable examples regarding the issue of institutional liability involves allegations of sexual harassment and assault surrounding the University of Colorado (CU) football program (*Simpson v. Colorado*, 2007). The U.S. Court of Appeals for the 10th Circuit reversed a grant of summary judgment to CU in September 2007, and the case was remanded for further proceedings. Colorado immediately settled with the two female plaintiffs rather than proceed to trial. Lisa Simpson and Anne Gilmore alleged they were sexually assaulted by CU football players and recruits in December 2001. They sued under Title IX, claiming the university deprived them of an equal education by allowing a pattern of sexual harassment to go unchecked within the football-recruiting program (Spies, 2006). The Federal Court of Appeals found there was an obvious risk that a sexual assault could occur (*Simpson*, 2007). The Court enumerated many instances in which CU football recruiting was a specific focus of concern. The oversight of the football recruiting program had garnered negative scrutiny from university administrators, local law enforcement agencies, and national media. The Court stated that the guidance of the player hosts and recruits regarding sexual harassment had been inadequate and CU had not made a sincere effort to effectively deal with the issue. The evidence showed that head coach Gary Barnett had general knowledge of the serious risk of sexual harassment, knew that assaults occurred during CU recruiting visits, and nevertheless maintained an unsupervised program to show recruits a "good time." The Court found there was no attempt on his or the institution's part to change the atmosphere conducive to this misconduct. Therefore, the Court reasoned that there was sufficient evidence for a jury to infer that the institution displayed deliberate indifference to the need for more or different training for football player hosts and recruits. The need for such training was obvious and the inadequacy was likely to result in further sexual assaults.

Universities should educate all student-athletes of the rising trends regarding sexual harassment. Universities must take appropriate steps in educating their athletes and protecting themselves from possible litigation.

National Christian College Athletic Association (NCCAA)

The NCCAA was established in 1968 as a Christian-based organization for the enhancement and promotion of intercollegiate athletic competition with a Christian perspective. The initial championship of the organization was a men's basketball tournament in Detroit, Michigan, in 1968. Other sports were eventually adopted and now 23 championships are held by the organization. Nearly 14,000 student-athletes compete in the NCCAA and approximately 60% of the members also have an affiliation with NCAA Division II or III or the NAIA (NCCAA, 2008).

A second division was added to the organization in 1975 when Bible colleges formed their own division. Membership has continued to grow to approximately 100 colleges and universities. The mission of the organization is more than competition, as it sees itself as a way to promote the Biblical teachings, impact communities and prepare student-athletes and coaches to make a positive impact for Christ (NCCAA, 2008).

The organization is divided into two divisions, with Division I providing athletic-based financial aid for its student-athletes while Division II does not. Division II members must also require all of its student-athletes to graduate with a minimum of 20 semester or 30 quarter hours in Bible-themed courses (NCCAA, 2008).

A board of directors oversees the operations of the organization, and from this group an executive committee is chosen. The NCCAA does have a national office led by an executive director, which conducts the daily business of the organization. The board of directors is elected to nine-year terms by member institutions with a limit of 20 members. Member institutions also choose a president, first vice-president, and second vice-president. They each serve three-year terms and rise in position every three years. So, the second vice-president is making a nine-year commitment when he or she is elected to the position. The board of directors selects a board chair and the president is by de facto the board vice-chair. A national sport chair is also elected by coaches of member institutions and the person is responsible for directing national competitions in his or her respective sport. Other committees within the NCCAA include an administrative council, a national sports council and an eligibility committee (NCCAA, 2008).

National Association of Intercollegiate Athletics (NAIA)

The NAIA had its beginnings with a basketball tournament in 1937 in Kansas City, Missouri. The organizers of the tournament, one of whom was James Naismith, wanted to bring an amateur basketball tournament to the area for the community and also wanted a venue for small colleges and universities to determine a national basketball champion. Accordingly, the National Association of Intercollegiate Basketball (NAIB) was formed (NAIA Constitution and Bylaws Committee, 2008).

The organization remained basketball oriented until 1952 when the name was changed to the NAIA. The name change also brought a wider spectrum of sports, as golf and track and field were added. Other sports, including football, baseball, swimming and diving, wrestling, and soccer, were adopted by the close of the decade. The organization has continued to grow and now crowns 23 national champions in 13 sports. Sports are only separated by divisions in football and men's and women's basketball, where two divisions exist in each. Nearly 300 institutions comprise the NAIA, which provides an outlet for athletic competition for approximately 48,000 student-athletes (NAIA Constitution and Bylaws Committee, 2008).

The NAIA's governance structure is led by the Council of Presidents, who are elected by fellow conference members, and who are chief executive officers of the organizations members. They are elected to three-year terms and are limited to two successive terms. From this group, an Executive Committee is chosen, which consists of a chair, chair-elect, and three members appointed by the chair. The Executive Committee is charged with conducting the business of the NAIA in between meetings of the Council of Presidents. The National Administrative Council is comprised of representatives with a background or position in athletic administration. This council consists of one representative from each affiliated conference along with representatives from the Athletic Directors Association and the Conference Commissioners Association. Institutions without conference affiliation also have representation on the council. The NAIA consists of 25 geographically aligned conferences plus the Association of Independent Institutions (NAIA Constitution and Bylaws Committee, 2008).

The NAIA is also very much a trailblazer in collegiate athletics. The organization was the first to allow blacks to compete for national championships as historically black universities were admitted as members in 1953. The NAIA also began fully incorporating women's athletics into the organization in 1980, and in 2000 began its Champions of Character program (NAIA Constitution and Bylaws Committee, 2008). The Champions of Character program promotes positive character values in student-athletes. It has an educational outreach component as well, which emphasizes integrity for student-athletes, coaches and community members (NAIA Constitution and Bylaws Committee, 2008).

National Junior College Athletic Association (NJCAA)

The NJCAA can trace its beginnings back to the late 1930s when a group of junior college representatives in California wanted to form a governing body to promote and supervise athletic competitions amongst themselves. A track and field competition was held in Sacramento, California, in 1939 and the NJCAA was off and running, so to speak. World War II hurt the organization's growth and expansion but a basketball tournament took place in 1947 with participants from as far east as Louisiana. At this time, other institutions wanted to participate but the organization was not yet ready to manage a national tournament (NJCAA Executive Committee, 2007).

These developments led the organization to dividing into 16 regions in 1949. The governance structure of the organization was a president, vice-president, secretary, treasurer, public relations official, and 16 regional vice-presidents. Policies for conducting regional and national competitions were established, and the first NJCAA Handbook was published. This provided the regulations and policies in which the organization would conduct business. The organization has continued to grow and add additional national championships in sports. A women's division was added in 1975 (NJCAA Executive Committee, 2007).

The NJCAA consists of 24 regions with more than 516 members. Athletic opportunities are provided for more than 50,000 student-athletes competing on more than 3,200 teams. Baseball alone has more than 10,000 participants. Basketball is second with more than 6,000 participants for the males. Softball is the highest participatory sport for females with approximately 5,000 participants while basketball has more than 4,500 female student-athletes. The NJCAA officially recognizes 24 sports in which its members can participate and compete for championships. The organizational structure is similar to one established in 1949. A full-time staff, headed by an executive officer, oversees the day-to-day operations of the organization. Member institution representatives comprise the executive committee and board of directors, both of which establish bylaws and policies for the organization (NJCAA Executive Committee, 2007).

Conclusion

Collegiate athletics is much more than the Notre Dames, Southern Cals, Oklahomas, and Tennessees of the world. Major college football and men's basketball are what most people associate with collegiate athletics but that is only a small part of collegiate athletics in the United States. The NCAA sponsors 89 national championships across its three divisions and has more than 450,000 student-athletes. So, the NCAA represents much more than a Michigan-Ohio State football game or a North Carolina-Duke basketball game. Other governing bodies include the NAIA, NJCAA, and the NCCAA and each provides a valuable contribution to collegiate athletics and student-athletes. The athletic abilities of student-athletes may differ in the levels of collegiate athletics but the quality of the experience and the opportunity to compete is important to each student-athlete.

References

Aurelia Davis v. Monroe County Board of Education ET. AL, 526 U.S. 629, 119 S. Ct. 1661 (1999).

Byers, W. (1995). *Unsportsmanlike conduct: Exploiting college athletes*. Ann Arbor, MI: University of Michigan Press.

Crowley, J. (2006). *In the arena: The NCAA's first century*. Indianapolis, IN: National Collegiate Athletic Association.

Davenport, J. (1985). From crew to commercialism: The paradox of sport in higher education. In D. Chu, J.O. Segrave, & B.J. Becker (eds.), *Sport and higher education* (pp. 5–16). Champaign, IL: Human Kinetics.

Davis v. Monroe County Board of Education, 526 U.S. 629 (1999).

Dougherty, N. (1976). Educators and Athletes: the Southeastern Conference, 1894–1972. Knoxville, TN: Department of Athletics.

Fulks, D. (2013). *2004–12 NCAA Revenues and Expenses of Division I Athletics Program Report*. The National Collegiate Athletic Association: Indianapolis, IN.

Gallico, P. (1938). *Farewell to sport*. New York: Knopf.

Heistand, M. (2004, August 19). 1984 TV ruling led to widening sweep of the college game. *USA Today*, p. D2.

Hums, M. A. & MacLean, J. C. (2009). *Governance and policy in sport organizations* (2nd ed.). Scottsdale, AZ: Holcomb Hathaway, Publishers.

Lisa Simpson and Anne Gilmore v. University of Colorado, 372 F. Supp. 2d 1229, LEXIS 5633 (2005/2007).

McChesney, R. (1986). *Sport, Mass Media and Monopoly Capital: Toward a Reinterpretation of the 1920s and Beyond*. Unpublished master thesis, University of Washington.

McQuilkin, S. (2002). Brutality in football and the creation of the NCAA: A codified moral compass in America. *Sport History Review 33*, 1–34.

Mott, F. (1962). *American Journalism, A History 1690–1960* (3rd ed.). New York: The MacMillan Company.

NAIA Constitution and Bylaws Committee (2008). *NAIA Official Handbook and Policy Handbook* (24th ed.). Kansas City, MO: National Association of Intercollegiate Athletics.

NCAA Membership Services Staff (2013a). *2013–14 NCAA Division I Manual*. Indianapolis, IN: National Collegiate Athletic Association.

NCAA Membership Services Staff (2013b). *2013–14 NCAA Division II Manual*. Indianapolis, IN: National Collegiate Athletic Association.

NCAA Membership Services Staff (2013c). *2013–14 NCAA Division III Manual*. Indianapolis, IN: National Collegiate Athletic Association.

NCCAA (2008). *NCCAA 2008–2009 Official Handbook*. Greenville, SC: National Christian College Athletic Association.

NJCAA Executive Committee (2007). *Official Handbook & Casebook of the National Junior College Athletic Association*. Colorado Springs, CO: National Junior College Athletic Association.

Osborne, B. & Duffy, C. (2005). Title IX, Sexual Harassment, and Policies at NCAA Division IA Athletics Departments. *Journal of Legal Aspects of Sport, 15*(1), 59–94.

Rader, B. (2008). *American sports: From the age of folk games to the age of televised sport* (6th ed.). Englewood Cliffs, NJ: Prentice Hall.

Rovell, D. (2005, Oct. 11). Once an afterthought, the Dance is big business. ESPN.com. Retrieved from http://sports.espn.go.com/ncb/columns/story?id=2186638.

Simpson v. University of Colorado, 500 F.3d 1170 (10th Cir. 2007).

Spies, J. S. (2006). Winning at all costs: An analysis of a university's potential liability for sexual assaults committed by its student athletes. *Marquette Sports Law Review 16*(2), 429–460.

Weinbach, J. (2007, October 19). Inside college sports' biggest money machine. *Wall Street Journal*, p. W1.

Chapter 4

The Business of Big-Time College Athletics

Kadence A. Otto, Western Carolina University

This chapter provides an overview of the transformation of college athletics as "participatory" to college athletics as a "big-time" commercial enterprise. Big-time athletics programs have been defined as select members of the National Collegiate Athletic Association (NCAA) Division I Football Bowl Subdivision (FBS) classification. This chapter consists of three sections: (1) the history of the NCAA; (2) issues in the NCAA; and (3) politics and the NCAA.

History of the NCAA

Founded in 1906, the Intercollegiate Athletic Association of the United States (IAAUS) was originally created to curb the violence in football. In 1910, the IAAUS changed its name to the National Collegiate Athletic Association (NCAA, 2012e). In its first constitution, the mission of the NCAA was to regulate and supervise college athletics in the United States, "in order that the athletic activities ... may be maintained on an ethical plane in keeping with the dignity and high purpose of education" (Falla, 1981, p. 21).

Following World War I, collegiate sports became integral to higher education as a business operation with new and expanding stadiums, the emergence of noted coaching personalities, extensive travel, and national radio broadcasts (Smith, 2000). As the amount of revenue in college football increased, university presidents were reluctant to turn down money from outside sources knowing that large amounts of revenue would benefit the entire university (Lapchick & Slaughter, 1994). Along with such growth, violations of the rules began to surface so the NCAA sought funding from The Carnegie Foundation to sponsor an independent commission to investigate college sports. After 13 years of reviewing university athletics programs, the Carnegie Report documented that rampant professionalism, commercialization, and exploitation were corrupting intercollegiate sports. University decisions regarding sports were made tailored to the consumer rather than students, athletes, faculty, or other members of the university community. A return to amateur sport was strongly recommended (Savage, Bentley, McGovern, & Smiley, 1929).

By the 1940s, with the United States coming out of the Great Depression, college sports took on even a greater meaning in American society. Just a year before the end of World War II, then-President Franklin Roosevelt enacted the Serviceman's Readjustment Act of 1944, which became known as the "G.I. Bill" (Reimann, 2004). The G.I. Bill entitled anyone with 90 days of military service to one year of higher education. With so many men having served in the war, there was a massive influx of male students into the nation's colleges and universities. Many of these men were former athletes, specifically football players. There was an indirect benefit for college football recruiting as a result of the G.I. Bill (Reimann, 2004).

The recruiting benefit for college football came with a cost—as the competition for the best football recruits escalated so did the corruption in the form of "under-the-table" payments to athletes in exchange for their services on the football field. With the presence of radio and the advent of television, college athletics now had a massive stage on which to sell its product. As a result of the new avenues of media attention for college football, corruption increased (Reimann, 2004). Former president of the Carnegie Foundation Dr. Henry Pritchett predicted such problems in 1925: "Competition produces a system of recruiting ... which is demoralizing and corrupt ... alumni devices for recruiting winning teams constitutes the most disgraceful phase of recent intercollegiate athletics" (Cowley, 1999, p. 495).

Due to increased under-the-table payments to athletes, the NCAA established the Sanity Code in 1948 (NCAA, 2012e). The Sanity Code permitted colleges and universities to award scholarships to athletes based on financial need with the intent of alleviating "the proliferation of exploitive practices in the recruitment of student-athletes" (Smith, 2000, p. 14). To ensure compliance with the Sanity Code the NCAA created the Constitutional Compliance Committee that interpreted NCAA rules and investigated possible violations (NCAA, 2012e). The only penalty the Committee could hand down was expulsion and since expulsion was such a severe penalty the committee's ability to enforce was ineffectual (Sack & Staurowsky, 1998). As a result of the failure of the Sanity Code, the massive popularity of college football, and the corruption that arose as a result of the competitive drive to recruit the best players, in 1952 the NCAA officially allowed financial aid in the form of a grant-in-aid athletic scholarship to students participating in athletics (NCAA, 2012e). Two other important changes took place in the NCAA in the early 1950s: former executive director Walter Byers strengthened the NCAA's enforcement division; and the NCAA contracted its first television deal for college football which was valued at more than $1 million (Sack & Staurowsky, 1998; Smith, 2000).

College sports boomed during the next two decades. As a result of the popularity of televised college sports, Division I football and men's basketball programs brought in increased revenue. Such popularity, however, came at a price because "from 1952 to 1985 the NCAA put more than 150 schools on probation for illegal recruiting, payments to athletes, or illegal benefits" (Lapchick & Slaughter, 1994, p. 11). Even though the NCAA had expanded its enforcement capacity in response to the commercialization and marketability of college football, critics alleged that the NCAA's enforcement practices were unfair (Smith, 2000). In response to these criticisms the NCAA established the Committee on Infractions in 1973 that was designed to divide the prosecutorial and investigative roles into separate groups. A primary problem with the Committee on Infractions was its inability to punish coaches for wrongdoings. While it was clear that coaches were giving monetary payments to prospective athletes, the Committee could only sanction the institution itself leaving the coach free to move on to another college (Lapchick & Slaughter, 1994).

Present-Day NCAA

With more than 1,050 active members, the NCAA is an unincorporated, not-for-profit educational organization whose purpose is to "initiate, stimulate and improve intercollegiate athletics programs for student-athletes and to promote and develop educational leadership, physical fitness, athletics excellence and athletics participation as a recreational pursuit ..." (NCAA Division I Manual, 2012–13, Bylaw 1.2, p. 1). For 2011–12 the NCAA generated $705 million in television revenue, which accounted for 81% of its revenue; an additional 18% came from the Division I men's basketball championships (i.e., gate receipts, merchandise, apparel) for a total of $871.6 million. While FBS members comprise just 11% of the total membership, they are responsible for generating 96% of the NCAA's annual revenue ("Annual Budget," 2013). Other NCAA Division I sports have also been successfully marketed, in fact the NCAA is currently engaged in a $500 million contract with ESPN through 2023–24 granting ESPN the rights to televise 24 men's and women's NCAA championships (*ESPN College Sports*, 2011). The NCAA maintains corporate sponsorship agreements with AT&T, AllState, Buick, Capital One, Enterprise, Infiniti, LG, Lowe's, Coca-Cola, Northwestern Mutual, Reese's, Unilever, UPS, Nabisco, and Buffalo Wild Wings (NCAA, 2012a). The NCAA also benefits from licensee agreements with 36 companies and owns the rights to 78 trademarks (NCAA, 2012b; NCAA, 2012f).

Annual revenues ($6.70 billion) and expenses ($6.35 billion) for NCAA FBS member institutions resulted in a profit of $350 million (Equity in Athletics Disclosure Act, 2011). The University of Texas at Austin has the largest athletics department budget of all FBS members ($163 million in annual revenues and $138 million in expenses, resulting in a net profit of $25 million). Fourteen FBS member schools' athletic department budgets exceed $100 million annually (see Exhibit 4.1); however, just 23 (19%) FBS athletics programs reported positive net generated revenues (Fulks, 2013).

Exhibit 4.1: The $100 Million+ Club: Top NCAA Member Institutions' Annual Revenue*

	School	Revenue (millions)	FBS Conference
1.	Texas	$163	Big 12
2.	Ohio State	$142	Big 10
3.	Michigan	$140	Big 10
4.	Alabama	$125	SEC
5.	Florida	$120	SEC
6.	Texas A&M	$119	SEC
7.	LSU	$115	SEC
8.	Penn State	$108	Big 10
9.	Oklahoma	$106	Big 12
	Auburn	$106	SEC
10.	Tennessee	$103	SEC
	Wisconsin	$103	Big 10
11.	Florida State	$100	ACC

*Data obtained from *USA Today* (refer to Berkowitz, S., Upton, J., & Brady, E. (2013, May 10) for complete report).

From its founding to its present status, the NCAA has shifted its focus *from* the student-athlete *toward* that of big-business. Is such a shift aligned with the values of higher education? The United States Department of Education, which is responsible for higher education, seeks to promote student achievement and foster educational excellence (U.S. Department of Education, n.d.). When students who also participate in intercollegiate athletics are treated as *commodities* the leadership of colleges and universities must be held accountable for allowing the values of intercollegiate athletics to be eroded; thereby, skewing the purpose of higher education.

Philosophical Differences of NCAA Divisional Membership

As of the fall of 2012, there were 120 members in the FBS, 122 in the FCS (Football Championship Subdivision, formerly known as Division I-AA), and 98 Division I members without football programs. In sum, there are 340 Division I members (32% of the total membership); Division II has 290 members and Division III has 436 member schools (NCAA, 2012c).

It may seem that Division I FBS members exist as financial enterprises seeking to generate revenue from their athletics programs as well as gain national visibility for their university. How can this be when the fundamental policy of the Association at each divisional level (I, II, and III) is the same?

> Bylaw 1.3—FUNDAMENTAL POLICY. 1.3.1 Basic Purpose. The competitive athletics programs of member institutions are designed to be a vital part of the educational system. A basic purpose of this Association is to maintain intercollegiate athletics as an integral part of the educational program and the athlete as an integral part of the student body and, by so doing, retain a clear line of demarcation between intercollegiate athletics and professional sports. (NCAA Division I, II, III Manuals, 2012–13, p. 1)

While the fundamental policy of each division is the same, the membership requirements are different. Each division has different NCAA requirements pertaining to: required number of teams sponsored for men and women; number of contests and participation in each sport; financial aid requirements for the overall program; and, sport specific scheduling and attendance requirements (NCAA Division I, II, III Manuals, Bylaw 20, 2012–13). It appears that the membership requirements for Division III most accurately reflect the NCAA's fundamental policy; whereas, the membership requirements for Division I stray from the fundamental policy and instead move in the direction of market-based principles.

Consider how these differences play out at the university level. The athletic department mission statement at University of Texas at Austin (the NCAA Division I FBS member with the highest annual revenue, $163 million) reads:

> The Athletics Departments at The University of Texas at Austin are committed to The University's mission of achieving excellence in education, research, and public service. Specifically, our mission is focused on three interrelated communities: Student-Athletes: To provide

opportunities and support for University student-athletes to achieve academically and compete athletically at the highest level, and provide programming and resources that help prepare them with skills for life. University Community: To operate with quality and integrity in our role as a focal point for school identity and spirit, while complementing the academic, cultural, and social facets of University life for the general student body, faculty, staff, and alumni. Citizens of the State of Texas: To support the community through public service and to be a source of pride and entertainment by representing the state of Texas with internationally successful sport programs and thereby benefit the state economy. (Texas Longhorns Official Athletic Site, 2012)

With the addition of the third segment of Texas' athletic department mission, "Citizens of the State of Texas," Texas opens the door to commercializing its athletics program and commodifying the athlete. In keeping with these market-based principles, the University of Texas recently signed a 20-year, $300 million contract with ESPN establishing the Longhorn Network, a 24-hour television network showing Longhorn sports (*ESPN.com*, 2011). Nowhere in the NCAA's fundamental policy is it stated that the purpose of college athletics is to be a source of entertainment or benefit the state economy.

On the flip side, consider the purpose and mission of the Texas Lutheran University's athletic department (a NCAA Division III member):

The intercollegiate athletics program exists for the sake of the students at Texas Lutheran University in promoting growth and development. That philosophy also promotes the concept of being the best person one can be in the classroom and on the field. Intercollegiate athletics provides equal opportunity for talented male and female students to participate in a nationally competitive sports program that is values-based and educationally sound. Two primary goals are of interest to the student-athletes who participate in the program: 1. Every student-athlete who completes his/her eligibility is expected to graduate. 2. Each sport should aspire to be competitive at the conference, regional, and national levels. (Texas Lutheran University Catalog, 2012–2013, p. 203)

Texas Lutheran's goals do not include an "entertainment focus" or "economic value"; rather, Texas Lutheran stresses a " … student-centered athletic department which is value-based and educationally sound …" (Texas Lutheran University Catalog, 2012–13, p. 203). Clearly, Texas Lutheran's athletics department mission is more closely aligned with the NCAA's fundamental policy than is the University of Texas.

Issues in the NCAA

Escalation of Coaches' Salaries

Over the past two decades coaches' salaries have drastically increased. In 1995 Florida State University was the first institution to offer then-head football coach Bobby Bowden a $1 million salary; 17 of the top 25 football programs followed suit. According to NCAA findings, overall athletic salaries and benefits rose 35% from the 1997 to 1999. According to the National Center for Education Statistics, the national average-wage index rose by less than 6% annually while the average college faculty member salary increased at the rate of 3.5% ("Digest," 2008). Between 1997–98 and 2007–08, the average college faculty salary increased by 5.5% ("Digest," 2008). In just two years, athletic department salaries soared 35%, while over a decade faculty salaries have increased just 5.5%. Such a rapid escalation of college football and basketball coaches' salaries has left critics questioning whether the leaders of higher education have strayed from their fundamental mission of teaching and research in exchange for an athletic reputation.

A *USA Today* (2013) special report revealed the coaches' salaries for the 62 schools that participated in the NCAA men's basketball tournament. Fifty-eight percent of coaches made more than $1 million; 24% made more than $2 million. Of note, Mike Krzyzewski (Duke University) made $7.2 million plus an additional $2.5 million from 2012; Rick Pitino's (University of Louisville) total university pay was $5 million (*see* USA Today Coaches Salary Database for all 62 coaches' salaries).

In keeping with the market-based system of capitalism, if there is demand for college athletics (the "product") then the owners (the member institutions through the NCAA) can control the price. This model certainly fits with professional sports because the purpose of professional sports is to make money by entertaining the public. College athletics is supposed to be unique when compared to professional sports because the purpose of college athletics is to contribute to the education of students through athletics such that participation is an avocation (something one does in one's spare time) and the athlete is an amateur (one who receives no form of compensation for their athletic participation). (*see* the NCAA's Principle of Amateurism).

> Student-athletes shall be amateurs in an intercollegiate sport, and their participation should be motivated primarily by education and by the physical, mental and social benefits to be derived. Student participation in intercollegiate athletics is an avocation, and student-athletes

should be protected from exploitation by professional and commercial enterprises. (NCAA Division I, II, and III Manuals, 2012–13, Bylaw 2.9, p. 4)

It is puzzling that NCAA bylaws restrict only the athlete from receiving any form of compensation. Why aren't coaches considered amateurs as well? Both coaches and athletes "participate" in college athletics. Coaches, however, can command salaries that the market will bear and are free to maximize their earning potential by engaging in endorsement deals with corporations to advertise products in exchange for money; whereas, athletes are barred from doing the same. The problem is that billions of dollars are being generated as a result of the "labor" of college athletes but the athletes are not allowed to reap any of the financial benefits. At this point in time the financial trickle-down-effect reaches everyone involved in college athletics *except* the athletes themselves. Is this fair? What exactly is the "product"? Who is the most important "commodity"? Consider who is more likely to win a game: a coach without his players or the players without their coach? The problems associated with the commercialization of college sports are not new. Consider the comments made by former president of the Carnegie Foundation Dr. Henry Pritchett in 1925:

> The question is whether an institution in the social order whose primary purpose is the development of the intellectual life can at the same time serve as an agency to promote business, industry, journalism, salesmanship, and organized athletics on an extensive commercial basis. The question is not so much whether athletics in their present form should be fostered by the university, but how fully can a university that fosters professional athletics discharge its primary function.... How far can an agency, whose function is intellectual, go in the development of other causes without danger to its primary purpose? Can a university teach equally well philosophy and salesmanship? Can it both sponsor genuine education and at the same time train raw recruits for minor vocations? Can it concentrate its attention on securing teams that win, without impairing the sincerity and vigor of its intellectual purpose? (Cowley, 1999, p. 495)

Exploiting Amateur Athletes

So what is really meant when someone says that college athletes are being exploited? Let's consider the following definitions: *commercialization* means "to manage on a business basis for profit, to exploit for profit, and to debase in quality for more profit," *commodification* is "to turn (as an intrinsic value or a work of art) into a commodity." A *commodity* is defined as "an economic good, something useful or valued, and one that is subject to ready exchange or exploitation within a market," and *exploit* is "to use, especially for profit." Has big-time college sports fallen victim to commercialization? Are college athletes treated as commodities? How can this be the case when the NCAA's Principle of Amateurism is in direct conflict with these market-based principles?

Are big-time college athletes being exploited? If so, what can be done to rectify this problem? As far back as 1989, Telander recommended that college football create a semi-professional league (Age Group Professional Football League—AGPFL). Athletes would not have to be registered students at their respective university, but rather would receive a compensation package to include room and board, and one year of college tuition for each of the four years of professional college sport the athlete completes. In this system, athletes would have 10 years to utilize the tuition credit (Telander, 1989). Davis (1991) suggested that athletes be treated as employees in the university system. These students should be provided the same benefits and protections that employees of the university receive, thereby establishing a legal contract between the student (who is also an athlete) and the university—in other words, an employment relationship.

More than just clarifying the relationship between the athlete and the university, Carsonie (1991) suggested that the student should play a role in governance decisions that university athletic departments' and the NCAA make. The idea of a student vote, whereby a student representative from each team would be elected and then attend a meeting in which they would relay information back to their teammates concerning reform proposals that the NCAA is considering would be a step in the right direction. Carsonie (1991) admitted that this type of vote may require a college players union similar to that of the National Football League Players Association (NFLPA).

The NCAA has made considerable progress toward giving athletes a voice with the formation of the Student-Athlete Advisory Committee (SAAC) in 1989. The intent of this committee is to allow student-athlete input on NCAA activities and proposed legislation that affected student-athlete welfare (NCAA, 2012d). In 1997, the NCAA modified the SAAC so that each division has its own representation (currently, there are 79 students serving amongst the three committees) (NCAA, 2012d). Each SAAC, acting as the student-athlete voice, is responsible for reviewing proposed NCAA legislation. All three SAAC's have input within the Association; however, only Divisions II and III SAAC's are permitted to speak to legislative issues on the NCAA Convention floor (NCAA, 2012d). The Division I SAAC should seek to obtain more of a voice regarding legislative issues since Division I FBS athletic programs are responsible for generating the majority of the NCAA's revenue.

So as to encourage athletes to stay in college and compete for four full years, in 1996 then-executive director of the NCAA, Cedric Dempsey put forth the option of athletes receiving financial incentives. Dempsey also proposed the possibility of anticipated earnings and endorsement opportunities (Sack & Staurowsky, 1998). While Dempsey admitted that paying athletes based on their on-field play is a "gray area ethically speaking, he believed that athletes should have the opportunity to earn athletically related income" (Sack & Staurowsky, 1998, p. 143). Under Telander's (1989) proposal college athletes would be compensated for their athletic prowess that would be commensurate with their revenue generating capabilities for the university that they serve.

So what is to be done with the "student-athlete"? While numerous scholars have suggested that student-athletes should be considered employees the courts have not. Based on *Waldrep v. Texas Employers Insurance Association* (2000) college athletes are not considered employees, the athletic scholarship is not considered "pay" or "income," and athlete injuries are not covered under workers' compensation. Even former NCAA president Myles Brand recognized that there is friction between intercollegiate athletics as "educational" verses intercollegiate athletics as a "business enterprise." Brand (2006) acknowledged that many people feel that it is not appropriate for college sports to be engaged in business activity. In response to such criticisms, Brand commented, "nonsense ... this type of thinking is both a misinterpretation and a misapplication of amateurism. 'Amateur' defines the participants, not the enterprise. We should not be ambivalent about doing the business of college sports" (Brand, 2006).

In an effort to clarify amateurism, Otto and Otto (2013) investigated the logical consequences of the common understanding of amateurism in the context of big-time college sports (see Exhibit 4.2).

Exhibit 4.2: "Clarifying amateurism:
A logical approach to resolving the exploitation of college
athletes dilemma" (excerpt from Otto & Otto, 2013, p. 2–5)

The Problem
    Myles Brand recognized that there is friction between intercollegiate athletics as "educational" versus intercollegiate athletics as a "business enterprise."

Such recognition stems from the fact that the very purpose of the NCAA is " ... to maintain intercollegiate athletics as an integral part of the educational program and the athlete as an integral part of the student body and, by so doing, retain a clear line of demarcation between intercollegiate athletics and professional sports" (NCAA Division I Manual, 2012–2013, Bylaw 1.3.1, p. 1). Indeed, in acknowledging that many people feel that it is not appropriate for college sports to be engaged in business activity, Brand (2006) insisted that "we should not be ambivalent about doing the business of college sports" (p. 1).

The problem with Brand's reference to amateurism is that it is misleading. How so? Professor Brand is not arguing that college players are (or are not) amateurs. His focus is on the "enterprise" of intercollegiate sports, which, as far as he's concerned, is, and ought to be, regarded as a business. If players are indeed amateurs, that does not mean that collegiate sport is not a business. Clearly, Brand's intent is to *decouple* participants from that in which they participate, so that the status of one does not necessarily apply to the other, and hence, we are entirely free to do "the business of college sports." But in such a context, what about the players—are they, or are they not, amateurs; and what about the NCAA, what is its role? We shall show that such a context, properly defined, does indeed make a significant difference.

The word *amateur* is commonly defined as one who engages in a pursuit, study, science or sport as a pastime or an avocation rather than a profession. Since players receive no compensation, it is assumed that they are amateurs, and given Brand's "decoupling principle" the NCAA and its member schools appear to be able to "have their cake and eat it too." However, the NCAA's Principle of Amateurism (wherein "student-athletes shall be amateurs in an intercollegiate sport ... participation ... is an avocation, and student-athletes should be protected from exploitation by professional and commercial enterprises") raises a red flag (NCAA Division I Manual, 2012–2013, Bylaw 2.9, p. 4). Consider the following analysis:

> Let *x* be a participant in a pursuit, study, science or sport as an avocation rather than a profession, receiving no remuneration.

Now suppose the product of *x*'s activity results in commercial profit which, although not shared by *x*, is received by others. Since it is also commonly understood that *exploitation* consists in taking the fruits of another person's efforts, that is:

> *x* is exploited if some *y* other than *x* unfairly receives commercial
> profit generated by *x*'s activity,

it follows that although technically (on the common definition) *x* remains
an amateur, <u>it is also the case that *x* is exploited</u>. Yet, NCAA Bylaw 2.9 states
explicitly that, "student-athletes should be protected from exploitation by
professional and commercial enterprises."

In other words, in certain commercial contexts, <u>an implication</u> of the
common definition of the word "amateur"—together with the common
definition of "exploitation"—runs headlong into conflict with a clear requirement of NCAA Bylaw 2.9! Consequently, Professor Brand's "decoupling principle" has to be rejected. One way to do this might be to adopt a
more rigorous definition of "amateur."

A More Rigorous Definition of "Amateur"

Keep in mind that the problem posed in the foregoing section might be
dealt with in some other way than by amending the definition of "amateur"
(e.g. one could pursue the possibility of adjusting the definition of "exploitation"), but, for the moment, it is enlightening to consider the implications associated with a change in the concept of "amateur" as follows:

> *x* is an amateur if, and only if, **no one** receives commercial profit
> from *x*'s play, performance or talent.

In other words, if *x*'s playing results in commercial profit, even if *x* doesn't
receive a share of it, *x*'s playing (like any other product) is part of a commercial transaction, and, as such, cannot be construed as an amateur activity. Although such a definition assures against exploitation, it has the
unfortunate consequence that, if *x* is to be an amateur, then the "business
of college sports" has to stop—an unthinkable turn of events!

It appears, therefore, that although any pair of the following can co-exist
logically, all three of them together cannot:

> (1) *x* is an amateur
> (2) *x* is free from exploitation
> (3) *x*'s play is the basis of the business of college sports

Thus, there seems to be three options: (1) & (2) but not (3); (1) & (3) but
not (2); and (2) & (3) but not (1). Of these, the first invites the unthinkable in a capitalistic society (giving up the business of college sports); the
second writes in stone the unconscionable (continuing to exploit student-
athletes); while the third seems to be the only rational way out (give up am-

ateurism, pay the players, and concede that your sports program is not amateur).

In sum, by definition, x's playing can no longer be called, with any accuracy, "amateur." By extension, then, x is no longer an amateur, for x is the producer of the product—the games, and by extension their derivatives (for example, EA Sports video games and multi-billion dollar television contracts with major networks)—precisely that which is being sold. The fact that the schools and businesses point out that none of the proceeds go to x, only makes matters worse. This amounts to an admission that one party to the commercial transaction is being deprived of a share of the proceeds. By trying to insist that x is an amateur because x receives no remuneration, is simply to admit to a very troubling level of exploitation.

The Good and Bad of NCAA Academic Reforms

As a result of a renewed focus on the "student"-athlete, in 2004 the NCAA passed legislation that requires that athletes maintain certain progress toward earning a college degree. Athletes must complete "24 semester hours of credit before the start of the second year; 18 semester hours of credit since the beginning of the preceding regular two semesters; and, 6 semester hours of credit during the previous regular term" (NCAA Division I Manual, 2012–13, Bylaw 14.4.3.1, p. 172). Athletes must also adhere the "40-60-80 rule" which requires athletes to complete 40% of the classes required for a specific degree at the beginning of their third year; 60% by the beginning of their fourth year; and, 80% at the beginning of their fifth year (NCAA Division I Manual, 2012–13, Bylaw 14.4.3.2, p. 175).

While the intent of the progress-toward-degree requirements is good, practically speaking the requirement can be detrimental to athletes. As a result of the stringency of the "40-60-80" requirement athletes are forced to choose a major early in their academic career. Should an athlete be interested in changing majors (like many college students do) they may be forced to choose between remaining athletically eligible (i.e., meeting progress-toward-degree requirements) or majoring in an area of academic study that they are truly interested in pursuing.

A problem that exists for transfer students relates to the number of credit hours a school accepts. For example, if the school a transfer student is seeking to attend does not accept all of the credit hours from their prior institution, they may not meet the minimum progress-toward-degree requirements (i.e., 40% of their coursework toward their chosen degree at the beginning of their third year) in order to be eligible to compete athletically. The intent of the progress-toward-degree requirements is good; however, the requirements are too rigid which has a negative effect the athlete's ability to earn an education in their desired field of study.

Similar to the progress-toward-degree requirements, the NCAA described its Academic Progress Rate (APR) as part of "a comprehensive academic reform package designed to improve the academic success and graduation of all athletes" (NCAA, 2004, p. 1). Implemented in 2005, the APR measures athletes' progress toward graduation each semester. Each athletic team's APR is calculated and then a cumulative total for each institution's entire athletic department is reported to the NCAA. Each member school's athletic program must score a minimum of 930 out of a possible 1000 points.

Numerous problems exist with the APR. First, when a new coach is hired they may be left to deal with athletes who may not meet the universities requirements as it pertains to maintaining a minimum grade point average (GPA). For example, a coach may inherent a team with a player whose GPA is below a 2.0. This coach may decide that this player should not have the privilege of being a member of an athletic team since the athlete cannot uphold the academic standards of the university. However because of the stringency of the APR requirements, a coach who wishes to dismiss this player from the team is oftentimes discouraged from doing so since this would have a detrimental effect on the overall athletic departments' APR. The notion behind this is "retention," the APR seeks to keep its athletes in "good academic standing." What follows is a second problem; namely, the coach may be forced to engage in "hand-holding" in order to "retain" the athlete. The negative outcome in this case is that the academically underachieving athlete is not punished for earning poor grades; rather, he/she is rewarded by being allowed to remain a member of the team so as not to negatively affect the teams' APR. Third, mandating retention affects a coaches' ability to dole out the appropriate punishment for athlete misbehavior (for example, an athlete who should be dismissed from the team for engaging in illegal behavior such as drug involvement or criminal activity). Finally, an athletic team is penalized if an athlete leaves school early (i.e., transfers, enters the professional ranks, takes break from school) without having obtained at least a 2.5 GPA. The problem is that the APR does not take into account special situations nor does it allow for logical reasoning on the part of the athletic administrator as it pertains to making an appropriate determination based on the particular circumstances of the athlete.

Major Violations

A report showing institutions placed on NCAA probation between 1997 and 1998 revealed that at least 50% of the sanctioned schools listed would not be considered big-time intercollegiate athletic programs (Davis, 1999). A more recent study revealed that 44% of big-time programs (53 out of 120) were found to have committed major violations from 2001–2010 and there was a sharp increase in the number of serious academic violations (up from eight in the 1990s to 15) (Lederman, 2011). Researchers have yet to determine why there has been such a drastic increase in serious academic violations but Gene Marsh, former director of the Division I Committee on Infractions from 2004 to 2006, suggested that such an increase could be due in part to universities " … admitting more people who really don't belong [in college] and spending millions on academic support to keep them there" (Lederman, 2011). Researchers have also discovered that sanctions handed down by the NCAA have revealed inconsistent rulings raising doubts as to the policies and procedures used to set penalties. As a result of such inconsistency, it is difficult to assess whether or not the NCAA acts equitably in its enforcement of the rules (Otto, 2005; 2006).

Politics and the NCAA

Critics argue that the corruption in big-time college athletics is actually symptomatic of a larger problem; namely, the commercialization and marketization of higher education itself. As far back as the early 1800s colleges were willing to modify their curricula and programs to meet the demands of their sponsors and students (Burke, 1982). Initially, the leaders of higher education were clergy and professional educators; however, the new leadership, which came into being in the mid- to late 1800s, was increasingly business-minded and their focus turned to sport (Chu, 1989). Some institutions of higher education have compromised academic integrity for the primary economic benefits produced by athletes as well as secondary benefits in the form of national visibility, prestige, and enhanced university image (Davis, 1999).

In 2006, Gerdy stated, "It is time to acknowledge that American education's experiment with elite athletics has failed. Its negative impact on our academic values, educational institutions, and cultural priorities can no longer be ignored or rationalized away" (p. 10). Indeed, reform is born out of frustration with the current system.

Reform Movements

There are four major reform organizations seeking to affect change in intercollegiate athletics: the Knight Commission on Intercollegiate Athletics (KCIA); The Drake Group (TDG); the Coalition on Intercollegiate Athletics (COIA); and, the National College Players Association (NCPA).

Established in 1989 by former university presidents, the Knight Commission on Intercollegiate Athletics stresses the importance of presidential control, academic integrity, financial integrity and certification (Knight Commission, n.d.). In 2001, the Knight Commission pointed out that reform must be a collective effort to include college and universities presidents and trustees, national higher education associations such as the American Council on Education (ACE) and the Association of Governing Boards of Universities and Colleges (AGB), the NCAA and its members, college and university faculty, athletic directors, coaches, and even college and university alumni ("A Call to Action," 2001).

The Knight Commission seeks reform in the following areas:

1. Athletes should be mainstreamed through the same academic processes as other students, to include, more specifically criteria for admission, academic support services, choice of major, and requirement governing satisfactory degree progress.
2. Athletic programs that do not graduate at least fifty percent of their players should not be eligible for conference championships or for post-season play.
3. Scholarships should be tied to specific athletes until they (or their entering class) graduate.
4. The length of playing, practice, and post-seasons must be reduced both to afford athletes a realistic opportunity to complete their degrees and to enhance the quality of their collegiate experiences.
5. The National Basketball Association (NBA) and the National Football League (NFL) should be encouraged to develop minor leagues so that athletes not interested in undergraduate study are provided an alternative route to professional sports careers ("A Call to Action," 2001, p. 27).

Concerning the de-escalation of the athletics arms race, the Knight Commission proposed that budgets of the athletic departments be subject to the same institutional oversight and control as other university departments. Specifically, schools should work to:

1. Reduce expenditures in big-time sports such as football and basketball (this includes a reduction in the total number of scholarships that may be awarded in Division I FBS football).
2. Consider coaches' compensation in the context of the academic institutions that employ them.
3. Require that agreements for coaches' outside income be negotiated with institutions, not individual coaches.
4. Revise the plan for distribution of revenue from the NCAA contract with Columbia Broadcasting System (CBS) for broadcasting rights to the Division I men's basketball championship. No such revenue should be distributed based on commercial values such as winning and losing. Instead, the revenue distribution plan should reflect values centered on improving academic performance, enhancing athletes' collegiate experiences, and achieving gender equity. ("A Call to Action," 2001, pp. 27–28)

Finally, colleges and universities must take control of athletic programs away from television and similar corporate interests. With respect to this proposal, the Knight Commission (2001) made the following recommendations:

1. Insist that institutions alone should determine when games are played, how they are broadcast, and which companies are permitted to use athletics contests as advertising vehicles.
2. Encourage institutions to reconsider all sports-related commercial contracts against the backdrop of traditional academic values.
3. Work to minimize commercial intrusions in arenas and stadiums so as to maintain institutional control of campus identity.
4. Prohibit athletes from being exploited as advertising vehicles. Uniforms and other apparel should not bear corporate trademarks or the logos of manufacturer's normal label or trademark. ("A Call to Action," 2001, p. 28)

Founded in 1999, the mission of The Drake Group is to defend academic integrity in higher education from the corrosive aspects of commercialized college sports. Comprised of current and former university faculty, administrators, coaches and other concerned citizens, The Drake Group aggressively lobbies the U.S. Congress concerning proposals that ensure quality education for college athletes. The Drake Group also supports faculty whose job security is threatened for defending academic standards and disseminates information on current issues and controversies in sport and higher education (The Drake Group, n.d.). The Drake Group urges faculty senates and other academic bodies concerned with the integrity of American higher education to endorse the following proposals:

1. Academic transparency: Ensure that universities provide accountability of trustees, administrators and faculty by public transparency of such things as a student's academic major, advisor, courses listed by academic major, general education requirements, electives, course GPA and instructor (without revealing the names of individual students). Report the average SAT and ACT scores for revenue producing sports teams, non-revenue sports, and scholarship students in other extracurricular activities. Comparisons should be made regarding the number of independent study courses taken, grade changes by professors, and classes missed because of extracurricular demands.
2. Academic priority: Require that students, who are participating in athletics, maintain a cumulative GPA of 2.0 each semester to continue participation in intercollegiate athletics. Make the location and control of academic counseling and support services for athletes the same as is for all students. Establish university policies that will ensure that athletic contests and practices do not conflict with scheduled classes.
3. Academic-based participation: Replace one-year renewable scholarships with need-based financial aid (or) with multi-year athletic scholarships that extend to graduation (five-year maximum). Require one year in residency before an athlete can participate in intercollegiate sport. This rule would apply to transfer students as well as first year students. (The Drake Group, n.d.)

Founded in 2002, the Coalition on Intercollegiate Athletics (COIA) is an alliance of 56 Division I FBS university faculty senates whose aim is to promote comprehensive reform of intercollegiate sports. COIA is concerned with issues such as academic integrity, athlete welfare, governance of athletics at the school and conference level, and finances and commercialization ("COIA," n.d.). COIA works collaboratively with external groups including:

> The NCAA, the Association of Governing Bodies (AGB), the Knight Commission, the American Association of University Professors (AAUP), the National Athletic Academic Advisors Association (N4A), the Division IA Faculty Athletics Representatives, the Division IA Athletic Directors Association, the Faculty Athletics Representatives Association (FARA), the College Sports Project, and others to promote serious and comprehensive reform of intercollegiate sports. ("COIA," n.d.)

The long-range goal of COIA is to preserve and enhance the positive contributions athletics can make to academic life by addressing longstanding problems in college sports that undermine those contributions.

Founded in 2001, the National College Players Association (NCPA) is an advocacy group started by former UCLA football player Ramogi Huma. The mission of the NCPA is to provide the means for college athletes to voice their concerns. The goals of the NCPA include:

1. Raise the scholarship amount—"full scholarship" does not cover the basic necessities for a college athlete.
2. Secure health coverage for all sports-related workouts.
3. Increase graduation rates—the ultimate goal for a college athlete is not a scholarship, it's a degree.
4. Allow universities to grant multiple year scholarships (up to 5 years) instead of 1-year revocable scholarships.
5. Prohibit universities from using a permanent injury suffered during athletics as a reason to reduce/eliminate a scholarship.
6. Establish and enforce uniform safety guidelines in all sports to help prevent avoidable deaths.
7. Eliminate restrictions on legitimate employment.
8. Prohibit the punishment of college athletes that have not committed a violation
9. Guarantee that college athletes are granted an athletic release from their university if they wish to transfer schools.
10. Allow college athletes of all sports the ability to transfer schools one time without punishment. ("NCPA," n.d.)

Thus far, the NCPA has:

1. Introduced the Collegiate Student Athlete Protection Act to the U.S. Congress.
2. Assisted football players at Northwestern University in filing for union status with the National Labor Relations Board.
3. Helped establish a $10 million fund to assist former athletes who wish to complete their undergraduate degree or attend a graduate program.
4. Eliminated limits on health care for college athletes.
5. Increased the NCAA death benefit from $10,000 to $25,000.
6. Expanded the NCAA Catastrophic Injury Insurance Policy so that college athletes who suffer permanent, debilitating injuries can receive adequate home health care.
7. Implemented key safety guidelines to help prevent deaths during workouts.
8. Played a key role in a legal settlement that made over $445 million in direct benefits available to athletes of all sports.
9. Increased in the type of scholarship money players can receive.
10. Eliminated the $2000 salary cap on money earned from part-time jobs. ("NCPA," n.d.)

Most recently a group of college athletes led by former UCLA men's basketball star, Ed O'Bannon, successful challenged the NCAA on antitrust grounds regarding the ownership rights of athletes' names and likenesses (*O'Bannon v. NCAA*, 2014). The *O'Bannon* decision has lessened the NCAA's control over revenues generated by athletes' participation in sporting events and has called into question the financial restrictions the NCAA places on the athletes in the name of "amateurism." Another lawsuit, *Jenkins v. NCAA* (2014) seeks to allow athletes to sell their services to universities in a free-market system (putting an end to the NCAA's athletic-scholarship price-fixing scheme). Actions such as these are the first steps toward the goal of achieving fairness for all parties responsible for the college sports product.

Summary

College athletics has undergone a significant philosophical shift; what began as an Association established to curb the excessive violence in football has become a major business enterprise. Due to the increase in major violations which have resulted in national scandals in higher education, the extreme escalation of coaches' salaries, and the cry of athlete exploitation it is important to examine the role that athletics should play in our institutions of higher learning. Indeed critics have called for the NCAA and its members to return to an athletics system that is aligned with the mission, philosophy, and values of higher education.

References

Berkowitz, S., Upton, J., & Brady, E. (2013, May 10). Most NCAA DI athletic departments take subsidies. *USA Today*. Retrieved from http://www.usa today.com/story/sports/college/2013/05/07/ncaa-finances-subsidies/2142443/.

Brand, M. (2006, September 11). President's message—Call for moderation is a complex message, not a mixed one. *The NCAA News Online*. Retrieved from http://www.ncaa.org/wps/portal/ncaahome?WCM_GLOBAL_CON TEXT=/ncaa/NCAA/Media+and+Events/Press+Room/News+Release+ Archive/2006/Official+Statements/NCAA+President+Delivers+State+Of+ The+Association+Address.

Burke, C.B. (1982). *American collegiate populations: A test of the traditional view*. New York, NY: New York University.

Carsonie, F.W. (1991). Educational values: A necessity for reform of big-time intercollegiate athletics. *Capital University Law Review, 20,* 661–690.

Chu, D. (1989). *The character of American higher education and intercollegiate sport.* New York, NY: State University of New York.

Coalition on Intercollegiate Athletics. (n.d.). Retrieved from http://blogs.comm.psu.edu/thecoia/.

Collegiate Student Athlete Protection Act. (2013, November 20). H.R.3545.

Cowley, W.H. (1999). Athletes in American colleges. *The Journal of Higher Education, 70,* 494–502.

Davis, R.N. (1991). Athletic reform: Missing the bases in university athletics. *Capital University Law Review, 20,* 597–609.

Davis, T. (1999). Sports law in the 21st century: Intercollegiate athletics in the next millennium: A framework for evaluating reform proposals. *Marquette Sports Law Journal, 9,* 1–20.

Digest of Education Statistics. (2008). Retrieved from http://nces.ed.gov/programs/digest/d08/.

Equity in Athletics Disclosure Act. (2011). Retrieved from http://ope.ed.gov/athletics/.

ESPN.com (2011, January 19). Texas, ESPN announce new network. Retrieved from http://sports.espn.go.com/espn/news/story?id=6037857.

ESPN College Sports (2011, December 15). NCAA, ESPN agree to new deal. Retrieved from http://espn.go.com/college-sports/story/_/id/7357065/ncaa-espn-agree-tv-deal-2023-24.

Falla, J. (1981). *NCAA: The voice of college sports.* Mission, KS: National Collegiate Athletic Association.

Fulks, D.L. (2013). 2004–2012 *Revenues and expenses of Division I intercollegiate athletics programs report.* Retrieved from http://ncaapublications.com/p-4306-revenues-and-expenses-2004-2012-ncaa-division-i-intercollegiate-athletics-programs-report.aspx.

Gerdy, J. R. (2006). *Air ball: American education's failed experiment with elite athletics.* Jackson, Mississippi: University Press of Mississippi.

Jenkins v. NCAA, Case 3:33-av-00001 (U.S. Dist. N.J. Mar. 17, 2014).

Knight Commission on Intercollegiate Athletics. (n.d.). Retrieved from http://www.knightcommission.org/.

Knight Foundation Commission on Intercollegiate Athletics. (2001). *A call to action: Reconnecting college sports and higher education.* Miami FL: John S. and James L. Knight Foundation.

Lapchick, R.E., & Slaughter, J.B. (1994). *The Rules of the game: Ethics in college sports.* Phoenix, AZ: American Council on Education and The Oryx.

Lederman, D. (2011, February 7). Half of big-time NCAA programs had major violations. *USA Today.* Retrieved from http://usatoday30.usatoday.com/sports/college/2011-02-07-ncaa-infractions_N.htm.

National College Players Association. (n.d.). Retrieved from http://www.ncpanow.org/.

National Collegiate Athletic Association. (2004). NCAA Board of Directors Adopts Landmark Academic Reform Package. *NCAA News*. Retrieved from http://www.ncaa.org/releases/divi/2004/2004042901d1.htm.

National Collegiate Athletic Association. (2012a). *Corporate Relationships*. Retrieved from http://www.ncaa.org/wps/wcm/connect/corp_relations/corprel/corporate+relationships/index.html.

National Collegiate Athletic Association. (2012b). *Licensee Agreements*. Retrieved from http://www.ncaa.org/wps/wcm/connect/corp_relations/corprel/corporate+relationships/licensing/licensees.html#Internal.

National Collegiate Athletic Association. (2012c). *Membership*. Retrieved from http://www.ncaa.org/wps/wcm/connect/public/NCAA/About+the+NCAA/Membership+NEW.

National Collegiate Athletic Association. (2012d). *Student-Athlete Advisory Committee*. Retrieved from http://web1.ncaa.org/committees/committees_roster.jsp?CommitteeName=1SAAC.

National Collegiate Athletic Association. (2012e). *The History of the NCAA*. Retrieved from http://www.ncaa.org/wps/wcm/connect/public/ncaa/about+the+ncaa/history.

National Collegiate Athletic Association. (2012f). *Trademarks*. Retrieved from http://www.ncaa.org/wps/wcm/connect/corp_relations/corprel/corporate+relationships/corporate+alliances/trademarks.html.

National Collegiate Athletic Association. *2012–2013 NCAA Division I Manual*. Retrieved Indianapolis, IN: National Collegiate Athletic Association.

National Collegiate Athletic Association. *2012–2013 NCAA Division II Manual*. Indianapolis, IN: National Collegiate Athletic Association.

National Collegiate Athletic Association. *2012–2013 NCAA Division III Manual*. Indianapolis, IN: National Collegiate Athletic Association.

National Collegiate Athletic Association. (2013). *Annual Budget*. Retrieved from http://www.ncaa.org/wps/wcm/connect/public/ncaa/finances/revenue.

National Labor Relations Board, Region 13, Case 13-RC-121359 (Mar. 26, 2014).

O'Bannon v. NCAA, No. C 09-3329 CW (N.D. Cal. Aug. 8, 2014).

Otto, K. A. (2005). Major violations and NCAA 'powerhouse' football programs: What are the odds of being charged? *Journal of Legal Aspects of Sport, 15*(1), 39–57.

Otto, K. A. (2006). Is the NCAA guilty of practicing "selective enforcement"? An analysis of Division I men's basketball rankings, investigations, infractions and penalties. *Sport Management and Related Topics Journal, 3*(1), 5–13.

Otto, K. A., & Otto, H. R. (2013). Clarifying amateurism: A logical approach to resolving the exploitation of college athletes' dilemma. *Sport, Ethics, and Philosophy, 7*(2), 259–270.

Reimann, P. A. (2004). The G.I. Bill and collegiate football recruiting after World War II. *International Sports Journal, 8*(2), 126–133.

Sack, A. L., & Staurowsky, E. J. (1998). *College athletes for hire: The evolution and legacy of the NCAA's amateur myth.* Westport, CT: Praeger.

Savage, H. J, Bentley, H. W., McGovern, J. T., & Smiley, M. D. (1929). *The Carnegie Commission Report.* The Carnegie Foundation. Retrieved from http://www.carnegiefoundation.org/publications/pub.asp?key=43&subkey=990.

Smith, R. K. (2000). A brief history of the National Collegiate Athletic Association's role in regulating intercollegiate athletics. *Marquette Sports Law Review, 11,* 9–22.

Telander, R. (1989). *The hundred yard lie: The corruption of college football and what we can do to stop it.* New York, NY: Simon and Schuster.

Texas Longhorns Official Athletic Department Site. (2012). *Mission Statement.* Retrieved from http://www.texassports.com/school-bio/mission-statement.html.

Texas Lutheran University Catalog. (2012–2013). *Intercollegiate Athletics Program.* Retrieved from http://www.tlu.edu/ftpimages/527/misc/misc_84004.pdf.

The Drake Group. (n.d.). Retrieved from http://www.thedrakegroup.org/.

United States Department of Education. (n.d.). Retrieved from http://www.ed.gov/index.jhtml.

USA Today Coaches' Salaries Database (2013). Retrieved from http://www.usatoday.com/sports/college/salaries/ncaab/coach/.

Waldrep v. Texas Employers Insurance Association, 21 S.W.3d 693 (Tex. App. 2000).

Chapter 5

North American Professional Sports: Creating a Competitive Balance

Mark S. Nagel & Matthew T. Brown,
University of South Carolina

Competitive Balance

Professional sport leagues operate differently than other businesses. While the main goal of most companies is to dominate and potentially eliminate competitors, individual franchises in professional sports' leagues such as the National Basketball Association (NBA), National Football League (NFL), National Hockey League (NHL), and Major League Baseball (MLB) exist as quasi-socialist franchisee-franchisor cartels (Scully, 1995). The main purpose of a league is to ensure that each individual franchise remains financially solvent and that profits continually increase. To reach these goals, leagues typically enact rules and regulations to maintain competitive balance so that no one team or small group of teams wins an inordinate amount of games or generates extremely high revenues relative to the rest of the league's teams. If a small number of teams dominate the league, competitive imbalance—the inability of certain teams to win enough games to attract fans and generate revenues—can occur. Competitive imbalance can have detrimental long-term effects since the stronger teams will eventually be unable to generate interest for their games against poorer-performing teams.

Attaining competitive balance, or parity, is often difficult because each franchise operates in a unique "local" market. Teams located in the largest metropolitan areas such as New York, Los Angeles, and Chicago will have an inherent advantage because these cities have more people to purchase tickets and other game-related products such as parking and concessions, a greater number of potential corporations to lease luxury suites and buy club seating, and many local media outlets bidding for the rights to broadcast the team's games. Though it may be exciting for fans in these large markets to see their team sign the best free agents and continually win the majority of their games, such an outcome does not necessarily create interest for the other teams in smaller markets or, potentially, enhance the overall value of the league's brand. There are a variety of rules that leagues have enacted to create an environment that fosters competitive balance. A player draft, first conducted by the NFL in 1936 ("Pro football draft...," n. d.) and later implemented by each of the other major North American professional sports leagues, "rewards" poorly performing teams by awarding them higher draft picks. Typically, the worst performing team during the season will "earn" the first pick in every round of the upcoming draft and the league champion will be awarded the last pick in each round. Every other team will draft in between the highest and lowest-performing team according to the inverse order of their success during the past season. In theory, this will allow the teams with the greatest "need" for an infusion of new players the best opportunity to acquire them since drafted players may only negotiate with the team that made the selection. Although there have been rare instances where selected players have refused to sign, in the vast majority of cases drafted players begin their careers as soon as possible after the draft. Of course, each team must be responsible for determining the best players to pick and there are no guarantees that they will make the "correct" selections. Each league uses a draft to assign incoming high school, college players, or international players. Some leagues, such as MLB, also utilize other drafts to disburse current minor league players throughout the league.

Exhibit 5.1: NBA Draft Lottery

Unlike the other major North American professional sports leagues, franchises in the National Basketball Association can be instantly and dramatically changed with the addition or subtraction of one superstar player, since there are only five players on the court at one time and the best players will usually play more than three-quarters of every game. In the late 1970s and early 1980s, some teams perceived that their best opportunity to achieve long-term success was to acquire the highest draft pick possible by losing games. The NBA awarded the first pick in the draft to the winner of a coin flip between the teams with the worst record in Western and Eastern Conferences, so "unsuccessful" teams with poor records often decided to "tank" games by limiting their best players' minutes or by sitting "injured" players late in a season once a playoff berth was not a possibility ("Why does tanking…," 2007).

During the 1983–1984 NBA season, the Houston Rockets attracted attention from the NBA, the media and fans as it made a series of questionable playing-time decisions during the second half of the season ("Coin flip to…," 2008). Many suspected that the Rockets worked to lose games to have a chance to win the coin-flip to then pick University of Houston center Akeem Olajuwon. After the Rockets did win the coin-flip and selected Olajuwon first, the NBA announced that the 1985 draft order for the seven non-playoff teams would be determined by a "draft lottery." The 1985 lottery created considerable excitement as the winner would likely select Georgetown University center Patrick Ewing. Despite having the worst record in the league, the Golden State Warriors "lost" the lottery and selected seventh in the 1985 draft. The New York Knicks, who had a better 1984–1985 record than the Warriors, won the lottery and eventually did select Ewing. The 1985 lottery did create some controversy as some pundits continue to claim that the NBA had a vested interest in seeing its signature franchise in New York draft the best player (Simmons, 2007).

Though it has denied any conspiracy, the NBA did make numerous changes to its lottery process. In 1987, the lottery only identified the teams selecting in the first three positions. Every other team would draft according to the inverse order of their record starting with the fourth selection. In 1990, the lottery was altered to allow the 11 teams not making the playoffs to have a number of chances related to their record. The worst team received 11 chances and the best non-playoff team received one chance. This format was changed in 1994 after the Orlando Magic won the lottery two years in a row, the second after having the best record of the non-playoff teams. The current format provides the team with the worst record a 25% chance to win while the team with the best non-playoff record has a .5% chance to win. Though these changes have occurred, there is still a question regarding the "best" possible lottery format. The NBA has recently investigated a "wheel" proposal that would allocate each franchises' draft slot for the next 30 years in advance to remove any incentive to "tank" (Lowe, 2013).

Professional sports leagues have also implemented rules that make drafted players the "property" of teams for a set period of time. For many years, players in each professional sport's league had few rights to determine their employment conditions. Leagues utilized "reserve rules" that tied a player to its team in perpetuity. Fortunately for the players, starting in the 1960s, *play-*

ers associations began to exert more pressure upon the owners during the *collective-bargaining* process. The Major League Baseball Players Association (MLBPA) became the most-powerful sports' union under Marvin Miller. Though Miller's initial demands involved working conditions, increasing pension payments, and the rights for players to profit from their likenesses, by the 1970s the players had also won the right to free agency (Miller, 1991). Free agency typically permits players to determine their "true" market value as every team has the potential opportunity to sign free agents. Once a player has been drafted he cannot become a free agent until he has attained the required service time (typically 4 to 6 years in the North American professional leagues). Before becoming a free agent, most players have their salaries artificially depressed because they typically have no leverage (beyond retiring prematurely or playing overseas if that is available) in salary negotiations with their team.

Unlike other professional sports, in Major League Baseball players have the right to *salary arbitration*, a process whereby an independent "judge" determines if the team's submitted salary or the player's salary will be chosen. The MLBPA initially negotiated the right to arbitration in 1973 and has consistently insisted that arbitration remain a key component of the MLB Collective Bargaining Agreement (Haupert, 2007). Every player with at least three years of MLB service time, as well as the top 17% of players (by service days in MLB) with two plus years of experience are eligible for salary arbitration if they are unable to reach a salary agreement with their team (Ray, 2008). Though most players come to an agreement with their club before proceeding to arbitration, the limited number of arbitration cases each year is closely monitored by both the players and owners to determine if there are any arbitration "trends."

Exhibit 5.2: Antitrust Law in Professional Sport: *Flood v. Kuhn*

Curt Flood was an outstanding outfielder for the St Louis Cardinals in the 1960s. He was a key member of the 1964 and 1967 World Series Champions and also appeared in three All-Star Games and won seven Gold Glove Awards. Despite his numerous on-field accomplishments, Flood will always be remembered for his failed attempt to institute free agency in baseball via the courtroom.

At the end of the 1969 season, the Cardinals traded Flood and other players to the Philadelphia Phillies. Flood refused to report to the Phillies despite his $100,000 playing contract and demanded that he be declared a free agent in direct opposition to MLB's established *reserve clause* that bound a player to a team forever—even after his contract had been fulfilled. Baseball Commissioner Bowie Kuhn denied Flood's request citing the provisions of the MLB standard playing contract. MLBPA President Marvin Miller and the union supported Flood's refusal to report and provided financial assistance for Flood's lawsuit, which claimed that MLB's reserve rules were a violation of *antitrust law* because they unfairly restricted the ability of players to bargain for their services (*Flood v. Kuhn*, 1972). Baseball Commissioner Bowie Kuhn and the owners fought the lawsuit all the way to the United States Supreme Court where, in a 5–3 decision, the owners prevailed as the court upheld a 1922 ruling that had declared MLB immune from antitrust scrutiny (*Federal Baseball Club v. National League*). Though Flood did return to play for the Washington Senators in 1971, his one-year hiatus and the time devoted to the lawsuit had diminished his skills. After playing poorly in 1971, Flood retired. Free agency would not be allowed in MLB until 1975 when arbitrator Peter Seitz ruled that players who played an additional year past the completion of their contracts were eligible for free agency.

Though Flood was unsuccessful in his lawsuit, he has been remembered as an important figure in professional sports history. Flood's stance began to alter many fans' perceptions of baseball's employment rules. Though Flood died in 1997, the United States Congress passed the Curt Flood Act of 1998 that removed MLB's antitrust exemption with regards to certain labor issues.

One of the main concerns for leagues is the individual team's pursuit of free agents. Certainly, any employee utilizes a variety of factors such as location, work environment, and the potential relationship with colleagues and supervisors, when evaluating job opportunities. However, for most, potential salary is a primary concern. In professional sports, potential salary is even more paramount because the average playing career only lasts a few years. Since player salaries are paid by individual franchises, leagues must create an environment where each team has financial resources to scout future players, re-sign their own players, and potentially bid for free agents. This is done primarily through two mechanisms: salary caps and revenue sharing.

Salary Caps

A salary cap limits the compensation an employer may provide to its employees. In sports, a salary cap is designed to restrict salaries for teams across an entire league—ideally creating an economic environment where every team can be assured of cost containment as well as an opportunity to compete for player services. Professional sports' owners cannot unilaterally implement a salary cap; they must negotiate with the players through the collective bargaining process. Each league has negotiated a variety of formats regarding potential player compensation with their players.

NBA Salary Cap

Although there had been unofficial and official salary caps in professional baseball before the 1930s, the first modern salary cap was implemented in 1983 by the NBA (Nagel, 2005). Numerous NBA teams had been struggling financially in the late 1970s and early 1980s, and concern existed that teams in larger markets (such as New York, Los Angeles, and Chicago) would be able to outspend teams in smaller markets (such as Utah, Indiana, and Cleveland) to the point that smaller market teams would have considerably diminished on-court performances which might cause some franchises to declare bankruptcy and potentially cease operations. The NBA owners and players agreed to a salary cap to mitigate the potential for a small group of teams to sign all of the best players. Each year the NBA owners and players calculate the league salary cap based upon overall league revenues. Though the cap has typically increased each year, in 2009 the cap decreased slightly from around $58 million to roughly $57 million due to a loss of overall league revenues—partially related to the economic recession throughout the world (Abrams, 2009). From 2010 to 2012, the NBA salary cap remained at approximately $58 million each season, but it then increased to $63 million in 2013. It is expected to increase dramatically once the NBA signs its next series of television deals that commence after the 2015–2016 season (Lowe, 2014). The NBA salary cap was designed, in theory, to maintain a level-salary field for every team in the league. However, given the nature of the sport of basketball, it quickly became apparent that the loss of one or two players from a 15-player roster could radically alter the quality of a team's performance. For this reason, the NBA instituted a variety of rules that allowed individual teams to circumvent the cap. The most prominent rule, the "Larry Bird Exemption"—so named because the Boston Celtics were concerned that the potential loss of Larry Bird to free agency would devastate their team—allows teams, in most cases, to re-sign their "own" potential free agents for salaries that would otherwise cause the team to exceed the designated yearly salary cap. This has created an environment where teams drafting quality players typically have an advantage in salary negotiations, as free agents can usually re-sign with their team for greater compensation than they can receive from other franchises. The length and complexity of the NBA's salary cap often causes confusion among journalists and fans. To mitigate this confusion, the NBA has released detailed salary cap information (Coon, 2014).

The 1998–1999 NBA season was condensed due to a *lockout* of the players by the owners. One of the owners' concerns was the escalating salaries of the league's top players. For instance, during the 1997–1998 season Michael Jordan's salary was $36 million while the Chicago Bull's team salary cap limit was $26.9 million. The lockout resulted in the NBA and the players agreeing to limit individual player salaries in addition to team salaries. A certain number of players were permitted to have their current salaries that exceeded the individual cap grandfathered into the NBA collective bargaining agreement. The lockout also resulted in a draft salary slotting system, which was designed to limit the compensation of players' initial contracts. Players were limited in their initial salaries but once they achieved free agency, they could negotiate among all the teams, potentially dramatically increasing their salaries.

The NBA owners locked out the players at the start of the 2011–2012 season. The owners were seeking to institute a "hard" salary cap, limit the length of player contracts from seven years to four, and reduce the players' share of Basketball Related Income (BRI) (specific revenues allocated to the formulation of the salary cap) from 57% to less than 47%. The players resolved to negotiate a new collective bargaining agreement that did not dramatically alter the NBA player-compensation model. In December 2011, the players and owners announced a new collective bargaining agreement that retained a soft salary cap and established BRI at a rate between 49% and 51% depending on overall league revenues.

NFL Salary Cap

The NFL implemented a salary cap system in 1993 in an effort to maintain competitive balance among its franchises. The NFL cap system, similar to the NBA's, has a maximum team salary and is based each year upon the overall league revenues. The NFL's system also has a team salary floor (minimum amount paid in salaries per team) that was created to appease the concerns that players had regarding the unwillingness of some NFL owners to participate in the bidding for player services. Unlike the NBA salary system where numerous loopholes exist to exceed the cap, the NFL cap has a "hard" ceiling that must be maintained each year.

However, the NFL salary cap can be manipulated with the use of signing bonuses. If an NFL player signs a four-year, $4 million contract, each year his salary will count $1 million against the NFL teams' salary cap, and the player will receive $1 million during each season. Unfortunately, since NFL contracts are usually not guaranteed, the player risks not receiving all of the money if he is released (due to injury, ineffectiveness, etc.) by the club before each year of the contract is fulfilled. For this reason, players like bonuses that are paid immediately upon signing the contract. If the aforementioned example is augmented with a $4 million signing bonus in addition to the $4 million for the four-year contract, the player receives $5 million in the first year of the contract, and the team is able to allocate $2 million a year to its salary cap total. If this player were to be cut after playing two years, he would only "lose" $2 million. Though the team will not have to pay the remaining years of salary on the contract, it will have to account for the remaining $2 million from the signing bonus on its salary cap. NFL teams have relied upon the continued escalation of the salary cap to provide additional space for "dead" salary cap money. Numerous long-term NFL contracts that provide large up-front signing bonuses are signed with both parties knowing that there is a small likelihood that the contract will be completed but that both parties will be satisfied with the agreement. As long as revenues continue to escalate, the salary floor and ceiling will also escalate, enabling teams to continue to manipulate the salary cap limits. After many years of dramatic NFL salary cap increases, since 2011 the salary cap has increased at a slow rate from $120.3 million to $120.6 million and then to $123 million in 2013. This has caused many NFL veterans to have to restructure their contracts or be cut due to NFL teams assuming consistent, year-over-year increases in the salary cap (Barnwell, 2013).

Even during times of rapid salary cap growth, the use of signing bonuses to circumvent the NFL cap in the short term is not without repercussions. In the 1990s, the Dallas Cowboys and other teams utilized signing bonuses to pay numerous players large salaries in the hopes of winning championships. The Cowboys were able to field successful teams in the short term, but as players retired, became injured, etc. the team was unable to sign other players under the cap as they had "mortgaged" their future with past signing bonuses (Nagel, 2005).

The NFL owners locked out the players prior to the 2011 season because they wished to retain a greater share of the overall revenues, create an 18-game schedule, and to institute a more restrictive rookie wage scale. Though the owners and players held contentious negotiations throughout the late spring and early summer of 2011, they eventually agreed to an amicable split of the $9 billion in NFL revenue. Though a new rookie wage scale was implemented and there were some minor changes in other areas of the collective bargaining agreement, the overall revenue sharing and player compensation models were retained.

NHL Salary Cap

For many years, the National Hockey League owners had desired to implement a salary cap. The players had previously resisted the implementation of a salary cap during collective bargaining negotiations. The 1994–1995 season was nearly canceled when the owners locked out the players, but a partial season was played after the owners reluctantly agreed to forego demands for a salary cap. However, the 2004–2005 season was canceled when the owners demanded a salary cap and the players refused to acquiesce. After the owners canceled the first complete season in North American professional sports history, the players reluctantly agreed to return for the 2005–2006 season with a salary cap in place. In addition, the players allowed the value of every contract to be decreased by 24% (Fitzpatrick, 2005).

The NHL's salary cap is similar to the NFL's as it has a floor and ceiling that are based upon league revenues. However, the NHL's cap does not allow the use of many "creative accounting" methods. Signing bonuses and other incentives are not as likely to be included in an NHL contract. Further, teams must be careful when signing long-term deals as the Collective Bargaining Agreement limits a team's ability to restructure an existing contract and specific rules can penalize a team for having an older player retire while under contract (Fitzpatrick, n.d.).

MLB Salary Cap

Despite having official and unofficial salary caps during various times during the early part of MLB's history in the 19th century, the Major League Baseball Players Association (MLBPA) has adamantly opposed any salary cap system. On August 12, 1994, the MLB players went on strike to protest a potential salary cap. The strike eventually caused the cancelation of the World Series for the first time since 1904. Though the players "won" the dispute since they avoided a salary cap, the cancelation of the World Series and the perceived greed of the players and owners caused outrage among fans. Major League Baseball players have remained adamant that they will work to avoid the implementation of a salary cap in the future (Bloom, 2009).

Revenue Sharing

Though the potential implementation and operation of salary caps are an important concern for professional sports' owners and players, of equal importance is revenue sharing. A salary cap attempts to balance the potential spending on players, while revenue sharing is designed to narrow the potential financial resources' gap of the participating teams. Though revenue sharing can be applied to team and league revenues, individual owners may have various sources of revenue from other businesses. The inequality of these non-league revenue sources can become a concern since some owners may be able to lower their team's profit margin or potentially take a yearly financial loss since the team may not need to be financially successful to maintain the owners' current lifestyle. For instance, since Robert Sarver bought the team in 2004, the Phoenix Suns has sold two first round draft picks to the Portland Trailblazers and have practically "given away" players such as Kurt Thomas and other first round draft picks in order to save money (Coro, 2007; Haller, 2007). Sarver operates his team with the financial bottom-line as his primary concern. This certainly can be frustrating for fans who want to see their team consistently strive to win championships (Simmons, 2008). Though it is difficult for leagues to maintain a completely equal financial environment, they do utilize a variety of revenue sharing methods to mitigate potential discrepancies. North American professional sports leagues equally share revenues from "national" media contracts. The sharing of national television revenue permits every team to generate the same revenue regardless of their number of national television appearances. Though every league shares national television revenues, this sharing mechanism has varying impacts. Since the NFL plays a 16-game once-a-week schedule, every game is broadcast through a national television contract resulting in a much greater percentage of overall league revenues being shared than in other leagues. The NBA and NHL play an 82-game schedule and Major League Baseball has a 162-game schedule, which means there are many potential games played each week of the season. Though some MLB, NBA, and NHL games are broadcast via an equally shared national television agreement, the vast majority of these games will be broadcast through an unshared "local" television agreement. Since the local television market of each team is a different size, the potential for generating revenue can vary considerably. For instance, the large population difference between the New York metropolitan area and the Minneapolis-St. Paul metropolitan area results in millions of additional potential media dollars for New York teams in MLB, the NBA, and the NHL. Market-size differences have been exacerbated by the recent proliferation of Regional Sport Networks (RSN). These cable stations generate money through advertising and subscription fees, and, unlike traditional over-the-air television stations, will typically elect to broadcast as many games as the local team permits. Regional Sport Networks have provided large-market franchises with a tremendous financial advantage over their small-market competitors.

Exhibit 5.3: Single-entity or franchise structure?

Though most North American professional sports leagues operate with a franchisor-franchisee structure, there have been attempts to utilize a single-entity structure where owners purchase shares in the league rather than in an individual franchise. A single-entity structure results in the league office handling all player transactions such as negotiating contracts and assigning players to individual teams. This insures that players are disbursed throughout the league in a manner that encourages competition, which should increase potential fan interest. In addition, under a single-entity structure, the league office will negotiate sponsorship and media contracts for the entire league and will insure that revenues are shared in a manner that maintains each team's ability to remain financially solvent.

A single-entity structure will typically lower potential league costs as individual owners are not able to sign players to salaries that do not conform to the overall goals of the league. In addition, the league office can insure cost containment for travel, equipment and team staff. Though a single-entity structure provides some financial benefits, critics have argued that it reduces the incentive for individual franchises to maximize their revenues (Mickle & Lefton, 2008). Most professional sport franchises generate a substantial portion of their revenues from "local" sources. Though the league office may be able to effectively negotiate national sponsorship agreements, local sponsorships are difficult to identify and foster. In addition, if there is no incentive for individual teams to increase revenues, creative marketing activities that would attract additional customers are less likely to occur, negatively impacting the entire league. The Women's National Basketball Association (WNBA) initially operated under a single-entity structure, but soon switched to a franchisee-franchisor model to encourage the maximization of local revenues. The WNBA Commissioner at the time, Donna Orender, noted, "While the launch model was successful, it became evident that owners wanted more control" (Mickle & Lefton, 2008, para. 10). As individual owners exert greater marketing and financial control in a franchisee-franchisor model, the potential for large revenue discrepancies can occur, which could negatively impact overall competitive balance.

Major League Soccer (MLS) began play as a single-entity league in 1996. Though the single-entity model enabled the league to build their fan base slowly, some of the players argued that the league structure unfairly decreased player salaries. In *Fraser v. Major League Soccer* (2000), a group of players filed an antitrust suit against the MLS claiming that the league's structure unfairly restrained trade since players could not bargain their services among the different MLS teams. The league countered that the single-entity structure prevented any unfair restraint of trade because one individual entity cannot conspire with itself to hurt the marketplace ("Court accepts...," 2000). In addition, the league argued that competition for player services had increased since the MLS was founded as before 1996 there was no viable Division I professional soccer league in the United States. The court eventually ruled in favor of MLS, determining that its single-entity structure, though unusual for North American professional sports, was legal under antitrust laws. Though the players lost the case, the attention generated by the lawsuit led to the league and the players negotiating increased player benefits in the future. In addition, as the MLS became profitable, greater player salary flexibility was implemented, new investors were attracted and the league began to discuss the possibility of switching to a franchisee-franchisor model (Wagman, 2008).

Maintaining Financial Viability

The recent growth of the Internet has provided North American professional sports leagues with an opportunity to equally share revenue streams from "emerging" media sources. The Internet is certainly one of the most powerful marketing tools ever invented. However, the use of the Internet to generate revenues is still in its infancy. In 2000, Major League Baseball created Major League Baseball Advanced Media (MLBAM) to investigate and manage future new media opportunities in areas such as online game streaming. MLBAM controls each of the team's websites and generates revenues that benefit the entire league. Though the MLB owners voted unanimously to create MLBAM, the National Hockey League encountered resistance from the New York Rangers when it attempted to control every team's website. In 2007, the Rangers sued the NHL when the league threatened to fine the Rangers $100,000 a day for failure to relinquish control of the nyranger.com website. The Rangers eventually lost the case and the NHL was able to recreate the Rangers' website to match the format of the other teams ("Madison Square Garden sues...," 2007).

Though the Rangers' dispute with the NHL created tremendous headlines, it did reinforce a common concern among some owners of professional sports teams. The Rangers believed that the loss of control of their website eliminated some of their incentive to maximize their marketing efforts. Teams that receive revenue sharing dollars from the league may elect to *free ride* on the efforts of more successful teams. For instance, the four major North American sports leagues all equally share revenues from licensed merchandise sales. The only money that is retained solely by teams is from sales of products in a team's facility or local team stores (Brown et al., 2010). In addition, revenues from league national sponsorship deals are shared equally. This creates a scenario where poorly performing teams or teams that elect to minimize their marketing efforts receive financial benefits from the "extra" efforts of the more successful teams. Dallas Cowboy owner Jerry Jones has been critical of many other NFL owners who he feels have failed to maximize their revenue opportunities (Helyar, 2006). While Jones invests heavily in marketing endeavors to advance the Dallas Cowboy brand, other owners appear content to retain a smaller marketing staff and a lower advertising budget while they financially benefit from Jones' efforts.

The Cowboys are certainly not the only large market team in the four major professional sport leagues to complain about the detriments of revenue sharing, but their complaints are certainly the "loudest" since the NFL shares much more of its revenues than other leagues. The NBA and NHL do not share any revenue generated from gate receipts, while the National League of MLB shares 5% and the American League of MLB shares 20% with the visiting team (Dobson & Goddard, 2001; Zimbalist, 1992). The NFL not only shares 40% of its gate revenues with the visiting team, but it also allocates the revenues across the entire league, so the actual visiting team that may attract fans does not generate any additional revenue (Brown et al., 2004). Even though the Cowboys are heavily marketed and are one of the more popular teams, Jerry Jones does not realize any added financial benefit when the Cowboys play a road game in front of capacity crowds, and the 40% of the ticket sales for sold out Cowboy home games are redistributed throughout the league.

In addition to sharing revenues from national television contracts, emerging media, licensed merchandise, and national sponsorships, North American professional sports leagues also utilize other revenue sharing mechanisms.

After the lockout canceled the 2004–2005 NHL season, the players and owners agreed to a complex revenue sharing plan that would augment the newly implemented salary cap. The bottom 15 revenue-producing clubs receive additional revenue-sharing dollars beyond the equally shared sources such as national television contacts (Bernstein, 2005). However, lower revenue producing clubs in metropolitan markets that have at least 2.5 million households are ineligible to receive revenue sharing dollars. In addition, the NHL agreement requires clubs to achieve predetermined attendance levels to be eligible to receive these revenue-sharing dollars. NHL Deputy Commissioner Bill Daly noted, "You don't want a revenue-sharing program that doesn't incentivize performance" (Bernstein, 2005, para. 18). The NHL's complex revenue sharing formula has worked to stabilize the league, but there are concerns that too much money is being shared with teams in untenable positions. The majority of revenue-sharing dollars have been directed to teams in the southern portion of the United States (such as Florida, Tennessee, Arizona), causing many in Canada to question why they are subsidizing teams in areas that have traditionally not been interested in hockey ("NHL owners growing wary…," 2008). In 2009, despite receiving revenue sharing dollars, the NHL had to take over financial control of the Phoenix Coyotes due to their mismanagement and failure to attract a sufficient fan base to generate enough revenues to cover costs (Sunnucks, 2009).

In addition to individual player and team salary caps, the NBA also utilizes a luxury tax on high spending teams to "encourage" teams to limit their player salaries. Prior to the 2011 NBA Collective Bargaining Agreement, the NBA salary cap was set at roughly 51% of the Association's BRI, and the luxury tax was set at roughly 61% of BRI (Coon, 2009). Teams that had salaries that exceeded the 61% threshold had to pay a dollar-for-dollar tax that was then distributed evenly to all of the non-taxed teams. Teams close or at the luxury tax level often avoided paying any additional salaries since the dollar-for-dollar tax essentially meant that any contract awarded to a player that causes the team to exceed the limit costs "double" the actual value of the contract. Further, exceeding the luxury tax limit prevents the team from receiving any luxury tax revenues. Though the luxury tax has helped to restrict some team's team salaries to a level above the salary cap but below the luxury tax limit, a handful of teams typically exceeded the luxury tax each year. The New York Knicks consistently exceeded the luxury tax limit and paid taxes equaling $45.1 million in 2007, $19.7 million in 2008, and $23.7 million in 2009 ("#1 New York Knicks," 2007; "Final 2007–2008 luxury…," 2008; Garcia, 2009).

Under the new CBA, the luxury tax is much more punitive. Teams will now pay $1.50 for every dollar over the luxury limit up to $5 million. For teams that have salaries that exceed the cap between $5 million and $10 million, a $1.75 tax per dollar will be charged. The tax increases to $2.50 per dollar between $10 million and $15 million and $3.25 per every dollar in salary between $15 million and $20 million. There are additional taxes that are paid for team salary levels that exceed the luxury tax limit by $20 million (Parasuraman, 2011).

Though the Major League Baseball Player's Union has adamantly opposed a salary cap, they have permitted the owners to implement a luxury tax. The luxury tax was first utilized in the 1997–1999 seasons and then was phased out. It was then implemented once again starting in 2003. The luxury tax penalizes a first-time offender 22.5% of their amount that exceeds the tax limit. When a team exceeds the cap a second time the penalty rate increases to 30%. For the third and any succeeding violation the rate increases to 40% (Brown, 2007). In addition to a luxury tax, Major League Baseball has also implemented a revenue sharing formula where the top 13 revenue-producing teams contribute to the bottom 17 revenue-producing teams based upon the team's distance from the revenue mean (Bloom, 2006). Revenue sharing and luxury tax dollars are supposed to be utilized by receiving teams to improve their on-field product. There have been some concerns that a few MLB clubs simply take their revenue sharing dollars and retain them as profits. The Milwaukee Brewers, formerly owned by Commissioner Bud Selig and his family, received tens of millions of dollars in revenue sharing while fielding low payroll teams in the early 2000s. The Brewers situation caused some to speculate that Selig would not fine the team for pocketing revenue sharing dollars that were designed to improve the quality of a team, rather than simply make the owner richer ("HBO's Real Sports examines…," 2004).

Conclusion

Though leagues recognize and understand the importance of competitive balance, no "perfect" revenue sharing and salary cap model currently exists. Of the four main North American professional leagues, the NFL shares the most revenue and provides the greatest level of competitive balance. An easily identified indicator of the NFL's success is the existence of the Packers in Green Bay, Wisconsin. The team not only survives but also has financially and competitively thrived in the NFL's smallest metropolitan market due to the NFL's revenue sharing formula. However, the same formula that shares money generously in the NFL can also permit teams to free ride off the effort of others. The Cincinnati Bengals have been notorious for maintaining low salaries for players and limiting their front offense expenses for scouting and marketing (Daugherty, 2008).

League officials and academic researchers have extensively studied competitive balance with no definitive answer regarding how best to structure a league.

Ultimately, the league offices must balance the individual owners' varying desires to succeed financially and on the playing field. Further, a league cannot maximize its marketing opportunities if fans perceive that a specific number of teams have little-to-no opportunity to ever compete to win a championship. However, league owners will not maximize their marketing efforts if they perceive some of their fellow owners will have few negative repercussions if they do not attempt to compete.

References

#1 New York Knicks. (2007, December 6). *Forbes*. Retrieved from http://www.forbes.com/lists/2007/32/biz_07nba_New-York-Knicks_328815.html.

Abrams, J. (2009, July 8). N.B.A.'s shrinking salary cap could shake up 2010 free agency. *New York Times*. Retrieved from http://www.nytimes.com/2009/07/09/sports/basketball/09nba.html.

Barnwell, B. (2013, March 11). Pawn stars. *Grantland*. Retrieved from http://grantland.com/features/bill-barnwell-changes-nfl-free-agent-landscape/.

Bernstein, A. (2005, August 1). Inside the complex NHL deal. *SportsBusiness Journal*. Retrieved from http://www.sportsbusinessjournal.com/index.cfm?fuseaction=article.main&articleId=46287&requestTimeout=900.

Bloom, B. M. (2009, March 10). Fehr does not foresee a salary cap. Retrieved from http://mlb.mlb.com/news/article.jsp?ymd=20090310&content_id=3961482&vkey=news_mlb&fext=.jsp&c_id=mlb&partnerId=rss_mlb.

Bloom, H. (2006, October 27). Inside the latest MLB CBA. *Sports Business News*. Retrieved from http://sportsbiznews.blogspot.com/2006/10/inside-latest-mlb-cba.html.

Blum, R. (2008, December 23). Yankees hit with $27 million luxury tax. *New York Post*. Retrieved from http://www.nypost.com/seven/12232008/sports/yankees/yankees_hit_with_27_million_luxury_tax_145590.htm.

Brown, M. (2007, December 25). Breaking down MLB's luxury tax: 2003–2007. *The Biz of Baseball*. Retrieved from http://www.bizofbaseball.com/index.php?option=com_content&task=view&id=1805&Itemid=41.

Brown, M., Nagel, M. S. McEvoy, C. D., & Rascher, D. A. (2004). Revenue and wealth maximization in the NFL: The impact of stadia. *Sport Marketing Quarterly, 13*(4), 227–235.

Brown, M. T., Rascher, D. A., Nagel, M. S., & McEvoy, C. D. (2010). *Financial management in the sport industry*. Scottsdale, AZ: Holcomb Hathaway Publishers.

Coin flip to lottery: Did the Rockets tank to get Olajuwon? (2008, January 19). Retrieved from http://reclinergm.wordpress.com/2008/01/19/coin-flip-to-lottery-did-the-rockets-tank-to-get-olajuwon/.

Coon, L. (2014). NBA salary cap FAQ. Retrieved from http://www.cbafaq.com/salarycap.htm.

Coro, P. (2007, June 29). Suns sell pick, choose Tucker. The Arizona Republic. Retrieved from http://www.azcentral.com/arizonarepublic/sports/articles/0629suns0629.html.

Court accepts Major League Soccer's single entity defense in players' antitrust suit. (2000, Summer). Retrieved from http://law.marquette.edu/cgi-bin/site.pl?2130&pageID=494#5.

Daugherty, P. (2008, November 2). Doc calls Mike Brown out. Retrieved from http://news.cincinnati.com/article/20081102/COL03/811020446.

Dobson, S., & Goddard, J. A. (2001). *The economics of football*. Cambridge, UK: Cambridge University Press.

Federal Baseball Club v. National League. (1922). 259 U.S. 200.

Final 2007–2008 luxury tax numbers. (2008, July 9). Retrieved from http://myespn.go.com/blogs/truehoop/0-33-31/Final-2007-2008-Luxury-Tax-Numbers.html.

Fitzpatrick, J. (n.d.). Retrieved from http://proicehockey.about.com/od/learnthegame/a/nhl_salary_cap.htm.

Fitzpatrick, J. (2005, July 13). NHL and players make a deal. Retrieved from http://proicehockey.about.com/od/thelatestonthelockout/a/cba_agreement.htm.

Flood v. Kuhn. (1972). 407 U.S. 258.

Fraser v. Major League Soccer. (D. Mass. April 19, 2000). 97 F.Supp.2d 130.

Garcia, A. (2009, July 8). Knicks and Mavericks hit hardest by luxury tax. Retrieved from http://www.nba.com/2009/news/features/art_garcia/07/08/salarycapinfo/index.html.

Haller, D. (2007, July 20). Kurt Thomas traded to Seattle. The Arizona Republic. Retrieved from http://www.azcentral.com/sports/suns/articles/0720kurttraded-CR.html.

Haupert, M. J. (2007, December 3). The economic history of Major League Baseball. EH.Net Encyclopedia. Retrieved from http://eh.net/encyclopedia/article/haupert.mlb.

HBO's Real Sports examines plight of the Brewers. (2004, February 25). *SportsBusiness Daily*. Retrieved from http://www.sportsbusinessdaily.com/article/83052.

Helyar, J. (2006, March 6). Labor peace threatened by rift between owners. Retrieved from http://sports.espn.go.com/nfl/news/story?id=2354095.

Lowe, Z. (2013, December 23). The NBA's possible solution for tanking: Good-bye to the lottery, hello to the wheel. Retrieved from http://grantland.com/the-triangle/the-nbas-possible-solution-for-tanking-good-bye-to-the-lottery-hello-to-the-wheel/.

Lowe, Z. (2014, July 23). Eric Bledsoe's long, hot, restricted summer. Retrieved from http://grantland.com/the-triangle/eric-bledsoes-long-hot-restricted-summer/.

Madison Square Garden sues NHL over promotion terms. (2007, September 28). *USA Today*. Retrieved from http://www.usatoday.com/sports/hockey/nhl/2007-09-28-msg-suit_N.htm.

Mickle, T., & Lefton, T. (2008, August 4). Several leagues later, debate on single-entity model still lively. *SportsBusiness Journal*. Retrieved from http://www.sportsbusinessjournal.com/article/59720.

Miller, M. (1991). *A whole different ball game*. New York: Birch Lane Press.

Nagel, M. S. (2005). Salary caps. In Encyclopedia of World Sport (Vol. 3, pp. 1322–1323). Great Barrington, MA: Berkshire Publishing.

NHL owners growing wary of league's revenue sharing system. (2008, October 13). *SportsBusiness Daily*. Retrieved from http://www.sportsbusinessdaily.com/article/124637.

Parasuraman, V. (2011, December 3). Everything you could ever want to know about the new NBA labor deal. Grantland.com. Retrieved February 28, 2012 from http://www.grantland.com/story/_/id/7303114/everything-ever-want-know-new-nba-labor-deal.

Pro football draft history: 1936. (n.d.). Retrieved from http://www.profootballhof.com/history/general/draft/1936.aspx.

Ray, J. L. (2008, February 23). How baseball arbitration works. Retrieved from http://baseball.suite101.com/article.cfm/how_baseball_arbitration_works.

Scully, G. W. (1995). *The market structure of sports*. Chicago, IL: University of Chicago Press.

Simmons, B. (2007, April 19). Links while tossing around conspiracy theories. Retrieved from http://insider.espn.go.com/espn/page2/blog/entry?id=2842986&searchName=simmons&campaign=rsssrch&source=bill_simmons.

Simmons, B. (2008, May 5). A requiem for the S.S.O.L. era in Phoenix. Retrieved April 27, 2009 from http://sports.espn.go.com/espn/page2/story?page=simmons%2F080501.

Sunnucks, M. (2009, May 6). NHL takes over Coyotes web site. *Phoenix Business Journal*. Retrieved from http://phoenix.bizjournals.com/phoenix/stories/2009/05/04/daily46.html.

Wagman, R. (2008, January 5). Garber's leadership has solidified MLS future. *SoccerTimes*. Retrieved from http://www.soccertimes.com/wagman/2008/jan05.

Why does tanking occur in the NBA but seemingly not in other leagues? (2007, April 9). *Sports Law Blog*. Retrieved from http://sports-law.blogspot.com/2007/04/why-does-tanking-occur-in-nba-but.html.

Zimbalist, A. (1992). *Baseball and billions*. New York, NY: BasicBooks.

Chapter 6

Moving Towards Equity: Women in Sport

Heidi Grappendorf, University of Cincinnati

Participation rates for girls and women in sport continue to increase. Further, women continue to make strides towards management and leadership positions within sport. These strides would not have been possible without the numerous strategies and initiatives that have been created to eliminate gender discrimination, promote opportunities and to ensure gender equity in sport.

Movements that began at the grassroots level have prompted many of the laws and legislation that exist today. These grassroots movements were crucial in the quest for gender equity and they continue to be for reform. The movement for gender equity by grassroots organizations nationally, as well as internationally, has a steadfast history. Grassroots level activity and the push for policies and procedures to ensure equity range from female physical educators organizing participation opportunities for women in sport to the formation of numerous national organizations that are dedicated to the advancement of women and elimination of gender inequity and discrimination in sport. For example, the Commission on Intercollegiate Athletics for Women (CIAW), which later became the Association for Intercollegiate Athletics for Women (AIAW), was created. Additionally, organizations such as National Association for Girls and Women in Sport (NAGWS) and the National Association of Collegiate Women Athletics Administrators (NACWAA) were formed by women who believed in opportunity and equity for women in sport. These and similar organizations continue to keep the pressure on politicians, as well as trying to keep gender equity on the forefront of the public eye.

Numerous initiatives, laws, and policies have been created to try to ensure equity for women in sport. The push for policies and procedures, as well as the enforcement of them, has and will continue to be an important factor in the battle to attain gender equity. Regarding laws, Title VII of the Civil Rights Act of 1964 prohibits employment discrimination on the basis of race, color, national origin, sex or religion. Furthermore, the Equal Pay Act of 1963 requires that men and women in the same organization receive equal pay for equal work. However, one of the most prominent laws in the United States history related to gender equity is Title IX. Title IX was enacted on June 23, 1972, and stated that "No person in the United States shall, on the basis of sex, be excluded from participation in, be denied the benefits of, or be subjected to discrimination under any education program or activity receiving Federal financial assistance." Other countries have passed similar legislation, as they too face many of the same challenges related to gender equity. The Brighton Declaration on Women and Sport, for example, was a set of principles established to assist those in sport to create guidelines and policies to increase the involvement and access for women in sport at all levels. These initiatives and others have had a tremendous impact in the pursuit of gender equity for girls and women in sport.

Despite the growth in participation levels and strides made by girls and women, gender inequity persists. The management and leadership ranks in collegiate and professional sports continue to be dominated by men. The shrinking number of women coaches continues to be a concern in intercollegiate athletics. Women continue to battle for equity in financing, marketing, pay, and media opportunities. More than 40 years after the passage of Title IX, there is a continued need for policies, legislation, and enforcement of these to ensure that gender equity is achieved.

Historical Background

Historically, opportunities for girls and women in sport have been limited. Gender equity has always been, and continues to be a controversial issue in society.

> An athletics program can be considered gender equitable when the participants in both the men's and women's sports programs would accept as fair and equitable the overall program of the other gender. No individual should be discriminated against on the basis of gender, institutionally or nationally, in intercollegiate athletics (NCAA, 2009).

Traditionally, participation opportunities, budget allocations, operating expenses, salaries, and the representation of female coaches and administrators have not been equitable for girls and women in sport. The pursuit of gender equity for girls and women in sport has been an ongoing struggle. However, the commitment of female physical educators and advocates of women in sport has been strong as they strive to ensure gender equity.

Leadership and Governance

Girls and women have consistently faced barriers and resistance to their participation and involvement in sport. Myths, stereotypes, and traditional expectations regarding women's roles have long impeded women's efforts in the sports realm. However, due to the early efforts of women leaders even before Title IX, the road was being paved for future policies and laws that would impact girls and women in sport for years to come.

During colonial times, women's participation in sport was minimal. Prior to the Civil War there was a movement in feminism in which women were demanding greater opportunities for physical education. Following the Civil War, there was an even greater demand from women to participate in physical education and sport, and thus more colleges began offering competitions. The difference in women's sports is that whereas students typically ran men's sports, female physical educators ran women's sports (Rintala, 2001; Swanson & Spears, 1995). Female physical educators rejected the competitive and commercial male model of sport (Rhode & Walker, 2007).

Due to the violent nature of football and a need for organization, the Intercollegiate Athletic Association was created in 1905 to oversee men's sports only. This organization changed its name to the National Collegiate Athletic Association (NCAA) in 1910 (Couturier & Chepko, 2001). For women's sport, volunteer female physical educators led by Sandra Berenson wrote the first rules for women's basketball. Eventually this committee became the Committee on Women's Athletics (CWA) and they began writing rules for other sports as well (Chepko & Couturier, 2001). This organization and several others, such as the Amateur Athletic Union (AAU), continued to create rules and advocate for women's sports as interest and participation grew.

The United States was undergoing significant social and political changes in the 1960s and 1970s. With these changes came a call for a more organized governing body to oversee women's participation in athletics. In 1967, the Commission for Intercollegiate Athletics for Women (CIAW) was founded to encourage development of sport programs for all (Hult, 1980). In 1971, due to the continued growth of intercollegiate sports for women, female physical educators established the Association for Intercollegiate Athletics for Women (AIAW) (Hultstrand, Park, & Hult, 1993; Swanson & Spears, 1995), which was an outgrowth of the CIAW. The AIAW was created by women for two primary reasons: (a) they believed women had been deprived of the sporting learning experience; and (b) they believed there were better approaches than the men's model in the NCAA (Uhlir, 1987). In 1971–1972, 278 institutions were members of the AIAW. By 1981, there were more than 900 institutions that belonged to the AIAW (Hultstrand, 1993). The AIAW continually worked to sign television contracts and gain corporate sponsorships, as they held national championships and continued to grow. The AIAW accomplished many things for women's athletics, yet one of the greatest contributions the AIAW had was related to its role in helping get Title IX passed.

Title IX

Title IX was passed in 1972 as an amended part to Title VII of the Civil Rights Act of 1964 and institutions were given until 1978 to comply (Anderson, Cheslock, & Ehrenberg, 2006; Epstein, 2003). Title VII protects people on the basis of race, color, religion, sex or national origin. Institutions were initially unsure if Title IX applied to athletics. A three-prong test was established to evaluate compliance. The test is: (1) participation opportunities for male and female athletes that are in proportion to enrollments at their university; (2) that schools demonstrate a history and continued practice of program expansion for athletes of the underrepresented sex; and (3) that schools demonstrate that programs offered are congruent with the interests and abilities of the underrepresented sex (Cunningham, 2011; Dougherty, Goldberger, & Carpenter, 2002; Epstein, 2003). It is important to note that for a school to be in compliance with Title IX, they need to only meet one of the aforementioned prongs. Essentially, the three-pronged approach gave women a legal basis for filing lawsuits.

Because the law was not specific in how administrators were to provide equal opportunities and funding to both men and women, the Office of Civil Rights (OCR) was charged with interpreting and developing polices that would help administrators implement Title IX (Cunningham, 2011; Epstein, 2003). Though schools were given until 1978 to comply, many did not. There are still schools not in compliance with Title IX (Carpenter & Acosta, 2005). The OCR in an attempt to further clarify Title IX determined that the following areas must be taken into account:

1. Equipment and supplies
2. Scheduling of games and practice times
3. Travel and per diem
4. Tutoring
5. Coaching
6. Locker rooms and facilities
7. Training and medical services
8. Housing and dining facilities and services
9. Publicity

10. Support services
11. Recruitment of student athletes
12. Athletic financial assistance
13. Accommodations of interests and abilities (Cunningham, 2011; Dougherty, Goldberger, & Carpenter, 2002; Epstein, 2003).

Utilizing these areas, equitable treatment relates to the benefits the athlete receives; not the dollar amount. In other words, these requirements do not examine how much was spent on outfitting a football player versus a female volleyball player; it would examine that both received an equal opportunity for the uniform. The only exception to this is in the areas of financial assistance and recruitment (Dougherty, Goldberger, & Carpenter, 2002).

The interpretation and application of Title IX has resulted in much debate, and ultimately numerous lawsuits. In 1984, in one of several court cases that attempted to clarify Title IX so that institutions would be certain to comply, the Supreme Court ruled in *Grove City College v. Bell* that Title IX only applied to those programs that specifically received financial aid. Though a setback to Title IX, Congress did pass in 1988 the Civil Rights Restoration Act that clarified that Title IX be applied to all programs at federally funded institutions (Anderson, Cheslock, & Ehrenberg, 2006). Therefore, if a university athletic program was not in compliance with Title IX, the entire university could lose all federal funding.

Court cases continued as the efforts to explain, and to ensure that institutions complied with, Title IX continued. In 1992, the Supreme Court ruled in *Franklin v. Gwinnett County Public Schools* that monetary damages could be awarded (Anderson, Cheslock, & Ehrenberg, 2006). This case was crucial in that it now provided financial "encouragement" to get schools to comply. Furthermore, in 1992 the NCAA created the Gender Task Force to address issues related to Title IX (Epstein, 2003), and in 1994 the Equity in Athletics Disclosure Act was passed that mandated that schools make information about the operations of their men's and women's athletic programs available to the public (Anderson, Cheslock, & Ehrenberg, 2006).

Another substantial case related to Title IX was *Cohen v. Brown University* (1992). In 1991, Brown University announced that it was going to eliminate women's gymnastics and volleyball. In 1996, the courts found Brown violated Title IX as it failed all three tests under the law. An agreement was reached and Brown University never lost its federal funding. Eventually, the women's teams were restored to university-funded status (Dougherty, Goldberger, Carpenter, 2002; Epstein, 2003).

The clarification efforts and lawsuits continued regarding Title IX into the 21st century. However, during the 1970s a change in the governance of women's sports was also taking place. The passage of Title IX, as well as the growth of the AIAW had gotten the interest of the National Collegiate Athletic Association (NCAA), who actually had opposed the passage of Title IX. In fact, Walter Byers, Executive Director of the NCAA, believed that Title IX was going to be the death of men's sports. However, eventually the NCAA recognized that women's sport was going to continue to grow, and that they should get involved. Thus, the NCAA began holding national championships for women (Hums & MacLean, 2004: Park & Hult, 1993: Swanson & Spears, 1995). Prior to the growth of the AIAW and the passage of Title IX, the NCAA showed little interest in women's athletics, and actually opposed the passage of Title IX, requesting an exemption from the law. The NCAA viewed women's sports as a threat to the funding of men's sports, in additional to not viewing women's athletics as ever profitable (Hultstrand, 1993; Park & Hult, 1993; Swanson & Spears, 1995). Eventually, the NCAA sought out colleges and universities who were with the AIAW by offering them incentives and national television coverage (Hult, 1994). The AIAW did not have the resources and could not compete with the NCAA. According to Hums and MacLean (2004), this event was a "hostile takeover" (p. 183) and, ultimately, the AIAW dissolved in 1982.

Ongoing Issues Related to Gender Equity

Gender equity continues to be an issue that plagues women's sports. More than 40 years have passed since Title IX was enacted, yet gender equity has yet to be achieved in various areas. Participation and leadership opportunities, equal pay, operating budgets, and facility issues are just a few concerns that still need to be addressed. Lawsuits and criticisms continue as the struggle to achieve gender equity continues. It is likely that these challenges to Title IX will continue until it is realized and embraced by society that Title IX mandates that discrimination on the basis of gender will not be tolerated, and that equal opportunities for both men and women be equally provided (Cunningham, 2011; Epstein, 2003).

The compliance to Title IX, the enforcement of Title IX, and the efforts made by some to weaken Title IX have all been barriers for girls, women, and advocates of Title IX. Despite the tremendous growth in participation, gender disparities remain. Rhode and Walker (2007) noted that, despite Title IX's remarkable legacy, frustration continues as to how Title IX has, or actually has not been implemented.

Predominantly, Title IX and the intent of Title IX have been challenged over the years by male sport programs and the athletes and coaches of those teams.

These challenges for the most part, have occurred due to the decrease in certain men's athletic teams with the simultaneous growth in women's teams (Epstein, 2003). Universities have cut non-revenue producing men's sports in attempts to comply with Title IX. As Dougherty, Goldberger, and Carpenter (2002) noted, "Title IX does not rank the importance of sports" (p. 90) and nowhere within Title IX does it require or encourage the cutting of non-revenue producing sports. Title IX regulates the overall equity in athletics. Title IX allows individual schools to decide how best to implement its regulations. "Nonetheless, the cuts led to widespread protests, a wave of largely unsuccessful litigation, and pressure to reconsider Title IX interpretations" (Rhode & Walker, 2007, pp. 10–11). It has to be noted though that most schools comply with Title IX by adding athletic opportunities for women without cutting teams, yet lawsuits highlight those that have cut programs. The National Wrestling Coaches Association has been heavily involved in bringing legal action against the Department of Education in an attempt to show who collegiate wrestling programs have been eliminated in attempts to comply with Title IX.

Existing Disparities

Even though it has been more than 40 years since the passage of Title IX, gender disparities remain. Despite more financial resources being provided to women's sports since Title IX, the numbers have not kept up with what has been allocated to men's sports. Thus, the gap continues, as resources for women's athletic programs continue to lag behind men's. While women make up 53% of the student body at NCAA Division I colleges, they are only 41% of the athletes. Additionally, they receive only 32% of recruiting dollars while getting only 36% of overall athletic operating budgets (NAGWS, n.d.). Lastly, women continue to be under-represented in athletic administration, particularly at the upper levels of administration, while the number of female coaches continues to decrease (Carpenter & Acosta, 2012).

Participation, Yet Under-Representation of Women in Leadership

Arguably, Title IX has helped changed the landscape of women's athletics. There is no doubt that Title IX has provided more girls and women at both the high school and intercollegiate levels more opportunities to participate in athletics. At the interscholastic level, the number of girls participating in sport is at an all-time high with 3.1 million girls participating in sports (National Federation of State High School Associations, 2008). At the collegiate level in 1972, the average number of women's teams offered per university was 2.5. In 2012, that number was at 8.73, the highest ever (Carpenter & Acosta, 2012). Despite the tremendous participation opportunities, there has unfortunately been a downside to Title IX. One of the unintended negative consequences or backlash effects of Title IX has been the number of women in leadership positions, particularly in coaching and administration. Prior to Title IX being passed more than 90% of female teams were coached by a female and more than 90% of women's athletic programs had a female athletic director. Acosta and Carpenter (2012) found 42.9% of female teams coached by female coaches (see Exhibit 6.1). Additionally, only 20.3% of all athletic directors are female compared to more than 90% of the administrators that headed women's programs in 1972 (see Exhibit 6.2) (Acosta & Carpenter, 2012).

Exhibit 6.1

Percentage of female head coaches for all divisions, in all sports

Year	% of head coaches
1972	90+
1978	58.2
1988	48.3
1998	47.4
2008	42.8
2010	42.6
2012	42.9

(Acosta & Carpenter, 2012)

Exhibit 6.2

Percentage of female athletic directors

Year	% All Divisions
1972	90.0+
1980	20.0
1988	16.1
1998	19.4
2008	21.3
2010	19.3
2012	20.3

(Acosta & Carpenter, 2012)

Numerous reasons have been hypothesized and researched attempting to explain the under-representation of athletic administrators. Initially, when Title IX was passed, schools typically had a separate men's athletic director for men's athletics, and a women's athletic director for women's athletics. After the passage of Title IX, athletic departments merged with the female athletic director position being eliminated (Grappendorf, Lough, & Griffin, 2004). Many schools believed this would help them be more efficient and would help with cost containment (Cahn, 1994; Delpy, 1998; Fox, 1992; Uhlir, 1987). Essentially, women were pushed out of key leadership positions as it was seen as the most logical choice for athletic directors to choose a male as they believed men to be more competent as leaders. Furthermore, regarding coaches, as the profile of women's sports grew, so did the financial lure of the job, and it became more enticing to males in the coaching profession (Wilson, 2007).

Since the numbers of women in coaching and administration have yet to rebound to their pre-Title IX state, other research has been conducted on the reasons for under-representation of female administrators and coaches in athletics. According to Shaw and Hoeber, the reasons are "overwhelming" (p. 348). Everything from homologous reproduction (which is the tendency to hire those most like ourselves) (Knoppers, 1994; Stangl & Kane, 1991) to hegemony (the power and dominance of one group over another—i.e. men over women) (Coakley, 2007; Sage, 1998; Whisenant, Miller, & Pedersen, 2005) to those listed is Acosta and Carpenter's (1988) work: (a) lack of support systems for women, (b) failure of the "old girls" network, (c) female burnout, and (d) failure of women to apply for job openings. Stroh, Langland, and Simpson (2004) examined the glass ceiling effect, which refers to an invisible, but real barrier that prevents women from moving upward in administration. Cunningham (2011) identified three categories to explain the underrepresentation: (a) stereotypes, (b) structural forces, and (c) personal characteristics. Stereotypes affect people's beliefs about women's abilities to lead and what roles they are capable of being successful in. Structural forces are those that constrain or prevent women from advancing in athletics, and can include the lack of social networks, discrimination, or the hours and days associated with careers in sport. Lastly, personal characteristics, though influenced by stereotypes, and structural forces, include things such as attitudes and intention to move up, or the decision to leave one's career (Cunningham, 2011). Rhode and Walker (2007) suggested three main reasons for under-representation amongst coaches: (a) adverse stereotypes, (b) in-group favoritism in hiring and support networks, and (c) work/family conflicts.

Family and Medical Leave Act

The Family and Medical Leave Act is a federal law that entitles employees to up to 12 work weeks off for childbirth, adoption, employee health issues or family related medical emergencies. The law applies to those businesses with 50 or more employees and can apply to women for maternity leave or men for paternity leave (Epstein, 2003). What had not been known is if athletes would be covered under this law. In the fall of 2008, the NCAA suggested some guidelines, but stopped short of implementing any legislation to protect pregnant student athletes (Chronicle of Higher Education, 2008). The NCAA created a Model Policy that member institutions can adopt as their own approach for dealing with pregnant and parenting student athletes. The Model Policy notes that athletic departments cannot make athletes sign contracts not to get pregnant and that they cannot revoke an athlete's scholarship due to pregnancy. Male athletes (as fathers) as well as female athletes are protected. Essentially, Title IX already protects students from discrimination or exclusion of an extracurricular activity based upon pregnancy, so the Model Policy set forth by the NCAA is more of a clarification tool more than anything else (Chronicle of Higher Education, 2008). There is also a provision in the NCAA bylaws that allows an institution to approve a one-year extension of the five-year eligibility period for female student-athletes who become pregnant.

Equal Pay Act

The Equal Pay Act of 1963 is a federal law mandating equal pay to those who perform substantially the same work (Epstein, 2003; Fitzgerald, 2001). Five criteria are utilized to determine if the Equal Pay Act has been violated. These include:

1. Skill;
2. Effort;
3. Responsibility;
4. Working conditions; and
5. Place of Employment.

Despite the tremendous growth in women's sports, there is still a significant gap between men's and women's salaries (NCAA, 2005). Though several cases have been brought forward utilizing the Equal Pay Act, Title IX, and Title VII of the Civil Rights Act of 1964, there has not been a significant amount of precedent setting cases on pay equity for women in intercollegiate athletics to determine or state exactly how the courts are deciding on pay issues (Carpenter, 2001). In *Stanley v. University of Southern California* (1994), Marianne Stanley, the head women's basketball coach at USC, sued under the Equal Pay Act and Title IX that she was entitled to receive the same salary as the head men's basketball coach, George Raveling. She argued that skill, effort, responsibility, and working conditions were similar. Despite having a more successful record than the men's team, and the fact she had been named a Pac-10 (now Pac-12) Conference Coach of the Year, the courts found that a difference in the experiences of a head men's and women's coach, different responsibilities, and different market value dictated a need for a difference in pay (Carpenter, 2001; Rhode & Walker, 2007). This was a tremendous setback for female head coaches and their quest for equal pay.

In *Pitts v. Oklahoma State University* (1994), the head women's golf coach sued the university under the Equal Pay Act, Title IX, and Title VII because her salary was approximately $28,000 less than the men's head coach. The jury found that the university had violated Title VII and Title IX, but not the Equal Pay Act (Carpenter, 2001; Rhode & Walker, 2007). It is fair to suggest that due to a lack of legal precedents that some ambiguity still exists in clearly defining how the law will impact gender equity related to salary issues.

International Leadership

The women's sports movement has not been limited to the United States. Many countries have faced many of the same issues that women's sports have faced in the United States. Participation, access, funding, under-representation in coaching and management are global issues that have and continue to impact women in sport. In response to these issues, a global women's movement was created to promote and ensure opportunities for women in sport.

Brighton Declaration

In 1994, a conference in Brighton, England, was held, entitled "Women, Sport and the Challenge of Change." Eighty-two countries were represented to discuss the issues women face in sport, and it was supported by the British Sports Council and the International Olympic Committee (IOC) (International Working Group on Women and Sport, n.d.). From this conference, The Brighton Declaration was created to facilitate a culture that values and commits to the involvement of women in all aspects of sport. The Brighton Declaration had 10 principles. These include:

1. Equality in society and sport;
2. Facilities;
3. School and junior sport;
4. Developing participation;
5. High performance sport;
6. Leadership in sport;
7. Education, training, and development;
8. Sport information and research;
9. Resources; and
10. Domestic and international cooperation.

From 1994–1998 more than 200 international organizations adopted the Brighton Declaration (Shelton, 2001).

> The Brighton Declaration acknowledges that physical education, sport, and sporting activities are an integral aspect of the culture of every nation, but it highlights the inequalities that exist in participation levels and opportunities for women and girls compared to men and boys. It also acknowledges the fact that women are still underrepresented in management, coaching, and officiating, particularly at the higher levels. (Shelton, 2001 p. 425–426)

The International Working Group on Women and Sport (IWG) was another outcome of the Brighton Conference. The IWG consists of representatives of government and non-government agencies all over the world and it was created to oversee the International Women and Sport Strategy (Shelton, 2001). The International Women and Sport Strategy was established to be an organizing body on issues related to women in sport. This strategy coordinated the sharing of successful initiatives amongst varying international sport organizations (Shelton, 2001).

International Gender Equity

Internationally, the recognition of the importance of sport in women's lives also has been acknowledged. Several countries (i.e., Canada, Norway) have passed legislation to ensure equal treatment for women in sport, and various groups are also monitoring the participation and leadership percentages in their respective countries. Further, getting the International Olympic Committee (IOC) on board supporting and advocating how sport can contribute to improving women's status and quality of life has also occurred (Shelton, 2001).

One issue that has received considerable attention in recent years, have been the cultural and religious barriers to women participating or being involved in the governance of sport. For example, Muslim nations have struggled with reconciling sport participation with traditional women's roles and dress. Concerns by some Muslims over uniforms and females' skin showing and fear of sexual glances being made have constrained Muslim women from participation in physical education and sport (Sfeir, 1985; Shelton, 2001). Despite the constraints, some change is occurring as a result of the spread of socialist ideas that have contributed to some attitudes changing as countries try to navigate modern society and traditional religious views (Sfeir, 1985). Advocates of women's participation and involvement in sport note that sport should be a human right, and that it could be used to promote positive social change, including empowerment for women in many countries.

Future Considerations

Gender equity has yet to be fully achieved in the athletic realm. Women still receive fewer opportunities to participate in sport, less in collegiate scholarships, and less in operating expenses. Lack of compliance with Title IX by administrators, and lack of enforcement by the government continue to be a barrier for girls and women in sport. The lack of compliance and the failure of the government to hold universities accountable for Title IX have contributed to the tumultuous history of it. Ultimately, equality for women in sports has been and continues to be a struggle.

Title IX Policies and Legal Action

There continues to be resistance to Title IX. Solomon (2002) estimated that only 20% of intercollegiate athletic programs were in compliance with Title IX. However, not one school has ever lost federal funding due to not being in compliance with Title IX. The threat of funding cutoffs appears to be more theory than reality.

Title IX has been contested partly due to the fact that athletic administrators have cut men's sports to comply with Title IX. Title IX is often blamed for these cuts despite the fact that expenses for football, men's basketball, and salaries for men's coaching continue to skyrocket. The perceived revenue sports of football and men's basketball continue to consume the majority of men's total athletic budgets in Division I-FBS schools with them taking 72% of the total budget (NAGWS, n.d.). Many believe that putting more money into football and men's basketball will increase their revenue, yet it is rare to find athletic programs that actually make money (Coakley, 2007). Ultimately, this forces the other men's programs to compete for the remaining funds, with the women's program also getting only a small share of the total athletics budget. To reduce the backlash against Title IX, it will be important to examine, and possibly create policies that do not cut men's sports and make Title IX the scapegoat for those cuts. Athletic directors and universities must be held responsible for their decisions. Financial responsibility, including limiting the expenditures specifically to football will be necessary for the ideals of Title IX to be fully embraced.

Continued Participation Growth without Representation

Despite the dramatic increase in the numbers of girls and women participating in sport, women have not shared the same success in obtaining leadership positions within sport. " ... although more girls are playing athletics, they are playing in programs controlled by men" (Whisenant, 2003). Furthermore, the percentage of female coaches at the intercollegiate level continues to decrease. Administrators must make a solid commitment to the promotion and advancement of women. Policies regarding hiring practices to eliminate any discrimination, particularly based upon stereotypes, could be implemented. Additionally, policies related to the structural issues in an organization could be examined, and laws should be enforced.

Advocacy

Advocacy is an important component to changing the attitudes and alleviating the inequities for women in sport. Advocacy can include mentoring, networking, and systematic planning (DePauw, Bonace, & Karwas, 1991). Further, according to Rhode and Walker (2007), equity in sport can be achieved through political efforts and pressure by women's organizations. It will be important for advocates of women's sports to continue to strive for gender equity. Organizations like the Women's Sports Foundation, the National Association for Girls and Women in Sport (NAGWS), the National Association of Collegiate Women Athletic Administrators (NACWAA), and others will continue to play a vital role in advocating for equity. Additionally, these organizations can assist women in building networks, which could potentially assist them in the careers.

Conclusion

Efforts towards gender equity in sport have been numerous, and are ongoing as more women continue to participate and play in sport, as well as work their way towards more leadership positions. From the early efforts of physical education instructors and the women of the AIAW, to laws passed, and lawsuits being filed, the push for achieving gender equity continues. For women pursuing careers in coaching and administration, the continued push is essential as they strive to gain their place back in the locker rooms and boardrooms of athletics.

As noted in this chapter, there are many issues and barriers that still need to be overcome before true gender equity is met. It will take enforcement of Title IX. It will take policies and procedures to uphold laws and eliminate of discriminatory practices. It will take a concerted effort to recruit and hire more women into the leadership ranks. It will take discipline for schools to become financially responsible. It will take administrators willing to support gender equity. It will take educating the public about the necessity of gender equity. It will take an overall commitment, and continued movement to achieve gender equity.

References

Acosta, R. V., & Carpenter, L. J. (1988). *Perceived causes of the declining representation of women leaders in intercollegiate sports—1988 update.* Unpublished manuscript. Brooklyn College, Brooklyn, NY.

Acosta, R. V. & Carpenter, L. J. (2012). *Women in intercollegiate sport: A longitudinal, national study.* Retrieved from http://www.acostacarpenter.org/2008%20Summary%20Final.pdf.

Anderson, D. J., Cheslock, J. J., & Ehrenberg, R. G. (2006). Gender equity in intercollegiate athletics: Determinants of Title IX compliance. *The Journal of Higher Education, 77*(2), 225–250.

Cahn, S. K. (1994). *Coming on strong: Gender and sexuality in twentieth century woman's sport.* New York: Macmillian.

Carpenter, L. J. (2001). Gender equity: Opportunities to participate. In, D. Cotton, J. Wolohan, T. Wilde (Eds.), Law for recreation and sport managers (pp. 561–584). Dubuque, IA: Kendall-Hunt.

Carpenter, L. J., & Acosta, R. V. (2005). *Title IX.* Champaign, IL: Human Kinetics.

Chepko, S., & Couturier, L. (2001). From intersection to collision: women's sports from 1920–1980. In, G. Cohen (Ed.), *Women in sport: Issues and controversies* (pp. 79–110). Oxon Hill, MD: AAHPERD Publications.

Chronicle of Higher Education. (2008). After long battle, NCAA publishes guidelines to protect pregnant athletes. Retrieved from http://chronicle.com/ news/article/5493/after-long-battle-ncaa-publishes-guidelines-to-protect-pregnant-athletes.

Coakley, J. (2007). *Sport in society: Issues and controversies* (9th ed.). Boston: McGraw-Hill.

Couturier, L., & Chepko, S (2001). Separate world, separate lives, separate sporting models. In G. Cohen (Ed.), *Women in sport: Issues and controversies* (pp. 57–78). Oxon Hill, MD: AAHPERD Publications.

Cunningham, G. B. (2011). *Diversity in sport organizations.* (2nd ed). Scottsdale, AZ: Holcomb Hathaway.

Delpy, L. (1998). Career opportunities in sport: Women on the mark. *Journal of Physical Education, Recreation, & Dance, 69*(7), 17–21.

DePauw, K. P., Bonace, B. J., & Karwas, M. R. (1991). *Women and sport leadership. Journal of Physical Education, Recreation, & Dance, 62,* 32–34.

Dougherty, N. J., Goldberger, A. S., & Carpenter, L. J. (2002). *Sport, physical activity, and the law* (2nd ed.). Champaign, IL: Sagamore Publishing.

Epstein, A. (2003). *Sports law.* Clifton Park, NY: Thomson Learning.

Fitzgerald, M. P. (2002). Gender Equity: Coaching and administration. In D. J. Cotton, J. T. Wolohan, & J. T. Wilde, (Eds.), (2nd Ed), *Law for recreation and sport managers* (pp. 561–570). Dubuque, IA: Kendall-Hunt Publishing.

Fox, C. (1992). Title IX & athletic administration. *Journal of Physical Education, Recreation, & Dance, 53*(3), 48–52.

Grappendorf, H., Lough, N., & Griffin, J. (2004). Profiles and career patterns of female NCAA Division I athletic directors. *International Journal of Sport Management, 5*(3), 243–261.

Hult, J. S. (1994). The story of women's athletics: Manipulating a dream 1890–1985. In D. M. Costa, & S. R. Guthrie (Eds.), *Women and sport: Interdisciplinary perspectives* (pp. 83–106). Champaign, IL: Human Kinetics.

Hult, J. S. (1980). The philosophical conflicts in men's and women's collegiate athletics. *Quest, 32*(1), 77–94.

Hultstrand, B. J. (1993). *The growth of collegiate women's sports: The 1960's. Journal of Physical Education, Recreation, & Dance, 64*(3), 41–43.

Hums, M. A., & MacLean, J. C. (2004). *Governance and policy in sport organizations.* Scottsdale, AZ: Holcomb Hathaway Publishers.

International Working Group on Women and Sport. *The Brighton Declaration on Women and Sport.* Retrieved from http://www.iwg-gti.org/index.php?id=63.

Knoppers, A. (1994). Gender and the coaching profession. In S. Birrell & C. L. Cole (Eds.), *Women, sport & culture* (pp. 119–133). Champaign, IL: Human Kinetics.

National Federation of State High School Associations. (2008). *High School sports participation rises again: Boys, girls, and overall participation reaches all time high*. Retrieved from http://www.nfhs.org/web/2008/09/ high_school_sports_participation.aspx.

NAGWS. (n.d.). *Title IX quick facts*. Retrieved from http://www.aahperd.org/ nagws/template.cfm?template=titleix/facts.html.

NCAA. (2009). *NCAA gender equity*. Retrieved from http://www1.ncaa.org/ membership/ed_outreach/gender_equity/index.html.

NCAA. (2005). *NCAA 2002–2003 gender equity report indicates slight gains for women participating in intercollegiate athletics*. Retrieved from http:// www.ncaa.org/wps/ncaa?ContentID=4670.

Office of Civil Rights. (1979). *A policy interpretation: Title IX and intercollegiate athletics*. Retrieved from http://www.ed.gov/about/offices/list/ocr/ docs/t9interp.html.

Park, R. J., & Hult, J. S. (1993). Women as leaders in physical education and school based sports, 1865–1930s. *Journal of Physical Education, Recreation, & Dance, 64*(3), 35–40.

Rhode, D.L, & Walker, C. J. (2007). *Gender equity in college athletics: Women coaches as a case study*. Retrieved from http://law.bepress.com/cgi/viewcontent.cgi?article=9336&context=expresso.

Rintala, J. (2001). Play and competition: An ideological dilemma. In G. L. Cohen (Ed.), *Women in sport: Issues and controversies*, (pp. 37–56). Oxon Hill, MD: AAHPERD Publications.

Sage, G. H. (1998). *Power and ideology in American sport: A critical perspective (2nd Ed.)* Champaign, IL: Human Kinetics.

Sfeir, L. (1985). The status of Muslim women in sport: Conflict between cultural tradition and modernization. *International Review for the Sociology of Sport, 20*, 283–306.

Shaw, S., & Hoeber, L. (2003). "A strong man is direct and a direct woman is a bitch:" Gendered discourses and their influence on employment roles in sport organizations. *Journal of Sport Management, 17*, 347–375.

Shelton, C. M. (2001). International challenges for women in sport: The quiet revolution. In. G. Cohen (Ed.), *Women in sport: Issues and controversies* (pp. 421–439). Oxon Hill, MD: AAHPERD Publications.

Solomon, J. (June 23, 2002). Title IX, 30 years later: Sexes still unequal in Athletics: Title IX changed the playing field but it's still not level. *Houston Chronicle*, p. A1.

Stangl, J. M., & Kane, M. J. (1991). Structural variables that offer explanatory power for the under representation of women coaches since Title IX: The case of homologous reproduction. *Sociology of Sport Journal, 8*(1) 47–60.

Stroh, L. K., Langland, C. L., & Simpson, P. A. (2004). Shattering the glass ceiling in the new millennium. In. M. S. Stockdale & F. J. Crosby (Eds.), *The psychology and management of workplace diversity* (pp. 147–167). Malden, MA: Blackwell.

Swanson, R., & Spears, B. (1995). *The history of sport & physical education in the United States.* Burr Ridge, IL: McGraw-Hill.

Uhlir, G. A. (1987). Athletics and the university: The post-woman's era. *Academe, 73*(4), 25–29.

Whisenant, W. A. (2003). How women have fared as interscholastic athletic administrators since the passage of Title IX. *Sex Roles, 49*(3/4), 179–184.

Whisenant, W. A., Miller, J., & Pedersen. (2005). Systematic barriers in athletic administration: An analysis of job descriptions for interscholastic athletic directors. *Sex Roles, 53*(11/12), 911–918.

Wilson, R. (2007). Where have all the women gone? *Chronicle of Higher Education.* Retrieved from http://chronicle.com/cgi2-bin/printable.cgi?article=http://chronicle.com/free/v53/i35/35a04001.htm.

Chapter 7

The Olympic Movement

Lisa Delpy Neirotti, George Washington University

For all the positive impacts and iconic memories the Olympic Games produce, for better or worse, the Games also serve as a platform for political and social agendas and are continually faced with internal and external challenges. The Modern Olympic Movement was founded in 1894 by a French aristocrat, Pierre de Coubertin, who had long studied the Ancient Olympic Games (776 B.C.–393 A.D.) and its philosophies of sound mind and body. De Coubertin was disappointed in France's weak physical nature as evidenced by the loss of the Franco-Prussian War, and believed that the rebirth of the Olympic Games would provide the impetus to strengthen his countrymen.

The Olympic Family

The Olympic Movement is composed of a number of different Olympic sport organizations (OSOs) ranging from the international to the local level. The structure of the Olympic Movement is that of a diamond with the International Olympic Committee (IOC) at the pinnacle, the International Sport Federations (IFs) and National Olympic Committees (NOCs) at each horizontal point, and the National Sport Federations (NSFs) or National Sport Governing Bodies (NGBs) at the lower point. The Organizing Committees of the Olympic Games (OCOGs) fit nicely in the middle of this diamond (see Exhibit 7.1).

The IOC owns all rights to the Olympic Games and is responsible for promoting sport in accordance with the Olympic Charter. The IOC is composed of a maximum of 115 co-opted members whose primary responsibilities are to select Olympic host cities; maintain and enforce the Olympic Charter; and represent the IOC and the Olympic Movement in their countries. This final point is important to understand as, unlike the United Nations where members represent their country and respective interests, not all countries participating in the Olympic Games have an IOC member.

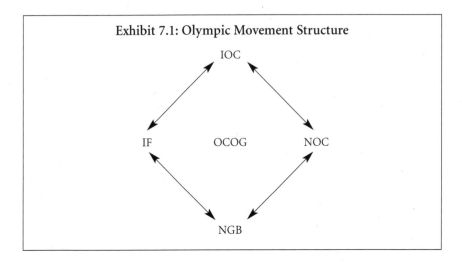

Exhibit 7.1: Olympic Movement Structure

The International Federations (e.g., Federation International Football Association (FIFA)) determine the rules of their respective sport competitions and athlete qualifications. For example, it was the Federation International Basketball Association (FIBA) that elected to allow professional players to compete in the 1992 Summer Olympic Games, not the IOC. Similarly, it is FIFA that restricts Olympic soccer competition to players less than 23 years of age as one way of differentiating the World Cup from the Olympic Games (FIFA, 2012).

In 2009, there were 33 IFs (7 Winter and 26 Summer) representing 54 disciplines and 400 events on the Olympic Program. These federations are organized under the Association of Summer Olympic International Federations (ASOIF) and the Association of the International Olympic Winter Sports Federations (AIOWF). The IOC is unique in that it defines sport as a single or group of disciplines. For example, the Fédération Internationale de Natation (FINA/International Swim Federation) governs the disciplines of swimming, diving, synchronized swimming, water polo, and open water swimming, all of which appear on the Olympic program. Together, these five disciplines make up the Olympic sport of "aquatics." For the swim discipline alone there are 17 events for men and women ranging from 50 meter freestyle to 4×100 medley relay. The IOC also recognizes 32 other IFs not on the Olympic program. Seven of these sports (golf, rugby, roller sports, squash, karate, softball, and baseball) bid to be added to the 2016 Olympic program with golf and rugby succeeding in their effort (Powers, 2009). The Olympic Program Commission, composed of IOC members, representatives of International Federations and National Olympic Committees as well as experts, evaluates the bids based on 33 criteria, with an emphasis on universality, popularity, and image. Since reforms in 2002, the IOC conducts a systematic review of the Olympic program after every edition of the Games to ensure that it remains exciting and relevant. Sports have to show merit to join the program and to remain on it and the number of sports in the Summer Games is limited to 28. In 2012, there were 26 sports on the Summer program in London as baseball and softball were eliminated from the Olympic Games after the 2008 Beijing Games. For the 2016 Games in Rio de Janeiro, the Olympic program will be full again with rugby and golf added. The IOC is sometimes faced with a difficult decision when classifying a sport as either a "sport" or a "discipline." Competitive snowboarding was conceived in the 1980s and pioneered by the International Snowboard Federation (ISF) that established competitions and developed standardized rules. The ISF prided itself as an independent governing body focused on the welfare of the athletes. The sport's popularity grew rapidly and before the ISF could gain IOC recognition of snowboarding as an autonomous sport, a rival tour of competitions was established in 1994 by the IOC recognized, Federation International de Ski (FIS). Soon thereafter, Snowboarding was admitted to the Olympic Program for Nagano 1998 as a discipline of skiing under FIS along with Alpine, Nordic, and Freestyle skiing. This proved to be a controversial decision as the 1998 Olympic competition was boycotted by several of the sport's most successful athletes who were loyal to the ISF over the "very bureaucratic" FIS. After laying the groundwork for snowboard to become an Olympic sport, the ISF eventually ceased operations in July 2002 (Natives News, 2002).

National Olympic Committees

The National Olympic Committees (e.g., United States Olympic Committee (USOC)) are responsible for developing and protecting the Olympic Movement and its values in their countries and for sending a delegation of athletes to the Olympic Games that conform to International Federation criteria and meet the principles of the Olympic Charter. Two such principles include Rule 42 related to the nationality of athletes and Rule 45 excluding discrimination of any kind (Olympic Charter, 2007).

The NOCs oversee and collaborate with the various National Sport Federations (NSFs), or Nationals Sport Governing Bodies (NGBs) as referred to in the United States, on training and selecting athletes for the Olympic Games. Each NGB (e.g., U.S. Gymnastics, USA Track and Field) identifies and prepares top athletes in their respective sports who then join the USOC to form the U.S. National Team. As of 2012, there were 205 NOCs representing both sovereign nations and other geographical areas (e.g., Palestine, Puerto Rico, Bermuda) recognized by the IOC. The issue surrounding if and/or how to recognize Taiwan (the Republic of China) versus the People's Republic of China (PRC) led to various boycotts between 1952 and 1976 as both entities wanted to represent China in the Olympic Games. Taiwanese athletes first refused to participate in the 1952 Helsinki Games due to the invitation of the PRC who sent 40 athletes. Next, the PRC boycotted the 1956 Melbourne Games on account of the presence of Taiwanese athletes and the recognition of the National Olympic Committee of Taiwan by the IOC. In 1958, the PRC broke off all relations with the IOC as they believed Taiwan was part of China and thus the recognition of two Olympic Committees for one country was in violation of the Olympic Charter. In 1976, Taiwan withdrew from the Games when the PRC pressured Canada, a trading partner, to deny the Taiwanese the right to compete as the Republic of China. The PRC returned to the Games in 1980 after the IOC voted in favor of recognizing the PRC Olympic Committee over the Republic of China. Since then, Taiwan competes in the Olympic Games under the Chinese Taipei name similar to the independent recognition of Hong Kong in the Games. ("China Orbit," 2009).

Hosting Cities

NOCs also nominate cities within their respective areas as candidates to host future Olympic Games. In the case of the USOC, since there are typically four to seven cities interested in hosting the Games, a domestic bid competition is established to select the best possible candidate to compete against other international cities. The IOC Executive Board then reviews all applicants submitted by NOCs and narrows the field to four to give candidate cities based on technical capabilities. For the 2016 Games, Chicago, Rio de Janeiro, Madrid, and Tokyo made it to the second or candidate phase of the bidding process. In the second phase, each of the candidate cities responds to a 250-page questionnaire that covers 19 major areas including transportation, accommodations, media operations, marketing, government support, general infrastructure, public opinion, and Olympic Village. An Evaluation Commission, composed of IOC members, representatives of the IFs, NOCs, the IOC Athletes' Commission and the International Paralympic Committee (IPC), as well as other experts, then analyze the detailed documents and visits each potential host city for four days. These visits are tightly scheduled with specific guidelines on what the candidate city can show and offer to the Evaluation Commission including limits on the number of guests invited to any receptions or dinners. Such restrictions were implemented as part of the 2002 Reforms, which also prohibits IOC members not on the evaluation committee from visiting candidate cities.

Following the visits, the Evaluation Commission prepares a report for the IOC listing its recommendations. This report is made public one month before the host city is selected at an IOC general assembly meeting held seven years in advance of the Olympic Games. During the IOC General Assembly seven years in advance of the Olympic Games, active IOC members listen to final oral presentations from each candidate host city representatives and cast secret ballots. If there is no city that receives an absolute majority of votes in the first round, the city with the fewest votes is eliminated and another round of voting begins. If there is a tie for the fewest votes, a special runoff is held with the winner proceeding to the next round. Once a winner is declared, the mayor of the host city and the President of the NOC sign a contract with the IOC. In the end, it is the NOC that is responsible to make sure the OCOG is formed and the Games are held successfully. Although not publicly acknowledged, candidate cities are wise to forge alliances with IOC members who may vote for a city eliminated early in order to have those votes shifted toward their city in subsequent rounds. Although IOC members should be voting on objective criteria, the candidate cities often have different strengths and weaknesses that are hard to compare and eventually it is left to the heart of each IOC member to vote how they feel on that specific day.

In the case of Beijing (selected to host the 2008 Games after the second round of voting), there were a number of factors in its favor, including the size of the country, improvements in Chinese anti-doping enforcement, its promise to enhance environmental conditions, and its two vote loss to Sydney, Australia, eight years earlier in the final round. For many, it was hard to deny a sport-loving country of 1.3 billion people, representing 20% of the world's population, the right to host the Games along with the hope that the Games may lead to progress on human rights. After all, the Games are not designed to be about politics but rather a forum to bring the world together to build a more peaceful universe. Unfortunately, some of the promises regarding freedom of the media and open Internet access made during the bid process were not carried out as hoped; however, the pride of the Chinese was never stronger than during the Olympic Games. The net social impact is difficult to measure. In the case of the 2016 Summer Olympic bid, Rio was the sentimental favorite as the Games have never been held in South America. Although Chicago had a very strong bid, they were the first to be eliminated. There are a number of reasons why this happened, including those who wanted Rio knew that Chicago was the strongest competitor and voted to eliminate them first. Tokyo also did not want to lose face by being eliminated first, and thus are said to have made agreements in exchange for subsequent round votes. Finally, USOC's favorable revenue split with the IOC and American politics also hurt Chicago's chances (Radford, 2009).

The NOCs are all members of the Association of National Olympic Committees (ANOC), which is split among five continental associations: Association of National Olympic Committees of Africa (ANOC); Pan American Sports Organization (PASO); Oceania National Olympic Committees (ONOC); European Olympic Committees (EOC); and the Olympic Council of Asia (OCA). These Continental Associations play a major role in the distribution of Olympic Solidarity fund to be discussed later in the chapter.

Organizing Committee of the Olympic Games

The final piece of the Olympic diamond is the Organizing Committee of the Olympic Games (OCOG), which at any one time could include two to three organizations (e.g., Sochi 2014, Rio 2016 Organizing Committees). OCOGs are analogous to temporary Fortune 500 companies that are created for the explicit purpose of organizing the Games and are disbanded shortly after. The IOC selects and entrusts the Games to the NOC of the host city, as well as the host city itself, seven years in advance. It is the responsibility of the NOC to establish an OCOG with the IOC serving in a supervisory and more recently a consultant role to the OCOG. The NOC is held jointly and severely liable, together with the OCOG and host city, for all commitments concerning the organization and staging of the Games, excluding the financial responsibility for the organization and staging of the Games.

Each OCOG works closely with the IFs to make sure the competition and practice venues are to their standards and that the competition schedule is appropriate. The NOCs coordinate ticket requests, housing in the Olympic Village, transportation, practice times, and security. The IOC ensures protocol, as outlined in the Olympic Charter, is being followed as related to everything from opening, closing, and medal ceremonies to Olympic Family transportation and hospitality.

Another related organization not included in this diagram, yet integral to the Olympic Movement, is the International Paralympic Committee (IPC). The IPC is the equivalent of the IOC for the Paralympic Games that, since 1988, follow the Olympic Games in the same city. The Paralympic Games are a multisport event for athletes with disabilities and since 1992 have been organized by the same OCOG. Further details pertaining to Paralympic sport and other disability sport initiative are addressed in Chapter 9.

Funding the Olympic Movement

For the first 84 years of the Modern Olympic Games (1896–1980), the Olympic Movement struggled financially. It was not until the 1984 Summer Games in Los Angeles, under the direction and vision of Peter Ueberroth, that the Games realized a surplus of $223 million and led to a renewed interest in host cities and the creation of a new financial model for the IOC. Prior to 1984, hundreds of companies paid a relatively small fee (typically less than $20,000) to be associated with the Games. Ueberroth, facing great financial pressure, as no public money was dedicated to the Games, decided to reduce the number of corporate sponsors and charge a minimum of $4 million for more exclusivity. He also limited the amount of new infrastructure required by utilizing as many existing venues as possible (Eason, 1984).

For the 1985–1988 quadrennium, which included the Calgary and Seoul Olympic Games, The Olympic Partners (TOP) corporate sponsorship program was established by the IOC with nine international companies spending more than $10 million each for marketing rights in all the countries participating in the Games. Since this time, worldwide sponsorship revenue has increased from $96 million to $957 million for the 2009–2012 quadrennium including Vancouver and London Olympic Games ("Olympic Marketing Fact File," 2012). Of this revenue, half is distributed between the OCOGs (30% to Summer Games, 20% to Winter Games). Another 40% goes to NOCs based on the relative market share/consumer spending of each country (e.g., Germany receives more than Jamaica). The remaining 10% stays with the IOC. Prior to TOP, fewer than 10 NOCs in the world had a source of marketing revenue. Now all 205 NOCs receive some amount of marketing dollars.

One issue, however, is that in 1988 the USOC negotiated a separate arrangement with the IOC stating that they would receive 20% of the TOP revenue before distribution, and 12.75% of the U.S. broadcast revenue (Hersh, 2009). The IOC agreed to such a deal considering that all of the TOP sponsors at the time were U.S. based and the majority of broadcast revenue came from the U.S. rights. In 1988, NBC paid $300 million to broadcast the Seoul Olympics in the U.S., while the rest of the world together contributed $90.5 million. In 2012, however, only half of the TOP Sponsors were U.S. based, and for the 2013–2016 quadrennium, although NBC paid more than $2 billion, the United States broadcast rights fees fell below 50% of total IOC television revenue. ("Olympic Marketing Fact File," 2012; Mickle, 2012). Considering the smaller percent of IOC revenues derived from United States based companies and the ill-will that the long standing contract has caused between the USOC and the rest of the world, a new agreement is set to take effect in 2020 and run through

2040. At this point, the USOC will retain its current revenue, but its television rights share will be reduced to 7% on any increases in broadcast deals and its marketing share will be cut in half to 10% on any increases in sponsorship revenue. The U.S. will also contribute $15 million to the administrative costs for the Games through 2020 and $20 million after 2020 (Whiteside, 2012).

Revenues from the IOC agreement account for approximately half of the USOC budget. Since the USOC receives no federal subsidies, unlike most other NOCs in the world, it claims this money is vital for U.S. athletes. Others claim that the USOC is the wealthiest NOC and has an unfair advantage, such as establishing its own training centers during the Games. In Beijing and London, the USOC leased a university in order to offer U.S. athletes private practice facilities, a cafeteria with food from the U.S., and a medical unit, all at a price tag of more than $2 million each. Considering that the USOC brings the largest team (more than 600 athletes) to the Games, it believes such facilities are necessary in order to provide for the needs of the athletes. The question of "How much is enough?" is difficult to determine and depends on which side of the negotiating table a person sits.

One of the biggest bargaining chips the USOC holds is that the United States is the largest consumer market in the world, and how many companies would still pay more than $100 million for the marketing rights if the United States withdrew from the TOP program? According to the 1978 Olympic and Amateur Sports Act, a federal law, the IOC has to go through the USOC to do Olympic business in the United States.

In addition to the worldwide rights, each OCOG, in coordination with the IOC and local NOC, sells domestic sponsorships that grant marketing rights within the host country only. These funds, more than $1 billion for the 2012 London Games, help to support both the planning and staging of the Games as well as the host country's Olympic team. Since 1988, the IOC requires that the OCOG and NOC collaborate in order to centralize all marketing initiatives within the host country.

Another major revenue source for the IOC, accounting for more than 50% of all revenues, is broadcast rights fees including television, mobile, and the Internet. According to Rule 48 of the Olympic Charter, "The IOC takes all necessary steps to ensure the fullest coverage by the different media and the widest possible audience in the world for the Olympic Games" (Olympic Charter, 2011, p. 90). In light of this objective, the IOC refrained from accepting higher rights fees from non-public broadcasters until 2009 when it signed a deal with Sportfive, a sports marketing agency based in Germany. This agreement, worth a reported $316 million, included rights for all media platforms from free and subscription television to Internet and mobile phones, across 40 countries in

Europe for the 2014 Winter Games in Sochi, Russia, and the 2016 Summer Olympics in Brazil. Sportfive replaced the European Broadcast Union (EBU), an umbrella body of public broadcasters that had held Olympic rights in Europe for more than 50 years. The increase in fees from Sportfive along with France, Germany, Italy, Spain, Turkey, and Britain, who were not included in the Sportfive deal, is expected to be 30% more than the $850 million EBU paid for 2010 and 2012. Sportfive will now seek broadcast partners with the obligation of ensuring at least 200 hours of free-to-air television coverage for the Summer Olympics and 100 hours for the Winter Games (Wilson, 2009).

A risk to consider when working with a private agency such as Sportfive, versus a public television entity, is that of bankruptcy. In 2001, International Sports & Leisure (ISL), the sports marketing agency responsible for broadcast and sponsorship deals for the 2002 World Cup, 2002 Asian Games, world athletic champions, ATP Masters tennis series, and formerly the Olympic Games, filed bankruptcy costing FIFA alone up to $56 million in losses ("FIFA boss Blatter," 2001). The agency ran into trouble when it guaranteed organizations high marketing fees and could not deliver.

When NBC negotiated its contract with the IOC for U.S. rights, the Internet was in its infancy, and included all digital rights. The question now is could the IOC earn more by selling television, Internet, and mobile rights separately.

The maximization of broadcast revenues not only helps to support the OCOGs and IFs but also provides the necessary resources to expand the universality of the Olympic Games, one of the core values of the Olympic Movement. OCOGs receive 49% of revenues from broadcast rights fees with the remainder divided between the IOC, IFs, and NOCs. For the majority of IFs, these funds are their largest single revenue source. Olympic Solidarity, a division of the IOC, is responsible for the administration and redistribution of the NOCs share of broadcast revenues (approximately 19%). The mission of Olympic Solidarity is to offer educational, technical, and financial assistance to those NOCs and their NSFs that have the greatest need thus increasing the opportunity for athletes from all countries to compete in the Olympic Games. Olympic Solidarity funds specific world programs for athletes, coaches, NOC management, and the promotion of the Olympic values including women in sport, sport and the environment, and sport for all. One of the most successful world programs is the Olympic Scholarship which offers more than 1,000 athletes access to adequate training facilities; specialized coaches; regular medical and scientific assistance and checkups; accident and health insurance; full-board accommodation; and financial help towards entry for and participation in Olympic qualifying competitions.

For the 2012 London Games, 52% of the 1,264 scholarship athletes qualified for the Olympic Games either through an IF qualification system or via an invitation from the IOC/ANOC/IF tripartite commission which was set up to assist the participation of smaller NOCs at the Games. Such wild card invitations are normally only allocated to NOCs which historically have six or less participants in the Games. All total, these scholarship athletes represented 165 countries and won 76 medals, many of which were the first for their country, thus providing a chance to stand on the podium as equals with the other medal-winning nations.

Olympic Solidarity also funds Continental programs which are decided upon by each of the Continental Associations depending on the specific needs of their respective NOC members. The amount of funds allocated to Continental programs has increased over the years as part of a decentralization effort (Olympic Solidarity, 2008).

Lastly, Olympic Solidarity allocates Olympic Games subsidies to NOCs to assist in covering their participation costs that includes reimbursement of airline tickets for six athletes and two officials for Summer Games and three athletes and one official for Winter Games. Olympic Solidarity also provides a subsidy to recognize the NOCs' contribution towards the success of the Games based on the number of athletes participating in the Games. For London, the amount was $2,000 per athlete. Based upon these figures, the USOC with 530 athletes in London received a subsidy of more than $1 million. Here again, the question is raised if the wealthiest NOC should accept such subsidies.

Besides the controversy over the USOC receiving 12.75% of broadcast rights and whether or not they should accept Olympic Solidarity funds, other issues or concerns related to the distribution of broadcast revenues includes the fact that many IFs have become dependent and content with the broadcast revenue creating somewhat static organizations. Furthermore, some of the wealthier NOCs harbor quiet resentment that their share of broadcast revenue is increasing competition on the playing field. There is concern as well over accountability of some of the programs but policies have been added throughout the years, such as distribution of funds only after certain benchmarks have been reached, to ensure successful outcomes.

Olympic Crisis or Progress

Host City Selection

In the late 1990s, evidence of unethical conduct by both IOC members and cities bidding to host Olympic Games was revealed. The scandal initially related to improprieties related to the Salt Lake City Olympic bid but evidence from previous bids was subsequently uncovered. With many parties admitting to either accepting or offering gifts, cash, and other favors, change was imminent.

Without defending unethical actions, it is important to understand that in many countries, such gift giving is accepted and considered part of everyday business. Even in the U.S., the idea of influencing opinion via favorable incentives is common practice. Pharmaceutical companies, for example, are notorious for wining and dining doctors, offering ski and golf vacations, or trips to mega-sport events including the Olympic Games.

Furthermore, the competition between cities to host the Olympic Games has increased dramatically since the success of the 1984 Olympic Games. In fact, the IOC had a difficult time finding a city to host the 1984 Games. The only other city bidding against Los Angeles was Tehran and in 1980, Lake Placid was the only city bidding to host the Winter Games. Now the competition consists of up to 10 cities vying for the right to host the Games.

The Olympic bidding process is also rather lengthy—often including both a domestic and international competition as previously discussed. With all this time for host cities to create impressions on decision-makers, desperation may lead to inappropriate actions. Another important consideration is the change of climate within the Olympic structure from an amateur organization to a commercial and profitable entertainment entity. While this transformation greatly augments the funding for sport development around the world, it also allows for more diversity of its membership (no longer are IOC members only of the nobility who could afford to pay their own expenses), and increases the potential for corruption.

Although the fact that some IOC members and bidding cities fell into an unethical business model may be explainable, it is not acceptable. The major problem is that those associated with the Olympic Movement have vowed to uphold Olympic standards. In fact, two of the roles of the IOC cited in the Olympic Charter are to "[s]upport and encourage the promotion of sports ethics" and to "oppose any political or commercial abuse of sport and athletes" (Olympic Charter, 2011).

At one point after the allegations around the Salt Lake City bid, there were five investigations in process (IOC, USOC, Salt Lake Organizing Committee, the FBI, and Utah's Attorney General), but the IOC made the first investigative report calling for the expulsion of six IOC members and a re-haul of the bidding process. With near unanimity a set of sweeping reforms were enacted, including the addition of 15 active athletes to the membership, a ban on visits by IOC member to candidate cities, an independent selection committee to screen proposed candidates for membership, an 8-year renewable term for members, and an 8-year term for the president, with only one renewable term of four years. Under the artful persuasion and leadership of President Juan Antonio Samaranch, the IOC aggressively worked toward cleaning house, restoring public confidence, and rebuilding its image. As part of this, for the first time in its history a global promotional program, entitled *Celebrate Humanity*, was designed to communicate the core values of the Olympic Movement including friendship, fair play, joy in effort, and hope. The campaign included television, radio, and print messages translated into 18 languages.

The turn of the millennium was a difficult time for the IOC, yet spectators and sponsors remained supportive. Attendance records were set for both the 2000 and 2002 Games and corporations realized that they needed the Olympic marketing platform as much as the IOC needed them thus encouraged a fast resolution.

Judging & Anti-Doping

In addition to the bidding scandal that brought organizational reform to the IOC, the Olympic Games also faced incidences of judging improprieties in boxing and figure skating, as well as an increased number of positive doping cases. Since 1972, officials take an "oath" during the Opening Ceremonies to judge fairly without any discrimination. IFs are responsible for the selection of officials and judges; thus, it is their responsibility to pursue disciplinary action and review the judging process. As for the doping problem, testing for drugs (narcotics and stimulants) has been instituted since the 1968 Games. In 1999, the IOC took a more aggressive stance and organized with governments from five continents an independent agency, the World Anti-Doping Agency (WADA), to promote and coordinate the fight against doping in all sports. Composed and funded equally by the Olympic Movement and governments of the world, WADA developed the World Anti-Doping Code (Code), a document that harmonizes anti-doping policies, rules, and regulations within sport organizations and among public authorities. Priorities for WADA includes implementation and compliance of the Code, coordination with law enforcement to gather and share evidence as well as enacting laws to combat the manufacturing, supply and possession of doping substances; support research to identify and detect doping substances and methods; maintain the Anti-doping Administration and Management System (ADAMS), a web-based database that coordinates anti-doping activities and helps stakeholders comply with the Code; connect countries within regions to pool anti-doping resources and maximize activities; provide anti-doping educational programs including prevention strategies; and directly touch athletes at events and through personal correspondence, answering questions and sharing information (WADA, 2009).

For the first two years of operation (2000 and 2001), WADA was funded entirely by the Olympic Movement, who gave a total of $18.3 million, in order to give governments time to secure approval for their agreed upon 50% of the funding. In 2012, contributions to WADA totaled $26.7 million with $13.2 million from the IOC and the rest from public authorities ("WADA's Budget," 2012).

Drug free sport faces numerous challenges including the expense of maintaining adequate testing and staying ahead of chemists and new doping techniques. The argument to compete fairly also becomes more difficult as financial and commercial rewards increase.

Controversies surrounding WADA are numerous, including the fact that U.S. professional athletes in the NFL, NBA, and MLB do not follow the Code despite basketball, and previously baseball, being part of the Olympic program (Woods, 2009).

All other athletes, under the "Whereabouts Rule" included in the Code, are obliged to provide details of where they can be located for a one-hour period each day, seven days a week, between 6 A.M. and 11 P.M. in order for WADA to conduct out-of-competition testing. Many professional athletes are unhappy about this "Whereabouts Rule" as they feel it is too much of an intrusion on their training and competition schedule.

Opponents also claim that positive results are not always valid. For those athletes who wish to contest results or have other legal concerns, the IOC established an independent Court of Arbitration for Sport (CAS) specializing in sports-related problems and authorized to pronounce binding decisions in a flexible, quick, and inexpensive manner.

Since 1983, CAS has resolved both commercial and disciplinary cases utilizing four distinct procedures: arbitration, appeals arbitration, advisory opinions, and mediation. Commercial disputes frequently involve the execution of contracts related to sponsorship and relationships between players, coaches, clubs, and/or agents, whereas disciplinary cases are most often related to appeals of a doping charge or a sports organizations decision such as disqualification or ineligibility. All Olympic International Federations, WADA, and most NOCs have recognized the jurisdiction of the Court of Arbitration for Sport and included in their statutes an arbitration clause referring disputes to the CAS. The International Council of Arbitration for Sport (ICAS) is the administrative and financial arm of CAS that safeguards its independence (TAS/CAS, 2012).

Keeping the Games Unique and Manageable

Throughout the years of the Modern Olympic Movement, the IOC has witnessed a series of highs and lows yet continues to grow. A major concern of the IOC is how to keep the Games unique and manageable. The first Games in 1896 attracted 245 athletes from 14 countries and in 2012 there were 10,903 athletes from 205 countries.

Soon after Jacques Rogue became IOC President, he initiated the Olympic Games Study Commission that offered 117 recommendations in 2003. The recommendations focused on five major areas: Games Format, Venues and Facilities, Games Management, Number of Accredited Persons, and Service Levels. The recommendations covered a gamut of issues from environmental sustainability (e.g., maximizing the use of temporary structures), to controlling the service levels for transportation of Olympic family members (buses rather than private cars) (Pound, 2003).

Although the IOC states that it wants to control the cost, size, and complexity of the operating budget of the Olympic Games, it continues to select host cities that require a considerable amount of new infrastructure with great travel distances between venues (e.g., Sochi and Rio). The 2014 Winter Olympic Games in Sochi were stated to cost a total of $51 billion, the most expensive Games to date, but this included the cost to completely upgrade Adler (the town where the Olympic Park, the Olympic Village, and numerous new hotels were housed) and to build three ski resorts in the Krasnodar region, including a new highway and rail system to the mountains. The actual Sochi OCOG budget accounted for $6 billion or less than 12% of the total stated (Yaffa, 2014). Similarly in London, the Olympic Games were used as a reason to develop East London from a desolate area to a vibrant commercial center (Moore, 2012).

Another program that the IOC initiated in 2000 to help OCOGs is the Olympic Games Knowledge Management (OGKM) program, previously referred to as Transfer of Knowledge. The objective is to provide a framework or reference point so that OCOGs do not need to reinvent the wheel each Olympic Games. Examples of documents include checklists, organizational charts, time lines, and budgets all based on previous Games. This is a great concept idea in theory, but limited in application as adaption depends on local politics, laws, culture, history, economics, and technology. Language barriers and unique sourcing and reporting processes also hinder collection of accurate data.

The relevance of the Olympic Games, especially among youth is another concern of the Games. The introduction of triathlon, snowboarding and BMX racing into the Games Program are examples of how the IOC is trying to make the Games more appealing to today's youth. The IOC also agreed to create the Youth Olympic Games (YOG), at the strong urging of Jacques Rogue, as a way to engage the younger generation and to give them an education based on Olympic values. These Games target athletes 14–18 years old and include sport, culture, and educational programming not just for participants, but spectators and youth around the world. There are great concerns, from IOC members and others, over the actual impact and implications of these Games. How will an unknown event, with small delegations of unknown athletes (3,600 from 204 countries), capture the interest of the media, nations, and the athletes themselves? The budget for the Games more than tripled from what was originally sold to IOC members and for most sports the qualification criteria is similar to other events, leaving many to wonder how athletes participating in the Youth Games differ from those in the World University Games, Junior World Championships, and even regional Games such as the Asian Games or Pan American Games. The only sure difference from the Olympic Games is that there are no national flags or anthems. The Olympic flag and anthem will exclusively be used during the Opening Ceremonies and medal ceremonies.

With such a heavy competition schedule already, IF leaders as well as parents of athletes express concern over how the Youth Games impact athletes' competition, training, and academics. The Winter Youth Games, held during the academic school year, requires more time away from the classroom, which is already substantial during a normal competition year. For most sports, the Youth Games do not count as a qualifier or contribute to competition points.

The inaugural 2010 YOG in Singapore grossly underestimated the cost to host the Games with the initial budget of $78 million increasing to $289 million ("Singapore Admits," 2010). With such a price tag, the question remains if the YOGs will make any lasting impact on the Olympic Movement or if the money would be better spent elsewhere. Host Cities are expected to pay for infrastructure and lodging while the IOC will pay the travel costs and room and board for all athletes and judges.

International Relations

Although the Olympic Charter clearly states that politics should not be involved in sport, the history of the Olympic Movement has provided several examples where the two have influenced one another (see Exhibit 7.2).

The IOC, NOCs and IFs, as independent and autonomous bodies, continue to work with governments and non-governmental organizations (e.g., United Nations) to ensure not only the development of sport worldwide but the development of wider human development goals reflecting the philosophy of Olympism.

> **Olympism** is a philosophy of life, exalting and combining in a balanced whole the qualities of body, will and mind. Blending sport with culture and education, Olympism seeks to create a way of life based on the joy found in effort, the educational value of good example and respect for universal fundamental ethical principles. The goal of Olympism is to place sport at the service of the harmonious development of man, with a view to promoting a peaceful society concerned with the preservation of human dignity (Olympic Charter, 2011).

According to IOC President Jacques Rogge, "More than ever, sport is a universal language and plays the role of catalyst in today's society as a means of improving quality of life and well-being" (Halvorsen, 2006, p. 4). Through the three core values of the Olympic Movement, excellence, friendship, and respect, sport has the power to help bridge cultural and ethnic divides, create jobs and businesses, promote tolerance and non-discrimination, reinforce social integration, and advocate healthy lifestyles.

Within the IOC, the Department of International Cooperation and Development, the Department of NOC Relations, and Olympic Solidarity work closely with other non-governmental organizations (NGOs) (e.g., World Health Organization), to organize conferences, write position papers, support programs, and provide general information on related policies and actions. One example of a program was the "Giving is winning" campaign in which all athletes and officials participating at the 2004 Olympic Games were invited to donate clothes to be distributed in collaboration with the United Nations High Commissioner for Refugees (UNHCR) to different refugee camps in the world. Several NOCs, as well IOC partners, donated batches of unused clothes as did the athletes. The program was so successful that the collection areas within the Olympic Village were overflowing.

Olympic Truce Foundation

In 2000, the IOC established the International Olympic Truce Foundation (IOTF), a non-governmental organization, to promote the Olympic ideals of peace, friendship and understanding in the world, especially the Greek tradition of the Olympic Truce, or Ekecheiria. During the Ancient Olympic Games, a ceasefire was called to allow safe passage of athletes and spectators to and from Olympia. Similarly, the Modern Olympic Truce calls for a worldwide cessation of all hostilities for the duration of the Games and was adopted by the member states of the UN General Assembly in 1993. Unfortunately, the Truce seems to be more rhetoric than real as witnessed when Russia, host of the 2014 Winter Games and strong supporter of the 2008 Olympic Truce, invaded Georgia on August 8, 2008, the Opening Day of the Beijing Games. The IOC's response was "The Olympic truce is an ideal (of the IOC) and how it is implemented is really through the UN" (Hayes, 2008, p. 2). Much criticism is cast on the IOC for not being more forceful in pressuring governments to live up to Olympic ideals such as peace and human rights, as in the case of Beijing. If the IOC becomes too political, however, it would risk the opportunity to gather athletes from around the world in a peaceful gathering at the Olympic Games, the ultimate goal of the IOC.

It was not the official U.S. government that kept the U.S. team from competing in the 1980 Games but surprisingly the U.S. Olympic House of Delegates, composed of 20% of current or recent athletes, voted to boycott the 1980 Olympic Games. President Jimmy Carter, however, made a very passionate address prior to the vote, and delegates obviously felt nationalistic pressure to support the commander-in-chief. Many regrettably commented after the vote that they were not sure what happened as they intended to oppose any boycott (DeFrantz, 2012).

The Olympic Games have endured numerous boycotts as well as IOC bans on NOCs for National policies conflicting with Olympic philosophies (see Exhibit 7.2). The verdict is still out on what affect, if any, such actions have made. Many believe boycotts do more harm to athletes than good for the cause.

Did 30 years of South African athletes not being allowed to compete in international sports influence or change the minds of their leaders? The hope of the Olympic Movement is that the Olympic Games provide an opportunity to bring people of all nationalities together, share common experiences, build friendships and heal wounds. Critics believe the IOC represents the hypocrisy of ignoring political problems in the name of entertainment and profit.

Although Olympism is a philosophy of life to be practiced 365 days per year, is it realistic to assume that the Winter and Summer Olympic Games, which each take place for 16 days once every two years, can resolve world problems? The actions of the IOC and events around the Olympic Games can and should play a contributing and supportive role, but the lead role in addressing such issues as human rights and political matters are more appropriate for governments and concerned organizations.

Exhibit 7.2: Olympics and Politics

1908
London

First time that athletes marched into Opening Ceremonies behind their country's flag. Finland, then ruled by Russia, was told that they could not march with their own flag. The furious Finns elected to march with no flag at all.

1916
Berlin

Cancelled due to WWI. This would have been the sixth in the four-year Olympic cycle and it was counted as such.

1920
Antwerp

Less than two years after the armistice, the Olympics resumed in Belgium, a symbolic and austere choice considering it had been occupied for four years by enemy forces. Twenty-nine countries sent athletes to the Games. Germany, Austria, Bulgaria, Hungary, Turkey, the defeated enemies of Belgium and the Allies, were not invited. The Athletes Olympic oath and the Olympic Flag, with its five multicolored, intersecting rings representing the 5 continents of the world and colors of all national flags, made their first appearance at the Antwerp Games.

1928
Amsterdam

These Games marked Germany's return to the Olympics after serving a 10-year probation for its "aggressiveness" in WWI. These Games also revived the Ancient Olympic tradition where the flame in the cauldron would burn throughout the games as a sign of purity, reason and peace.

1936
Berlin

Despite attempts of dictator Adolf Hitler and his Nazi followers to utilize the Games to demonstrate Germany's racial superiority, German crowds applauded thunderously, as world record-holder Jesse Owens, a black sharecropper's son from Alabama, stole the show, winning his three individual events and adding a fourth gold medal in the 4×100-meter relay. Hitler spent $25 million to ensure the finest facilities, the cleanest streets and the perfect atmosphere.

1940
Tokyo (canceled)
1944
(canceled)

By mid-1938, Japan was at war with China and withdrew as host. The venue was transferred to Helsinki; however, Finnish preparations were halted with the invasion of the Soviet Union in 1939. By then, Germany had invaded Poland, and WWII had begun. Games were canceled in both 1940 and 1944 due to war.

1948
London

Although much of the British capital had been reduced to rubble in the blitz, the games were held in London. Germany and Japan were not invited. Israel was also excluded to avoid a boycott by other nations. The Soviet Union was invited, but chose not to show.

1952 Helsinki

The Soviet Union returned to the Olympics after a 40-year absence. The Soviet Union had invaded Finland twice during WWII. Russian athletes were housed in a separate "village," due to fears of Cold War rivalries that were proved unfounded.

1956 Melbourne

The Soviet invasion of Hungary provoked some western countries such as Spain, Switzerland and the Netherlands to withdraw from the Games. Egypt, Lebanon and Iraq refused to participate in protest of the Franco-British Suez intervention. And the People's Republic of China refused to participate because of the presence of the Republic of China (Taiwan). Despite all the political unrest, the Games were a success. It was the first time athletes entered the stadium for the Closing Ceremony together, as a symbol of global unity, instead of behind national flags.

1960 Rome

Free of political entanglements, save the ruling that Nationalist China had to compete as Formosa, the 1960 Games attracted a record 5,348 athletes from 83 countries. This was the first Summer Games covered by U.S. television.

1964 Tokyo

Tokyo welcomed the world to the first Asian Olympics. The new Japan spent a staggering $3 billion to rebuild the city and prove to the world they were open for business. The IOC withdrew South Africa's invitation to compete in the Games for their refusal to condemn the practice of apartheid. This ban lasted 32 years until the 1996 Games.

1968 Mexico City

Ten days before the Olympic Games over 30 Mexico City university students were killed by army troops when a campus protest turned into a riot. Despite this, the Games began on time and were free of discord until black Americans Tommie Smith and John Carlos, who finished first and third in the 200 meter-run, bowed their heads and gave the Black Power salute during the national anthem as a protest against racism in the U.S. They were immediately suspended from the team by Avery Brundage, then President of the U.S. Olympic Committee and of the IOC. In 1936, however, Brundage made no issue of the Nazi salute which some felt was hypocritical. The Olympic Charter says in article 51 that 'No kind of demonstration or political, religious or racial propaganda is permitted in any Olympic sites, venues or other areas.' Violations can lead to disqualification and loss of Olympic accreditation.

1972 **Munich**	On Sept. 5, with six days left in the Games, The Palestine Liberation Organization (PLO), in hopes of capturing attention and support for its goals in the Middle East, attacked the Olympic village, and took hostages, resulting in the deaths of 11 Israeli athletes After suspending competition for 24 hours and holding a memorial, the games continued.
1976 **Montreal**	Right before the Games were scheduled to open, 32 nations, most of them from black Africa, walked out when the IOC refused to ban New Zealand because its national rugby team was touring racially segregated South Africa. Taiwan withdrew when Canada denied the Taiwanese the right to compete as the Republic of China.
1980 **Moscow**	Over 60 nations, including West Germany and Japan, stayed away from the Moscow games in support of the American-led boycott to protest the December 1979, Soviet invasion of Afghanistan. Others, such as Britain and France, while supporting the boycott, allowed their Olympic committees to participate if they wished.
1984 **Los Angeles**	The Soviet Union and 13 Communist allies boycotted the Games in what some say was a payback for the West's snub of Moscow in 1980. Mainland China returned to the Olympic Games along with Taiwan (competing under Chinese Taipei).
1988 **Seoul**	Cuba and Ethiopia stayed away in support of North Korea. The IOC turned down North Koreans' demand to co-host the Games, so they refused to participate.
1992 **Barcelona**	Germany competed under one flag for the first time since 1964. 12 nations from the Soviet Union joined forces one last time as the Unified Team. South African athletes returned to the Games since the start of the Apartheid Boycott. They participated under a "non-racial flag" instead of the "old" national flag.
1996 **Atlanta**	The Atlanta Games were the largest at that time with a record 197 nations competing. A bomb exploded in the Olympic Park killing two and injuring others. The person responsible was an anti-abortionist and charged with two additional bombings.
2000 **Athens**	North and South Korea marched into Opening Ceremonies as a joint team behind the Korean Unification flag although they competed as two separate teams. Afghanistan was not allowed to par-

	ticipate in the Games as the NOC was banned from the IOC due to discrimination against women under the Taliban rule.
2004 Sydney	Despite Iraq being in a war, its football team qualified and competed in the Games.
2008 Beijing	Protests against China's human rights, Tibet crackdown, and financial ties to Sudan occurred along the torch relay and raised concern about boycotts of the Games. Ultimately more countries and heads of state attended the Olympics than any other. It was the first time that a U.S. President attended the Games on foreign soil.
2012 London	The wrong national flag was hung for the North Korean women's football team in the women's football group match before the opening ceremony. Otherwise the Games were incident-free and, for once, politics and terrorism took a backseat as the world focused on the triumphs and tears of sport.
2014 Sochi	Leading up to the Olympic Games there were major security concerns with on-going unrest between the Russian government and Circassians. Human rights were also an issue in light of Russia's "gay propaganda" laws and treatments of workers.

(Adapted from TeacherVision, 2009; Griffiths, 2012; Nichol, 2014)

[*Note: See Appendix C for additional information pertaining to international politics in sport.*]

Leadership of Olympic Sports Organizations

Historically, sports activity has been organized around the commitment of volunteers who have provided both leadership and management. As the landscape of sport evolves, requiring the management of numerous partners (i.e., sponsors, public authorities, media) with multiple interests as well as fiscal accountability of often large sums of money, a more professional approach is required.

Mismanagement of funds, conflict of interest, lack of transparency, corruption, and internal political conflicts are some of the most common issues with which Olympic Sports Organizations struggle. Efforts are needed to improve transparency and increase effectiveness. The success of a sports organization can be reflected in various ways including growth of the organizations membership/participation base, financial stability and strength, and the organizational social and environmental impact. There is often a paradoxical mandate involving both public service and commercialization that requires a unique set of leaders to keep the organization steering straight.

Within the Olympic Movement, the organizational make-up runs from small one-person NOC and IF offices to a highly professional joint collaboration between USA Basketball and the National Basketball Association at the NGB level. The IOC has offered educational programs to increase the professionalism of both volunteer leadership and staff. At the impetus of President Juan Antonio Samaranch, the IOC also encouraged the inclusion of more women in leadership positions at all levels.

The first two female IOC members were elected in 1981 and, in 2009, 15% of IOC members were women. One female has also served on the IOC executive board since 1997. In 1996, the IOC established a goal that by the end of 2005 at least 20% of all decision-making positions within the NOCs, IFs, and sport governing bodies belonging to the Olympic Movement should be held by women. This goal turned out to be more ambitious than expected as seen in Exhibit 7.3 (IOC, 2012). By 2010 just more than 30% of the NOCs and 29% of the IFs achieved the 2005 target.

Exhibit 7.3: Percent of women in leadership roles within NOCs and IFs.		
	NOC	IF
Women on Executive Boards	17.6%	18.0%
Women Presidents	4.0%	3.2%
Women Secretaries General	9.0%	3.9%

In terms of gender equity on the field, the Olympic Games have come a long way since the Ancient Games, where only men were allowed to compete. The first female participation in the Modern Olympic Games occurred at the 1900 Games despite strong opposition from President Pierre de Coubertin who believed that the Games should remain a "Eulogy for men's sport" (IOC, 2009). At the 2012 Games, 44% of all athletes were female, every competing nation included at least one woman athlete and, with the addition of women's boxing, it was the first time that women competed in every sport on the Olympic Program. Thirty-four countries had teams with more women than men, including the United States where the women brought home more medals than the men (58 compared to 46) (Shambaugh, 2012).

The Olympic Movement is complex and ever evolving, impacting lives across the globe. With a large alumni base of more than 60,000 Olympians reconnecting through the World Olympians Association (WOA) and thousands of Olympic volunteers gradually being identified through on-line communities, the spirit of the Games grows stronger every day. It is the responsibility of current and future leaders to continue to balance and expand the three pillars of the Olympic Movement (Sport, Culture, and Environment) and to remember their role in supporting positive changes in the world. Looking forward, challenges for the Olympic Movement include: financial parity, especially as it relates to the USOC; equality in terms of gender and drug-free competition; relevance to youth; prosperity via media rights and corporate partners; and protection and promotion of Olympic values.

References

China Orbit. (2009). China—Olympic History. Retrieved from http://www.chinaorbit.com/2008-olympics-china/olympic-games-history.html.

Eason, H. (1984). The unstated message of the 1984 Olympics; the Los Angeles games will show U.S. private enterprise at work. *Nation's Business*. Retrieved from http://findarticles.com/p/articles/mi_m1154/is_v72/ai_3153763/.

FIFA. (2012, June 2). Formula for Competition. Retrieved from http://www.fifa.com/tournaments/archive/tournament=512/edition=8229/news/newsid=72831.html.

FIFA boss Blatter prepares for questioning by own board. (2001, June 12). Retrieved from http://sportsillustrated.cnn.com/soccer/news/2001/06/12/fifa_blatter_ap/.

Griffiths, F. (2012, July 25). North Korea Olympics Flag Flap: Women's Soccer Team Refuses To Take Field Against Colombia. Retrieved from http://www.huffingtonpost.com/2012/07/25/olympics-north-korean-flag-soccer-controversy_n_1703353.html.

Halvorsen, E. (2006). Safeguarding the Magic of the Rings. Retrieved from http://www.dnvusa.com/Binaries/_FORUM_0106_tcm153-191021.pdf.

Hayes, P. J. (2008, August 15). Kremlin crushes truce of the Games. *The Australian*. Retrieved from http://www.39essex.com/resources/article_listing.php?id=553.

Hersch, P. (2009, March 18). Globetrotting: IOC rattles a dull saber that could wound Chicago Olympic Bid. *Chicago Tribune*. Retrieved from http://newsblogs.chicagotribune.com/sports_globetrotting/2009/03/ioc-rattles-a-dull-saber-that-still-could-wound-chicago-olympic-bid.html.

IOC. (2009). Promotion of Women In Sport. Retrieved from http://www.olympic.org/uk/organisation/missions/women/activities/index_uk.asp.

IOC. (2012). Fact Sheet Women in the Olympic Movement Update—June 2012. Retrieved from http://www.olympic.org/Documents/Reference_documents_Factsheets/Women_in_Olympic_Movement.pdf.

Mickle, T. (2012, August 6). Revamped sales strategy helps IOC boost media rights fees. Retrieved from http://www.sportsbusinessdaily.com/SB-Blogs/Olympics/London-Olympics/2012/08/iocrevenue.aspx.

Moore, R. (2012, August 18). How the Olympics will shape the future of east London. Retrieved from http://www.theguardian.com/artanddesign/2012/aug/19/olympic-park-regeneration-rowan-moore.

Natives News. (2002, July 5). ISF Folds Operations. Retrieved from http://www.natives.co.uk/news/2002/0702/05fed.htm.

Nichol, J (2014, January 26). The 2014 Sochi Winter Olympics: Security and Human Rights Issues. Retrieved from http://www.fas.org/sgp/crs/misc/R43383.pdf.

Olympic Charter. (2011, July 8). Olympic Charter in Force as from 8 July 2011. Retrieved from http://www.olympic.org/Documents/olympic_charter_en.pdf

Olympic Marketing Fact File. (2008). IOC. Retrieved from http://multimedia.olympic.org/pdf/en_report_344.pdf.

Olympic Solidarity. (2008). Olympic Scholarships for Athletes "Beijing 2008" Results. Retrieved from http://multimedia.olympic.org/pdf/en_report_1397.pdf.

Pound, R.W., Q.C. (2003, July). Olympic Games Study Commission. Retrieved from http://multimedia.olympic.org/pdf/en_report_725.pdf.

Powers, J. (2009, October 10). Golf and rugby added for 2016 Olympics. *Boston Globe*. Retrieved from http://www.boston.com/sports/other_sports/olympics/articles/2009/10/10/golf_rugby_added_to_2016_olympics/.

Radford, P. (2009, October 4) Analysis-Olympics-Did Rio win or did Chicago lose 2016 Games? Retrieved from http://www.reuters.com/article/2009/10/04/olympics-bids-idUSL454817820091004.

Shambaugh, R. (2012, September 13). Summer Olympics Set the Example for Women in All Professions. Retrieved from http://www.huffingtonpost.com/rebecca-shambaugh/summer-olympics-set-the-e_b_1875049.html.

Singapore admits it got budget for Youth Olympics "wrong" after it trebles. (2010, September 16). Retrieved from http://www.insidethegames.biz/olympics/youth-olympics/2010/10526-singapore-admits-it-got-budget-for-youth-olympics-qwrongq.

TAS/CAS. (2012). History of The CAS. Retrieved from http://www.tas-cas.org/en/infogenerales.asp/4-3-236-1011-4-1-1/5-0-1011-3-0-0/.

TeacherVision. (2009). Olympics and Politics. Retrieved from http://www.teachervision.fen.com/world-politics/olympic-games/707.html.

WADA. (2012). Contributions to WADAs Budget 2012. t. Retrieved from http://www.wada-ama.org/Documents/About_WADA/Funding/WADA_Contributions_2012_update_EN.pdf.

WADA. (2009). World Anti-Doping Agency Mission & Priorities. Retrieved from http://www.wada-ama.org/en/dynamic.ch2?pageCategory.id=255.

Whiteside, K. (2012, May 24). USOC, IOC agreement opens door for possible bid. Retrieved from http://usatoday30.usatoday.com/sports/olympics/story/2012-05-24/usoc-ioc-revenue-sharing-agreement/55196490/1.

Wilson, S. (2009, February 18). IOC awards European broadcast rights to Sportfive. Retrieved from http://www.nytimes.com/2009/02/18/sports/18iht-olytv18.20285494.html.

Woods, M. (2009, February 25). Who are the real dopes in the NBA—the players or the policy-makers? Retrieved from http://www.guardian.co.uk/sport/blog/2009/feb/25/mark-woods-nba-basketball-drugs.

Yaffa, J. (2014, January 2). The Waste and Corruption of Vladimir Putin's 2014 Winter Olympics. Retrieved from http://www.businessweek.com/articles/2014-01-02/the-2014-winter-olympics-in-sochi-cost-51-billion.

Chapter 8

The Globalization of Sport

Lisa Delpy Neirotti, George Washington University

Sport plays a major role in societies around the world and people who study sport management must be able to embrace its global nature and understand its increasing power to transform lives and drive revenues. This chapter provides a historical overview of how different sports and professional leagues have grown internationally. It will also showcase both the social and economic impacts of the globalization of sport as well as tactics used by sport organizations to export sport and expand its marketplace. Although economic drivers may fuel the globalization of sport, the social and cultural impacts of sport are a source of secondary impetus to its international expansion efforts.

Sport is the one true universal language and bond between people from all corners of the world. Eitzen (2012) defines sport globalization as the "process whereby goods, information, people, money, communication, sport, fashion, and other forms of culture move across national boundaries" (p. 210). Through this exchange, political and social barriers may be diminished. One of the best examples of sport globalization occurred in 1971 when the U.S. Table Tennis team and its accompanying journalists became the first American sport delegation to set foot in the Chinese capital since the year 1949. This event marked a thaw in U.S.-China relations and paved the way for President Richard Nixon to visit Beijing. The impact of athlete exchange on international relations is referred to as Ping-Pong Diplomacy, a practice which remains today through globalization of the sport industry (Ping-Pong Diplomacy, 1999).

The globalization of sport continues to grow in parallel with increased communication and the evolution of transportation. The introduction of radio, television, and, more recently, Internet-based sport broadcasts enable fans from across the world to follow sports not native to their local area. Ground and air transportation allow athletes as well as fans the opportunity to travel greater distances to compete in and watch sport competitions.

Historical Overview of Sports Globalization

One of the first examples of sport exportation occurred in 1754 when Ben Franklin brought the 1744 laws of cricket from England to America. Cricket is experiencing a resurgence of growth in the United States at the turn of the 21st century due to the number of immigrants from Pakistan, India, and the Caribbean who know the sport and follow it. A cricket match held in 1844 between teams from the United States and Canada is listed as the first international sporting competition in the modern world, some 50 years before the Modern Olympics (Worral, 2006). The first recorded large-scale sport competition, however, was the first Modern Olympic Games in 1896 that showcased 241 athletes from 14 nations competing in nine sports and 43 unique events. To fully understand the globalization of sport, the historical exportation of some of the more popular sports internationally including soccer (football), baseball, and basketball will be explored more in-depth.

Globalization of Soccer

The contemporary history of soccer began in 1863 in England, when rugby football and association football (soccer) branched off on their different courses and the Football Association in England was formed—becoming the sport's first governing body (FIFA, 2014). The inaugural international match of association football between England and Scotland was held in Hamilton Crescent, at West of Scotland Cricket Yard, in 1872. Although this match was 20 months after the first international rugby match, it was the catalyst for the growth of soccer as an international game (Mitchell, 2005).

Association football was first documented in the United States in 1620, when the Pilgrims witnessed the American Indians playing along the coast of Massachusetts. The game grew in popularity throughout the states and was an organized sport at most universities by the mid-19th century. The American Football Association (AFA), founded in 1884, is recognized as the second oldest organized sports league in the United States after Major League Baseball. The AFA organized the first international soccer match held outside the British Isles in 1885 between United States and Canada (US Soccer, 2002).

Globalization of Baseball

As baseball became increasingly popular in the United States in the 1840s, more immigrants in the United States began learning and playing the game. Contrary to popular belief, the U.S. military did not bring the sport to foreign nations; it actually was the immigrants and academics that spread their love and passion for the game back to their home countries. Cuba, who remains an international baseball powerhouse, was the first Latin American country to be exposed to baseball. In 1864, Nemesio Guilló, on return from schooling at Springhill College in Mobile, Alabama, brought the first bat and baseball to the island of Cuba. Nemesio and his brother, Ernesto, founded the first baseball team in Latin America, the Habana Base Ball Club, but the team did not last long because Spanish colonial authorities outlawed the game during the Ten Years War from 1868–1878 (Echevarria, 1999). The game quickly spread throughout Latin America as Cubans fled during the Ten Years War to the Dominican Republic and other Caribbean nations. By the turn of the century, baseball became the most popular sport in countries of Cuba, the Dominican Republic, Venezuela, and Puerto Rico and their passion for the game rivals only the United States (Gillette, 2007).

The history of baseball in Japan began in 1872 when Horace Wilson, an American professor at Kaisei Gakko (Tokyo University), taught the game to his students because he felt they needed more physical activity. A year later, a professor at Kaitaku University, Albert Bates, organized the first game in Tokyo. Hiroshi Hiraoka, who learned the game in the United States while studying engineering, introduced baseball to his co-workers at Japan's national railways. He and his co-workers created the first baseball team, the Shimbashi Athletic Club in 1878 (Reaves, 2002). The game continued to spread throughout Japan and in 1910 it received a significant boost as American baseball players toured the country. Herbert Hunter, a Major League player, is credited with leading three such international tours and teaching the fundamentals of the game to thousands of Japanese boys. The Tokyo Giants were formed when a group of MLB All-Stars led by Babe Ruth and Lou Gehrig traveled to Japan in 1934 (Gillette, 2007). Baseball was then introduced in Taiwan by the Japanese who ruled the island from 1895 to 1945, while a missionary introduced the sport to Korea in the late 19th century.

Globalization of Basketball

Basketball was first developed by Canadian-born physical education professor Dr. James Naismith in 1891 in Springfield, Massachusetts. He invented the game to keep his class active on a rainy day and developed 13 rules to guide the game. Basketball spread quickly by the students he taught, and the first collegiate game was organized as an intramural competition by students from Geneva College outside of Pittsburgh in 1892. In 1904, the game was brought to Canada and the first interuniversity game was played between McGill University and Queens University (Naismith, 1941).

In 1930, the first officially recognized international basketball competition was held in Uruguay and included Argentina, Chile, Brazil, and the host country. The round robin tournament resulted with an undefeated record and championship for Uruguay. Basketball was officially recognized by the International Olympic Committee in 1930 following this tournament. The International Federation of Basketball Association (FIBA) was founded in 1932 by eight members: Argentina, Czechoslovakia, Greece, Italy, Latvia, Portugal, Romania, and Switzerland. At the 1936 Olympics in Berlin, James Naismith was named the honorary President of FIBA and the United States beat Canada in the championship game (FIBA, 2007). Although this was the first Olympics to officially include basketball, the St. Louis games in 1904 showcased the game to the world as a demonstration tournament among American teams (Hoffman, 2003).

The globalization of basketball took a major leap forward in 1979 when owner Abe Pollin took the Washington Bullets to China to tip off a new era in sports diplomacy (du Lac, 2009). Although the United States sent many amateur sports teams to China during the 1970s, the Bullets were the first U.S. professional sports team to visit China. The trip was able to occur because then President Jimmy Carter signed a normalization of relations document with Chinese leader Deng Xiao Ping on January 1, 1979, who then extended an invitation to Pollin (PBS, 1999). Team executives and current players, including NBA great Wes Unseld, traveled from Peking to Shanghai to Canton visiting the Great Wall, the Forbidden City, the Summer Palace, and Tiananmen Square (du Lac, 2009). The defending NBA Champion Bullets played both the Chinese national team and the People's Liberation Army's Bayi team, and from this diplomatic experience the popularity of basketball soared in China (Tang, 2009). In September 2009, the Wizards (formerly the Bullets) took another group of executives, current and former players to China to commemorate the 30th anniversary of their historic trip (du Lac, 2009). On this trip the team participated in a series of basketball clinics in universities and high schools, met with various Chinese corporations, and engaged in other philanthropic activities (Tang, 2009).

International Expansion of North American Professional Sport Leagues

The National Hockey League (NHL) is the most international league of the major professional sports in North America. The league's headquarters are split between Toronto and New York, which allows them to appropriately govern the seven Canadian-based franchises and the remaining 23 teams based in the United States. International expansion by a U.S.-based professional sports league first occurred in 1969 when Major League Baseball expanded to include the Montreal Expos franchise (now the Washington Nationals) and then the Toronto Blue Jays in 1977. Similarly, the NBA expanded to Canada in 1995 through the addition of franchises in Vancouver and Toronto. The Vancouver Grizzlies later relocated to Memphis prior to the 2001–02 season. MLB continued its global expansion in 2009 with a first ever exhibition series in China, and the third Opening Series in Japan.

It was not until the United States held the 1994 World Cup that support for a professional soccer league began to build in the United States. There were previous attempts at creating leagues but Major League Soccer (MLS), promised to FIFA as a condition of receiving the bid to host the tournament, has been sustained as a World Cup legacy. "Being involved in the 1994 World Cup (as a host of matches in Foxboro Stadium) was one the most thrilling experiences of my professional career and really opened my eyes to the potential for the growth of the sport in this country," said Bob Kraft, owner of the NFL's New England Patriots and founding MLS investor/operator of the New England Revolution, which has played in the MLS since its inaugural season in 1996 (Stedman, 2009, p. 4)

In 2005, MLS added Chivas USA, the only wholly Mexican-owned team in major professional sports in the United States, to its roster. Chivas USA is the sister team to Mexico's most beloved soccer club, Club Deportivo Guadalajara, popularly known as Chivas. MLS also has a team in Toronto, to compliment the expansion teams that arrived in Vancouver in 2011 and Montreal in 2012 (Stewart, 2012).

The National Football League was the first U.S. league to explore Europe by playing a pre-season game in London in 1986 and subsequently organized the World League of American Football in 1991, renamed to NFL Europa in 1998. The league ultimately folded in 2007 due to the negative cash flow the NFL Europa owners were experiencing. Since then, the NFL has marketed itself globally by holding pre-season and regular season games overseas so that the best teams and players in the world may be appropriately showcased. There are also talks of a NFL franchise in London sometime in the next decade (Thamel, 2009).

The NBA was the first U.S. sports league to hold a regular season game in Japan in 1990 between the Phoenix Suns and Utah Jazz. It currently has more global outreach programs than any other league with offices in 14 countries and the only one with representation in Africa.

In 2008, the NBA launched NBA China, a company, then valued at $2.3 billion, had 11%, or $250 million, of its initial investment come from five investor groups. The only non-Chinese firm of these five was Walt Disney Co. (de la Merced, 2008). In the first two years, NBA China claimed double-digit revenue growth primarily due to its 50 plus media deals. NBA China accounted for approximately half of the NBA's international revenue, valued by *Sports Business Journal* between $150 million and $170 million in 2010 (Lombardo, 2010).

Experts agree, however, that the key to further accelerated growth in China is more live programming, especially within the potential NBA affiliated league. The current Chinese basketball league, Chinese Basketball Association (CBA), is not considered very competitive compared to the NBA, therefore, many former NBA star players in the twilight of their careers decide to play in China. This has been beneficial for the CBA as the former stars draw bigger audiences to the arenas and television. As of 2012, the NBA is continuing to draw from its brand popularity in China to blend the CBA with a NBA affiliated league in China (Yardley, 2012).

In September 2009, the NBA was also the first to approve a foreign owner, Mikhail Prokhorov, deemed Russia's richest businessman, who bought controlling shares of the New Jersey Nets basketball team ("Russian buys controlling stake," 2009). Prokhorov's company, Onexum Group, invested $200 million for 45% of the Barclay's Center (new arena) and 80% of the team's capital. The commissioner of the NBA, David Stern, was content with the investment and promoted it as a way to help the globalization of the NBA ("Russian buys controlling stake," 2009).

Subsequently, the Cleveland Cavaliers signed an agreement in May 2010 with an investment group from China to become minority owners of the NBA franchise and its arena. This partnership is expected to not only provide an influx of needed capital to the team but serve as a direct pipeline to Chinese sponsors and fans. At the time, it was thought that both of these contributions may directly influence LeBron James' future with the team, especially the latter as Chinese ownership could open many commercial doors for James in China even more so than playing in a large market like New York (NBA, 2009). "You have to think globally," James said recently of his business interests. "I have a lot of fans in China and they're important to me" (Turner, 2009, p. 8).

The greatest impact to the growth of basketball during the 2000s was the emergence of Yao Ming. After being picked first overall in the 2002 NBA draft, Yao, a center who measured 7 feet, 6 inches tall, played nine years in the league, eight of which he was selected to the All Star Game. In his first season, the NBA debuted its fan voting All-Star selection ballot in Chinese to accommodate the Chinese fans who wanted to vote. Due to the demand in

China to see Yao play, the NBA started broadcasting games live in China in 2002. It drew 10 to 15 million people during games not featuring Yao and more than three times that when he did play (Yardley, 2012). He was also the face for advertising of multiple Chinese and American businesses, which were looking to use his global fame. The Yao Ming wave of enthusiasm for basketball in China has opened the basketball world to the possibilities of capitalizing on this new market.

Foreign Ownership

Not all international investment is well received. In 1992, Peter O'Malley of the Los Angeles Dodgers, along with other club owners, tried to veto a proposal by a Japanese group to purchase 37% ownership of the Seattle Mariners. The committee was not favorable to allowing ownership of American teams to someone residing outside of the United States and Canada (Chass, 1992). Similarly, Michel Plantini, president of the Union of European Football Associations (UEFA), spoke out in 2008 against foreign ownership of European soccer teams. Plantini suggested that wealthy Americans were buying too many clubs. Currently, 5 out of 20 English Premier League (EPL) clubs contain investments made by foreigners, including Manchester United, Liverpool, Arsenal, Aston Villa, Fulham, and Sunderland, which are all invested by wealthy Americans. English Premier League fans have further stated their discontent with American ownership, which could potentially hurt a team's bottom line if fans revolt by not attending games or buying merchandise.

In 2005, American businessman and owner of the National Football League's Tampa Bay Buccaneers, Malcolm Glazer, acquired a 98% stake in Manchester United. Although the club has achieved a large amount of success on the field and with sponsorship opportunities, the takeover by the Glazer family has left the club with more than $1.7 billion of debt (BBC News, 2010). This debt has led to an uproar from fans about the future of the club. In January 2010, the Red Knights, a group of Manchester United supporters, reached out to football financier Keith Harris to try to broker a deal to buy out the club from Glazer. They feel that the financial insecurity of the club is unhealthy and this will lead to the downfall of the club (BBC Sport, 2010). The Liverpool ownership of Tom Hicks and George Gillett was also under much scrutiny because of the poor relationship between Hicks and the team's managers. When Hicks purchased the team he planned to build a new stadium, which did not come to fruition (McNulty, 2008). In 2010, Liverpool was taken over by Fenway Sports Group, known primarily for their ownership of MLB's Boston Red Sox.

Growth of International Sports Leagues

The English Premier League (EPL) generates the highest revenue of any football league in the world, with total club revenues of €2.271 billion (more than $3 billion) in 2010–2011 (Deloitte, 2012). It was the first league to recognize its market size constraint and aggressively pursued fans internationally. The leagues initial push was through global media distribution, followed by exhibition matches, fan clubs, and commercial branding. The teams playing in the EPL now have a much larger fan base globally than domestically. Liverpool Football Club, for example, has 40,000 paying members in a fan club in Norway and has more fans in Australia than the Cleveland Indians have in all of the United States (D. Cipullo, personal communication, June 10, 2010). Manchester United has more than 300,000 subscribers to their fan magazine in Thailand (Reid, 2001).

Within the EPL, Liverpool and Manchester United benefited the most from sports globalization. They are recognized as Europe's pre-eminent clubs since they were the top performing teams during both the global cable expansion of the 1970s and 1980s and the satellite television boom in the 1990s (Schoenfeld, 2010). Manchester United lays claim to an unmatched global fan base of 333 million people—most of which reside in Asia (Schwartz, 2013).

European leagues that rival the EPL are Spain's La Liga, Italy's Serie A, France's Ligue 1, and Germany's Bundesliga. In a 2012 report by Deloitte Sports Business Group, the "Big Five" football leagues had a revenue increase from approximately $837 million to more than $9.2 billion. The report also stated that Real Madrid of Spain's La Liga has the highest revenue of any professional sports team in the world, $479 million (Deloitte, 2009). This total is even more than the highest grossing NFL and MLB team, the Washington Redskins and the New York Yankees, who brought in $345 million and $320 million, respectively (Phillips, 2009).

The Champions League brings together every year the top clubs from all of Europe's soccer leagues to compete to be crowned the best club in Europe. The Champions League final is the world's most watched annual sporting event bringing in an audience of more than 109 million people. The Super Bowl recorded a viewership of almost three million fewer people (BBC Sport, 2010). The Japanese J League is the most popular soccer league in Asia, but games are difficult to find and only broadcast in America through online telecasts (AFC, 2010).

Basketball is another sport with a significant presence overseas. The Euroleague is the second largest basketball league in the world, only behind the NBA. The Euroleague has teams from 18 different countries. Although this league is based in Europe, the country with the highest percentage of players is the United States with 26%. Lithuania is second with 2% of the players. Overall, European players make up 69% of the league (Talk Basketball, 2010).

Outside of the United States, the highest level of baseball competition is Japan's Nippon Professional Baseball League. The number of Japanese players moving to MLB, beginning with Hideo Nomo in 1995, significantly reduced the league's popularity and television ratings. Consequently, Japanese baseball and MLB agreed on a posting system for players under contract that serves to discourage player migration or at least compensates teams that lose players. MLB teams wishing to negotiate with a Japanese player must submit bids for a "posting fee," which the winning MLB team would pay the Japanese team if the player signs with the MLB team. Free agents are not subject to the posting system. Although the bid's amount is not publically released, estimates have exceeded $50 million. In 2002, with the approval of MLB, the New York Yankees signed a memorandum of understanding with the Yomiuri Giants that, among other things, includes the exchange of scouting reports on professional baseball players in the United States, Japan, and Latin America as well as an exchange of minor league coaches and staff (Bloom, 2002). Although no professional baseball league in Europe exists, there are 17 European Baseball Academies that producing MLB-level players. Germany, Netherlands, and Italy have the highest number of registered baseball players (Schaerlaeckens, 2011).

As of 2012, the largest non-North American hockey league is the Kontinental Hockey League (KHL) located in Russia. It is becoming a major player in the market for marquee athletes because of the tax-free salary incentive offered to players. The KHL has an exclusive TV/Internet deal with Sport TV that allows the games to be broadcasted both on television and the Internet internationally on RTR Planeta (Wyshynski, 2008).

Global Sports Marketing

The need to expand a sports market through global marketing became more prevalent to sport executives as U.S. professional sport leagues started to mature in the late 1970s, in tandem with, the globalization of sport through the broadcast of the Olympic Games and other international competitions.

With the commercial development of China and India, the two largest countries in the world population wise, executives are racing to create fans and grow their market share. Techniques used to develop fan bases abroad include: international broadcast rights, recruitment of foreign players, brand recognition through licensed goods, fan clubs, exhibition tours, youth academies, social media including localized websites, community service, and partnerships with regional market chains such as coffee shops or hotels.

International Broadcast Distribution and Websites

One of the most effective ways leagues have entered a market is through televised broadcasts. The 1956 Olympic Games were the first sporting event to be broadcast internationally from Melbourne, Australia (Cullen, 2010). In 1986, the NBA became the first major league to launch in-house international television distribution when the NBA and British Satellite Broadcasting reached an agreement to broadcast 40 games per season in the United Kingdom starting with the 1989–90 season. The games represent the first-ever weekly series of live NBA games to be broadcast overseas (Hoopedia, 2006). In 1999, the NBA debuted NBA-TV, which provided 24-hour viewing to 66 countries.

The National Football League led the way in 2012 with international broadcasts in 240 countries and territories. They are followed by MLB who broadcasts in 220 countries and 20 languages, the NBA with 215 countries and 47 languages, the EPL with 211 countries, and the NHL with 160 countries (Harris, 2010; Jessop, 2012; MLB International, 2012; NBA Global, 2012; NFL International, 2012). In 2008, MLS signed its first international television rights deal for an eight-figure sum to MP & Silva, a sports marketing agency. This five-year deal demonstrates an interest in the MLS internationally and allows MLS to gain the attention of future players in the league (Mickle, 2008).

Each of the leagues also has global websites offered in multiple languages. An analysis by comScore, Inc., an Internet market research company, found that visitors to the four largest leagues online sites had notable local and global differences. The sites examined were those for Major League Baseball (MLB.com), the National Basketball Association (NBA.com), the National Football League (NFL.com), and the National Hockey League (NHL.com). NBA.com has the most global Internet traffic, generating more than 52 million global monthly unique viewers, which is 47% of its total Internet traffic (Lombardo, 2010). The NBA's YouTube channel has accumulated more than 1 billion views since 2005 and about half of the league's Facebook, Twitter, and YouTube audience are based internationally (Jessop, 2012). The other major U.S. professional leagues are behind in international traffic; with the NHL having 88.2 %of traffic from the United States, MLB with 88.3%, and the NFL with 92.7 % (comScore, 2009). ComScore also completed a study of worldwide traffic figures for the top European football clubs' websites in March 2007. Manchester United attracted 2.2 million unique visitors to its website, making it the world's most popular football club online. The study also shows that roughly 60%, or 1.3 million, of Manchester United's 2.2 million monthly visitors do not reside in the U.K.—quantifying the global reach and appeal of the Manchester United brand franchise. The top seven most popular football teams online are Liverpool (1.5 million global unique visitors), Arsenal (1.4 million), Real Madrid (1.1 million), Barcelona (1.05 million), Chelsea (1.0 million), and A.C. Milan (0.8 million) (comScore, 2007).

International Exhibitions and Competitions

International exhibitions, pre-season, and in-season competitions are also used by leagues to introduce and grow their sport to new markets. International soccer clubs from England, Spain, and Italy frequently team with the MLS to hold tours of the United States prior to their season. In 2010, DC United played AC Milan, Seattle Sounders played Boca Juniors and Celtic, and the Philadelphia Union played Manchester United (MLS, 2010). Furthermore, the MLS All-Star game features players selected from the 16 teams in the leagues playing against an opponent from the English Premier League. Opponents have included Chelsea, Everton, West Ham, Fulham, and Manchester United in 2010 (Shore, 2010). The MLS also participates in the CONCACAF Champions League that crowns the North American and Caribbean Soccer Club Champion with the winner advancing to the FIFA Club World Cup.

The NFL held its first regular season game outside the United States in 2005 in Mexico City. Since 2007, the NFL has held a regular season game in London at Wembley stadium with the average attendance more than 80,000 (NFL, 2012). USA Football, the sport's U.S. governing body on youth and amateur levels, held the first "Team USA vs. The World" game during Pro Bowl Week in January 2010. The game matched USA Football's 2010 Junior National Team—45 of the country's top high school seniors—against a "World" team composed of the best players aged 19 and under from outside the United States, spanning four continents. USA Football was endowed by the NFL and NFL Players Association in 2002 and is their official youth football development partner (USA Football, 2010). The NBA has a series of programs to bring its team across the globe. Since 2006, NBA Europe Live is an annual event which pairs NBA teams with teams from Euroleague and Eurocup. In 2012, seven preseason games were played in Istanbul, Milan, Berlin, Barcelona, Shanghai, Beijing and Mexico City to a sold out crowd (NBA Global, 2012). MLB continued its international expansion in the spring of 2009 with its first-ever exhibition series in China (MLB International, 2012). In spring of 2012, the fourth Opening Series in Japan since 2000 took place, featuring the Seattle Mariners and Oakland Athletics. MLB also operates the World Baseball Classic (WBC), which brings teams from 16 countries together every three years for a tournament to decide the top national team in the world. The 2009 WBC had a significant international television rating increase compared with the inaugural 2006 classic. In Japan, the first game match up of Japan versus Korea earned a rating of 37.8 with more than 45 million viewers tuning in. This marked the highest rated sporting event of any kind in Japan, greater than either the 2002 World Cup in Korea/Japan and the 2008 Beijing Olympic Games. Similarly, an increase in viewership occurred in Canada for the 2009 WBC, with a 77% rating increase from the 2006 WBC (Baseball World, 2009).

The NHL is very active outside of North America, focusing primarily on the NHL Challenge Series, the Olympic Games, and the World Cup of Hockey. The NHL Challenge Series is a program that allows select NHL teams to travel outside of North American to hold training camps and play exhibition games. Hockey exhibits and fan festivals are also held in the host nations. Germany, Slovakia, Switzerland, Czech Republic, Finland, Sweden, England, and Japan have all been a part of the NHL Challenge Series (NHL International, 2010). In 2010 the NHL held a record 13 exhibition and regular season games in Europe (Lefton & Tripp, 2010).

Global competitions such as the Olympic Games and World Cup also help to grow a sport internationally, especially sports such as basketball, hockey, and soccer. The 2006 World Cup drew the highest cumulative audience to date of 26.29 billion viewers from 214 countries (FIFA, 2010).

Recruitment of Foreign Players

Drafting foreign players into a league and having them serve as ambassadors is another successful tactic. Leagues utilize foreign players to help market the team and league globally. In 2007, the NBA launched a marketing campaign with FedEx that utilized five international NBA players. The players selected were Andrei Kirilenko (Utah Jazz) from Russia, Manu Ginobili (San Antonio Spurs) from Argentina, Steve Nash (Phoenix Suns) from Canada, Tony Parker (San Antonio Spurs) from France, and Peja Stojakovic (New Orleans Hornets) from Serbia. This marketing campaign was another example of how the NBA promoted its vision to increase global popularity.

Transnational athlete migration is a dominant force in today's sport industry. The movement of transnational athletes may be seasonal, or may be due to tournaments such as the British Open or the Ryder Cup, and other major sport functions. Such events attract a host of international competitors hoping to make their presence known in the host country. Voluntary migration does not guarantee a shared experience for foreign athletes. Some athletes are welcomed anywhere with open arms, such as David Beckham or Alexander Ovechkin. Some athletes, however, report racist experiences in foreign countries. Others express feelings of culture shock and homesickness (Coakley, 2004). Landon Donovan, for example, played soccer in Germany early in his career, but returned to the MLS because of homesickness. U.S. athletes playing professional sports abroad also report feeling tremendous pressure as expectations to win are higher, rivalries stronger, and fan behavior more intense than in the United States.

Restrictions placed upon migrant athletes are a source of controversy in the sports industry. Today soccer leagues around the world have regulations limiting the amount of foreign-born players on their teams' rosters. Taken from the MLS Roster Regulations "Each team is allotted eight international slots, with the exception of Toronto FC who is allotted 13 international slots, five of which may be used on domestic U.S. players. All international slots are 'tradable,' therefore a team may have more or less than the eight International players on its roster" (MLS, 2010). During the 2010 season, there were a total of 165 players born abroad representing 58 countries in the MLS. This represents approximately 40% of the total players in the league, but many of these 165 are permanent U.S. citizens or green card holders, which do not count against the allotted eight international players per team. Of the MLS's 400 players, 97 are deemed as "internationals," meaning that they are not U.S. Citizens, Canadian citizens, or U.S. green card holders (W. Kuhns, Personal Communication, 2010).

The Barclays Premier League in England has a similar international player restriction as the MLS. Out of the 25 players on the roster, eight have to be "homegrown" players and no more than 17 can be older than 21 and not homegrown. "Homegrown" is described as a player that has been trained for three years under the age of 21 by someone within the English and Welsh professional system (Barclays Premier League, 2010). Therefore, a team may have a roster of all foreign born players as long as they have been trained by an English or Welsh club for more than three years. As of the 2009–2010 season, only 198 of the 499 players in the premier league were English born. This means that more than 60% of players in the English Premier League were not born in England. Compare this number to the 1989–1990 season where more than 75% of the 427 players were born in England (Williams, 2009). Globalization has significantly altered the makeup of the EPL over the past 20 years, and as seen in the MLS and other leagues across the world, this trend is continuously increasing.

Fans of baseball in the United States have been cheering for names like Ramirez, Martinez, Ichiro, and Nomo for decades without thinking twice about the origins of their favorite players. Roberto Clemente was the first Latin American player inducted into the baseball Hall of Fame in 1973. In 2012, the number of foreign-born baseball players at the major league level hit 28.4% on Opening Day. The league approximated that 50% of players across the major and minor league levels were not born in the United States (MLB, 2012). Signing international baseball talent is a rather simple process as opposed to acquiring athletes from the U.S., Canada, and Puerto Rico, who must first go through a draft process and subsequent hurdles under baseball's collective bargaining process. The only restriction placed on international talent is that the athlete must turn 17 before the end of the season in which he is signed. Without the oversight of actions of trainers and agents, the international scouting game has been referred to as an "economic free for all" (Helfgott, 2008).

International scouting divisions have developed in the Dominican Republic around the sport of baseball. The Dominicans are extremely passionate about baseball and talent is followed as early as 8 years old; support is granted to athletes through various training programs. Trainers called Buscones (literal translation "seeker") take care of all of the players' needs (i.e., meals, accommodations, training) in exchange for no less than 30% of any contract signed. A law was passed capping fees at 10%, but enforcement of the law is rare. Some professional baseball players are actually Cuban defectors.

Although baseball hosts the largest number of foreign-born players, 243 major players and 3,356 minor players, the NHL has reported even more; 273 or 33% of NHL's players are from outside of North America (NHL International, 2009). In the 2012–2013 season, the NBA documented 83 foreign-born players, the NFL noted 51 foreign-born players, and MLS identified 165 foreign-born players on rosters.

In 2004, the Ladies Professional Golf Association (LPGA) documented 280 registered golfers on its roster. Of that number, 98 were from countries other than the United States (Eitzen, 2006). In light of its large number of foreign players, the LPGA received much attention for its plans to implement English language requirements as a membership credential. Under the communication program by Commissioner Carolyn Bivens, a proposal was submitted which indicated that each participant must be able to communicate in English. This was to ensure that each player could competently communicate with sponsors and customers while in the United States. Players would have to pass a language proficiency exam. Failure to adhere to this policy was punishable by suspension of playing privileges (Bush, 2008). The proposal was abolished after protests occurred in September 2008 (Newport, 2008). Supporters of the proposal such as Tuyet Duong, staff attorney at the Asian American Justice Center, believed language-learning resources were an asset to the LPGA. However, it was deemed that the demand for such an exam was exclusionary. State Farm Insurance, a major sponsor of the LPGA, disagreed with the proposal and asked for alternatives. Senator Leland Yee of California announced an investigation of the proposal to determine if it was a violation of state or federal law. An official LPGA statement yielded that the Association would continue to implement the Kolon-LPGA Cross-Cultural Program, which would provide tutors, translators, and other assistance to its members (Bush, 2008).

In general, golf and tennis are two of the most global sports. Although American's long dominated the Professional Golfers Association (PGA), in 2012 international golfers occupied eight of the top 10 spots in the World Golf Rankings. Of the top 20 players competing in the Women's Tennis Association (WTA) and the Association of Tennis Professionals (ATP), only one player from the United States player is listed in each (Serena Williams and John Isner). There are a number of golf tournaments that promote international competition including the Ryder Cup, Walker Cup, Solheim Cup and Curtis Cup. The four grand slam tournaments in tennis are located across the globe: Australian Open, French Open, Wimbledon, and U.S. Open.

Global Brand Licensing and Sponsorship

Establishing brand recognition through licensed goods, store fronts, and cafes is yet another marketing tactic used by leagues to expand internationally. The NBA counted more than 300 licenses that manufacture, sell, and market NBA branded products that are sold to more than 100,000 retail locations in 100 countries on six continents (Hackler, 2011). Due to demand, two NBA stores opened in Beijing in July 2007, the first to open outside of North America. The two stores have far exceeded prior projections in sales by 70% and had 1,000 people waiting in line for the grand opening of one of the stores (Janoff, 2008). Thirty percent of all merchandise sales are generated from outside the United States. The NBA reported that for three consecutive seasons (2006–2009), Kobe Bryant of the Los Angeles Lakers had the top selling jersey in China, outselling Yao Ming, a Chinese native, of the Houston Rockets (NBA, 2009). In fact, Yao Ming was ranked 10th on the list for the top selling jerseys. The NHL generated more than $1 billion from their worldwide sale of NHL licensed products. They were able to spread their brand through partnerships with over 50 international corporate marketing partners.

MLB opened the world's first MLB Café in Tokyo featuring a restaurant, wedding chapel, MLB Shop, and a 500-inch giant TV monitor that constantly shows live and recorded MLB games. The MLB Cafe expects to have more than

100,000 visits to the facility each year and net around $8 million in sales (Japan Today, 2010).

Corporate sponsors also play a role in marketing leagues internationally while also contributing new revenue to the organization. Manchester United, claiming more than 300 million fans worldwide with more than 88 million people watching their games a week, is arguably the most marketable professional sports franchise in the world (Callahan, 2010). This has allowed it to make unique sponsor deals in the same industry with companies in specific countries. Achieving Official Telecommunications Sponsors of the MTN in six African nations, STC in Saudi Arabia, and Airtel in India, Manchester United is able to spread its brand recognition as well as gain valuable sponsorship revenue in markets around the world (Manchester United, 2010). Manchester United was also able to secure an unprecedented partnership with an American baseball club, the New York Yankees in 2001. The plan was to share marketing information to further spread each other's brand recognition. Although there were no major outcomes of this partnership due to ownership transition for both clubs, opportunities like this are only available to clubs that have both the international exposure and marketing initiative like Manchester United and the New York Yankees (Student Life, 2001). Sponsorships for the Premier League teams are primarily international focused versus local. The objective for these sponsors is global exposure compared to return on investment for most of the U.S.-based sport team sponsors. The Premier Football League is the world's most watched sporting league and the most lucrative football league, with combined club revenues of £2.5 billion ($1.6B) in 2010–2011 (Deloitte, 2012).

Grass Roots and Social Programs

Social programs are another way teams, leagues, and athletes are spreading their brands internationally while using its resources to make a difference. The MLS Works campaign has programs that partner with organizations like UNICEF to battle important international issues like child death and malaria (MLS, 2010). MLB supports an International Academy and a Development Center in China. As of 2012, MLB had a hand in baseball development programs in more than 60 countries (MLB International, 2012).

The NBA's social responsibility program, NBA Cares, has a large international presence. Since 2005, it has created 484 places where children and families can live, learn, or play, including 85 locations in 21 countries on five continents. These places include new and refurbished basketball courts, libraries, playgrounds, homes, fitness facilities and technology rooms (NBA Cares, 2010).

In addition, NBA Cares supports campaigns that address social issues, including the promotion of literacy, the eradication of malaria, and HIV/AIDS education. NBA Cares has also teamed with UNICEF to provide international ambassadors for their many programs. NBA stars such as Sam Dalembert, Pau Gasol, Manu Ginobili, Vladamir Radmonovic, Etan Thomas, and Amare Stoudamire work with UNICEF to spread awareness about many issues worldwide (UNICEF, 2010). Since 2001, the NBA's Basketball without Borders (BWB) program has served as a summer camp for young people designed to promote friendship, goodwill and education through sport. The first event was held in the former Yugoslavia and in 2010 BWB was held on three continents including Asia, Africa, and Europe. Previously camps were also held in South America (BWB, 2010). Current and former NBA players serve as camp coaches and leaders. As of 2010, 15 Basketball Without Borders participants had played in the NBA (B. Meeks, Personal Communication, July 6, 2010).

The NFL's Join the Team program offers many NFL youth programs and events in the United States and around the globe, including Canada, Korea, Japan, Germany, Thailand, Spain, France, and Netherlands. These programs provide children the opportunity to improve their basic athletic skills and learn about being a committed team member. Through camps, clinics, and tournaments, young players are given the opportunity to visit other countries while at the same time enhancing their football skills (Join the Team, 2008).

Numerous other social programs, such as Right to Play, utilize the power of sport for development, health, and peace in some of the most disadvantaged areas of the world. Founded in 1994 by four-time Norwegian Olympic speed skater Johann Olav Koss, Right to Play attracts athletes from more than 40 countries to assist in their programs. In December 2009, Right to Play became the official charity of Chelsea Football Club of the Barclays Premier League (Right to Play, 2010).

Implications of Globalization for the Sport Manager

Professional sport executives view sport globalization not only as a way to increase world understanding, but as a way to increase revenues through a larger market. Sport globalization is evident in most all sports and associated industries.

Global sport professionals may need to assist foreign players assimilate into a new culture. The term "global migrant workers" was coined by Coakley (2004) to reference a unique group of sport professionals who choose to explore international opportunities, and therefore change the dynamic of sport. Translators for foreign players may go unnoticed by the public but play vital roles in helping athletes both on and off the playing field. Translators must always be ready and anticipate their clients' needs, be it at practice to help communication between coaches and other players or in press conferences.

Global sport professionals must understand the need and process of travel visas for athletes. For the first World Baseball Classic in 2006, baseball's first worldwide professional tournament, the United States Treasury Department initially declined to license Cuba to play in the United States. Classic officials had to appeal the decision and submitted a new application assuring U.S. government officials that Cuba would not derive any revenue from the tournament. The Cuban government also sent a letter to event organizers stating that it would give any money it earned to victims of Hurricane Katrina (Chass, 2006). As a result of that pledge, the Cubans were allowed to play and ended up losing the final game to Japan. Few thought Cuba, one of the only teams without a Major League player on its roster, had a chance against the all-star lineups of other teams. The combined annual salaries of the United States, Dominican Republic, Venezuela and Puerto Rico teams totaled $471 million while Cuban players made $10–$15 per month working mandatory day jobs and playing baseball at night (Cuba Plays in World Baseball Classic, 2006).

For international sporting events held in the U.S., athletes from countries requiring visas must apply to their local consulate or embassy and progress through the regular visa process. To assist in this documentation procedure, national governing bodies hosting international events are encouraged to contact the United States Olympic Committee (USOC) governmental office in Washington, D.C., and are asked to provide details about the event, including a list of invited athletes, when possible. The USOC representative shares information with the State Department's intranet to facilitate crosschecking and verification of visa application information. The State Department values international exchange through sport and works to expedite the processing of athlete visas. For many countries, the "ease of entry" for athletes to the U.S. is viewed as difficult and may hamper future bids for major international events including the Olympic Games. Most other countries have a Ministry of Sport tied directly to the Ministry of Foreign Affairs who facilitate a more seamless visa process. However, for the Olympic Games, the visa entry process changes dramatically in the United States. An athlete's credential and passport may serve as entry documentation. Athlete and official delegation names are entered into a system as far in advance as possible and a dedicated state department staffer is assigned to manage the process and assist with any last minute requests. All Olympic-related workers must apply for special work permits through the U.S. government. When bidding to host an Olympic Games, the handling of athlete visas is a point of importance.

Sport manufacturing is also extremely global since it involves the sale of equipment, apparel, and goods around the world. According to the World Federation of Sporting Goods Industry (WFSGI), $315 billion was spent for sport equipment, apparel and footwear in 2010 (NPD Group, 2011). Nike is the global leader followed by Adidas ("Adidas keeps marketing," 2009). In the early 1990s, U.S. media reported that Nike and other sporting goods companies were using child labor to manufacture products in developing countries. In response, the WFSGI initiated efforts to stop child labor in all processes involved in making sporting goods including monitoring subcontractors. From a manufacturer's point of view, the wages paid, although extremely low compared to wages paid in developing countries, were far higher than other sources of income in these countries and if stopped could push children into other more dangerous and exploitive work. In response, the industry decided to commit to a social protection program and to provide educational opportunities for children who had been phased out of employment, along with provision of social and financial support for their families. As a result of these programs, 6,000 Pakistani children were phased out of production of soccer balls for export and returned to school. Similar programs are being implemented in India. The sporting goods industry also developed a Model Code of Conduct to assist companies to operate with the highest ethical standards in the global marketplace (WFSGI, 2000).

Sport event managers must also understand differences in cultures. In many Asian countries, relationships are extremely important and time must be spent on developing trust before anything can be accomplished. Differences in a culture's diet due to religious or geographic considerations are also important to know. When Aramark, the food service provider for the 1998 Winter Olympic Games, tried to explain to the food vendors that the buns were too big for the beef patties, the result was miniature buns versus larger burgers since beef was not that prevalent. Finally, an understanding of currency hedging is important as often millions of dollars are invested in foreign countries in preparation of mega sport events and as such it is important to follow currency exchange rates and understand how best to protect interests. Currency hedging is the act of entering into a financial contract in order to protect against unexpected, expected or anticipated changes in currency exchange rates.

Conclusion

Although some say sport globalization is an American invasion, based on history it appears to be more of a transformation of culture. As the world grows smaller through advanced communication and transportation mediums, and the opening of borders to facilitate the exchange of goods and people, cultural changes are to be expected. Marketing executives, however, speed up the process of cultural adaptation and transformation by enhancing the exposure of certain international products and services. Manchester United football club is considered the best at marketing their product and brand globally, however, U.S. leagues are closely following their lead. Future sport executives will need to understand and embrace the globalization of sports.

References

Adidas keeps marketing spending stable. (2009, June 6). Retrieved from http://us.fashionmag.com/news-64997-Adidas-keeps-marketing-spending-stable.

AFC. (2010). The Future is Asia. Retrieved from http://www.the-afc.tv/page/Home/0,,12620,00.html.

Barclays Premier League. (2010). Rules of the Premier League. Retrieved from http://www.premierleague.com/staticFiles/c5/47/0,,12306~149445,00.pdf.

Baseball World. (2009, March 23). World Baseball Classic Enjoys a Growth in Television Ratings and Attendance. Retrieved from http://baseballdeworld.com/2009/03/23/2009-world-baseball-classic-enjoys-growth-in-television-ratings-attendance-and-sponsorships/.

BBC News. (January 20, 2010). Manchester United Debt hits 716m. Retrieved from http://news.bbc.co.uk/2/hi/business/8470595.stm.

BBC Sport. (January 30, 2010a). Wealthy Manchester United Fans Approach Broker about Takeover. Retrieved from http://news.bbc.co.uk/sport2/hi/football/teams/m/man_utd/8488910.stm.

BBC Sport. (January 31, 2010b). Champions League Final Tops Super Bowl for Top TV Market. Retrieved from http://news.bbc.co.uk/sport2/hi/football/europe/8490351.stm.

Bloom, B. (2002, November 18). Yankees team with Yomiuri Giants. Retrieved from http://newyork.yankees.mlb.com/news/article.jsp?ymd=20021116@content_id=178064.

Bush, M. (2008, September 8). LPGA: Non-English speakers are allowed to play after all. *Advertising Age, 79*(33), 8.

BWB. (2010). Retrieved from http://www.nba.com/bwb/bwob_index.html.

Callahan, S. (2010, June 4). CMO Reports Aon's Sponsorship with Manchester United. *BtoB Online*. Retrieved from http://www.btobonline.com/apps/pbcs.dll/article?AID=/20100604/FREE/100609937/1417#seenit.

Chass, M. (2006, January 4). On Baseball; It's always all about the Yankees. Retrieved from http://query.nytimes.com/gst/fullpage.html?res=9406E4DA1 130F937A35752C0A9609C8B63.

Chass, M. (1992, February 7). Baseball; Committee rejected plan allowing foreign owners. Retrieved from http://www.nytimes.com/1992/02/07/sports/baseball-committee-rejected-plan-allowing-foreign-owners.html.

Coakley, J. (2001). *Sport in society: Issues and controversies* (7th edition). Boston, MA: McGraw Hill.

comScore. (2007, May 15). Top European Clubs Have Global Fan Base. Retrieved from http://www.comscore.com/Press_Events/Press_Releases/2007/05/European_Football_Clubs.

comScore. (2009, July). North American Pro Sports Score Local, Global Following. Retrieved from http://www.marketingcharts.com/television/north-american-pro-sports-score-loyal-global-following-10586/comscore-professional-sports-leagues-share-audience-worldwide-regions-july-2009jpg/.

Cuba plays in World Baseball Classic. (2006, March 10). History.com: This Day in History.

Cullen, K. (2010, February). IT and Telecom Olympics. Retrieved from http://www.powersourceonline.com/magazine/2010/02/it-and-telecom-olympics.

de la Merced, M. (2008, January 14). Disney Among Firms to Buy Stake in N.B.A.'s China Subsidiary. Retrieved from http://www.nytimes.com/2008/01/14/business/media/14nba.html.

Deloitte (2012). Annual Review of Football Finance 2012. Deloitte Sports Business Group. Retrieved from http://www.deloitte.com/view/en_GB/uk/industries/sportsbusinessgroup/sports/football/annual-review-of-football-finance/infographic/index.htm.

du Lac, J. Freedom (2009, September 13). 30 Years Later, Visit to China still Resonates. *The Washington Post*. Retrieved from http://www.washingtonpost.com/wpdyn/content/article/2009/09/12/AR2009091202267.html.

Echevarria, R. G. (1999). *The pride of Havana, A history of Cuban baseball*. New York: Oxford University Press.

Eitzen, D.S. (2012). *Fair and Foul: Beyond the Myths and Paradoxes of Sport*. Plymouth UK: Rowman & Littlefield Publishers.

FIBA. (2010). Basketball without Borders. Retrieved from http://www.fiba.com/pages/eng/fc/FIBA/fibaProg/fibaBwb.asp.

FIBA. (2007). FIBA History. Retrieved from http://www.fiba.com/pages/eng/fc/FIBA/fibaHist/p/openNodeIDs/987/selNodeID/987/fibaHist.html.

FIFA. (2014). *History of Football*. Retrieved from http://www.fifa.com/mm/document/fifafacts/organisation/02/13/11/06/03072013allaboutfifa_neutral.pdf.

FIFA. (2010). *TV Data*. Retrieved from http://www.fifa.com/aboutfifa/organ-isation/marketing/news/newsid=111247/.

Gillette, G. (2007). *The ESPN Baseball Encyclopedia*. New York: Sterling Publishing.

Hackler, T. (2011). Panini America Inks NBA Star Kevin Durant to Exclusive Trading Card and Memorabilia Deal. Retrieved from http://www.goodwin sports.com/tag/press-releases/page/16/.

Harris, N. (2010, March 23). Premier League Nets 1.6 Billion in TV Rights Bonanza. *The Independent*. Retrieved from http://www.independent.co.uk/sport/football/premier-league/premier-league-nets-16314bn-tv-rights-bonanza-1925462.html.

Helfgott, J. (2008, January 3). The International Game. *The Hardball Times*. Retrieved from http://www.hardballtimes.com/main/printarticle/the-international-game/.

Hoffman, A. R. (2003). The Buffalo Germans and the 1904 Olympic Basketball Tournament in St. Louis. *Journal of Olympic History, 11*(3), 19–21.

Janoff, B. (2008). Kobe Bryant Tops NBA Jersey Sales in China. Retrieved from http://www.adweek.com/news/advertising-branding/kobe-bryant-tops-nba-jersey-sales-china-104417.

Japan Today (2009). *World's 1st Official Major League Baseball Restaurant Opens in Tokyo*. Retrieved from http://www.japantoday.com/category/business/view/worlds-1st-official-mlb-restaurant-opens-in-tokyo.

Jessop, A. (2012, June 14). The Surge of the NBA's International Viewership and Popularity. Retrieved from http://www.forbes.com/sites/aliciajessop/2012/06/14/the-surge-of-the-nbas-international-viewership-and-popularity/print/.

Join the Team. (2008). Retrieved from https://www.jointheteam.com/about/.

Lefton, T. & Tripp M. (2010, June 7). *NHL Sharpens European Focus*. *Sports-Business Journal*. Retrieved from http://www.sportsbusinessjournal.com/article/65932.

Lombardo, J. (2010, May 24). *After Two Years, NBA China on Steady Course*. Retrieved from http://www.sportsbusinessjournal.com/article/65803.

Lombardo, J. (2010, April 19). *NBA's Revenue Exceeds Expectations*. Retrieved from http://m.sportsbusinessdaily.com/Journal/Issues/2010/04/20100419/This-Weeks-News/Nbas-Revenue-Exceeds-Expectations.aspx.

Manchester United. (2010) *Sponsors*. Retrieved from http://www.manutd.com/default.sps?pagegid={3479FBF4-753A-4BF4-8FDD-0F0BFCEA3FFF}.

McNulty, P. (2008, January 20) *Liverpool Braced for Takeover Bid*. BBC Sport. Retrieved from http://news.bbc.co.uk/sport2/hi/football/teams/l/liverpool/7197675.stm.

Mickle, T. (2008, December 22) *MLS Sells International TV Rights to MP & Silva*. The Sports Business Journal. Retrieved from http://www.sports businessjournal.com/article/61013.

Mickle, T. (2008, November 3). MLS attendance, TV viewership numbers slip. *Street & Smith's Sports Business Daily*, *11*(27), 10.

Mitchell, P. (2005). The First International Football Match. Retrieved from http://www.bbc.co.uk/scotland/sportscotland/asportingnation/article/0012/.

MLB International. (2012). Current Business Overview—2012.

MLS. (2014). Community. Retrieved from http://www.mlssoccer.com/community.

MLS. (2010). Roster Regulations. Retrieved from http://www.mlssoccer.com/regulations.

Naismith, J. (1941). *Basketball: Its Origin and Development*. New York: Associated Press.

NBA. (2009, May 24). Cavs Sign Ownership Deal with China Group. Retrieved from http://www.nba.com/2009/news/05/24/cavs.china.ap/index.html.

NBA (2009). Bryant's jersey remains top seller in China. Retrieved from http://www.nba.com/2009/news/10/08/bryant.jersey.china/.

NBA (2013). Basketball without Borders. Retrieved from http://www.nba.com/bwb/.

NBA Cares (2013). Retrieved from http://www.nba.com/nba_cares/global/global_programs.html.

NBA Global (2012). Retrieved from http://www.nba.com/global/.

New England Revolution Media Relations. (2009, July 7). MLS.net. Kraft joins USA bid committee board of directors. Retrieved from http://web.mlsnet.com/news/mls_news.jsp?ymd=20090707&content_id=5741682&vkey=news_mls&fext=.jsp.

Newport, J.P. (2008, September 13). How the LPGA Bungled on English. Retrieved from http://online.wsj.com/news/articles/SB122125269803829639.

News Ok. (2009). NBA Attendance Figures. http://newsok.com/actual-attendance/article/3391660.

NFL International. (2012). Retrieved from :http://www.nfl.com/international.

NHL.com. (2012). *NHL International*. Retrieved from http://www.nhl.com/ice/page.htm?id=26372.

NPD Group. (2011). Global Sports Estimate Report 2011. Retrieved from https://www.npd.com/wps/portal/npd/us/news/press-releases/pr_110915a/.

PBS Online (1999). Timeline of US-China Relations. Retrieved from http://www.pbs.org/wgbh/amex/china/timeline/timeline7nf.html#1979.

Phillips, M. (2009, December 21). *Tackling the Washington Redskins. Newsweek*. Retrieved from http://www.newsweek.com/2009/12/20/tackling-the-washington-redskins.html.

Ping-Pong Diplomacy (April 6–17, 1971). (1999). *Public Broadcasting Service, People and Events*. Retrieved from http://www.pbs.org/wgbh/amex/china/peopleevents/pande07.html.

Reaves, J. A. (2002). *Taking in a game: A history of baseball in America*. Lincoln, NE: Bison Books.

Reid, T. R. (2001, February 8). A joint grasp at worldwide reach; N.Y. Yankees, Manchester United agree on mutual promotion in home markets. Retrieved from http://www.highbeam.com/doc/1P2-416120.html.

Right to Play. (2010). Retrieved from http://www.righttoplay.com/International/Pages/Home.aspx.

Schaerlaeckens, L. (2011, September 13). American pastime rising in Europe as baseball gains in popularity, more MLB prospects coming from European nations. Retrieved from http://espn.go.com/mlb/story/_/id/6948276/mlb-baseball-europe-take-off.

Schoenfeld, B. (2010, May 3). Eyeing his exit. *SportsBusiness Journal*. Retrieved from http://sportsbusinessjournal.com/article/65598.

Schwartz, P. J. (2013, July 15). Real Madrid Tops the World's Most Valuable Sports Teams. Retrieved from http://www.forbes.com/sites/kurtbadenhausen/2013/07/15/real-madrid-tops-the-worlds-most-valuable-sports-teams/.

Schwartz, P. J. (2013, April 17) Soccer's Most Valuable Teams. Retrieved from http://www.forbes.com/sites/mikeozanian/2013/04/17/soccers-most-valuable-teams-real-madrid-dethrones-manchester-united-from-top-spot-at-3-3-billion/.

Shore, P. (2010, April 19). MLS Teams Negotiating High Profile Friendlies is a Win for the League. Retrieved from http://bleacherreport.com/articles/381087-mls-teams-negotiating-high-profile-friendlies-is-a-win-for-the-league.

Stedman, B. (2009, July 9). Kraft joins World Cup bid. *The Foxboro Reporter*. Retrieved from http://www.foxbororeporter.com/articles/2009/07/13/sports/local_sports/5267296.txt.

Stewart, M. (2012, October 21). Vancouver Whitecaps Become First-Ever Canadian Team In MLS Playoffs. Retrieved from http://www.huffingtonpost.ca/2012/10/21/vancouver-whitecaps-mls-playoffs-first-canadian-team_n_1998610.html.

Student Life (2001, February 9) New York Yankees Merge with Manchester United. Retrieved from http://www.studlife.com/archives/Sports/2001/02/09/NewYorkYankeesMergewithManchesterUnited/.

Talk Basketball (2010). Euroleague's Internationality. Retrieved from http://www.talkbasket.net/forums/index.php?/topic/2667-euroleagues-internationality/.

Tang, A. (2009, August 27). 30 Years Later, Wizards Go Back to China. Xinhua. Retrieved from http://news.xinhuanet.com/english/2009-08/27/content_11952174.htm.

Thamel, P. (2009, October 24). World is Beginning to Catch On as the N.F.L. Returns to London. Retrieved from http://www.nytimes.com/2009/10/25/sports/football/25london.html?_r=0.

Tope, J. (2008, November). Fighting the Second World War in Paradise with a bat and glove: Major league baseball comes to Hawai'i. *Hawaiian Journal of History, 42*, 265–276.

Turner, F. (2009, May 24) China investors make deal for stake in NBA Cavaliers. Retrieved from http://www.google.com/hostednews/afp/article/ALeqM5ierLqBIv5alVUEKXgOSZHT5ilY8.

UNICEF. (2010). Retrieved from http://www.unicefusa.org/partners/sports/the-national-basketball.html.

USA Football (2010). Overview. http://www.usafootball.com/pages/overview.

US Soccer (2002). US Soccer Timeline. http://www.ussoccer.com/About/History/Timeline.aspx.

WFSGI (2000, August). Code of Conduct. Retrieved from http://www.wfsgi.org/articles/71.

Williams, O. (2009, August 13). Where the English Premier League Players Come From. BBC Sport. Retrieved from http://news.bbc.co.uk/sport2/hi/football/eng_prem/8182090.stm.

Worrall, S. (2006, October). Cricket, anyone? *Smithsonian*, *37*(7), 56–64.

Wyshynski, G. (2008). It's Complicated but Russia's KHL Will Appear on US TV. Retrieved from http://sports.yahoo.com/nhl/blog/puck_daddy/post/It-s-complicated-but-Russia-s-KHL-will-appear-o?urn=nhl,98558.

Yardley, J. (2012, February 1). The N.B.A. Is Missing Its Shots in China. Retrieved from http://www.nytimes.com/2012/02/05/magazine/NBA-in-China.html?pagewanted=all.

Chapter 9

Adapted Sport: A Snapshot

Margaret Stran & Brent Hardin, University of Alabama

History of Adapted Sport and Athletics

People with disabilities have always been part of society, and their involvement in organized sport goes back more than 100 years, when Sport Clubs for the Deaf were established in Berlin in 1888 (DePauw & Gavron, 2005). As the prominence of people with disabilities has increased, so too have the sporting opportunities. From large-scale international competitions to small community exhibitions, sports for people with disabilities have expanded and grown to include a wide variety of activities and a range of competitive and recreational platforms (ICP, 2013a).

Today, individuals with a variety of disabilities ranging from physical to intellectual and mild to severe, play sports. Disability sport is generally organized by disability type: intellectual or physical with subcategories within each area. Within each disability category, organizations have been created that oversee and support individuals at all levels of competition.

Although some sporting events were designed specifically for persons with a disability and have no able-bodied equivalent, many of the sports that individuals with disabilities participate in, referred to as adapted sports, are previously established able-bodied sports whose rules and regulations have been modified to meet the needs of athletes with disabilities (Sherrill, 2004). Examples of adapted sports include wheelchair basketball, wheelchair curling, swimming, rowing and track and field events (Sherrill, 2004). Recently, the inclusion of more "extreme sports" into the catalogue of disability sports has gained popularity. Action sports such as rock climbing, skateboarding, kayaking, wakeboarding, and motocross are performed at the Extremity Games (EXG, 2013).

Other recent trends show the inclusion of disability sports with able-bodied sports. Sports such as tennis and rowing include athletes with disabilities in their events. Thus, at Wimbledon, tennis fans can see women's singles, men's doubles, women's wheelchair singles, and men's wheelchair doubles. Similarly, at the World Rowing Championships in Cheng Ju, Korea, in 2013, adaptive rowing events were part of the larger competition and held with the able bodied races. On a larger scale, the 2002 Manchester Commonwealth Games began fully integrating disability sports and disabled athletes into their medalling process (CGF, 2013). This is the first multi-sport event that fully included athletes with disabilities (CGF, 2013).

Disability Type

People are either born with a disability (congenital) or acquire their disability (Sherrill, 2004). Congenital disabilities can be due to many factors. For example, Down syndrome is an intellectual disability that is chromosome based, and spina bifida is a physical disability that affects the spinal cord and is caused when the neural tube fails to close properly (Kelly, 2011). Acquired disabilities come about from some type of trauma. They are more often physical in nature, such as amputation or spinal cord injury, but can also be intellectual such as a traumatic brain injury. Typically, those who have an acquired disability are more successful in sport because of their experience and exposure to standing sport prior to the onset of their disability (Sherrill, 2004). This, however, should not be used to limit the athletic potential or disregard the success of those athletes with congenital disabilities. For example, Jean Driscoll is a seven-time winner of the Boston Marathon and has a congenital disability.

Competitions and Opportunities for Athletes with Disabilities

There is a vast array of competitions for athletes with disabilities around the world. It would be impossible to list all competitions, but the largest are highlighted below.

Paralympics

The Paralympics, like the Olympics, are elite competitions for athletes with physical and visual disabilities. Held every four years, in the same cities and venues and a few weeks after the Olympic Games, the Paralympics has grown steadily since its inception (IPC, 2013b). Rome, Italy, was the host city for the

1960 Olympics-style competition; this is considered the first summer Paralympic Games (Hums & MacLean, 2008). The 1960 event hosted 400 athletes from 23 countries competing in eight sports while the 2012 London Games included 4,237 athletes from 164 countries participating in 20 different sports (archery, athletics, boccia, cycling, equestrian, football 5-a-side, football 7-a-side, goalball, judo, powerlifting, rowing, sailing, shooting, swimming, table tennis, volleyball [sitting], wheelchair basketball, wheelchair fencing, wheelchair rugby, and wheelchair tennis) (Hums & MacLean, 2008; IPC, 2013b, 2013c). The first winter Paralympics were held in Sweden in 1976 (IPC, 2013d) and the 2014 games were hosted by Sochi, Russia.

Individuals with intellectual disabilities have been included in the Paralympic games since 1992 (DePauw & Gavron, 2005). In 2000, it was found that members of the Spanish basketball, table tennis, swimming and athletics teams did not have intellectual disabilities (DePauw & Gavron, 2005). As a result of the cheating, individuals with mental limitations were suspended from the 2002 Winter Paralympic Games; basketball, table tennis, swimming and athletics were included as exhibition events in the 2004 games (DePauw & Gavron, 2005). In 2012, athletes with intellectual disabilities participated in athletics (track events), swimming, and table tennis (IPC, 2013e).

In 1948, Sir Ludwig Guttmann organized a wheelchair sporting competition at the Stoke Mandeville Hospital in Aylesbury, England for veterans wounded in World War II (Hums & MacLean, 2008). This competition was held at Stoke Mandeville in 1952 with Dutch veterans competing against the British, making it the first international event of its kind (DePauw & Gavron, 2005). The Stoke Mandeville Games grew to include non-veterans in 1960 and individuals with a variety of disabilities in 1976, and evolved into what is currently known as the Paralympic Games (IPC, 2013a).

Deaflympics

The Deaflympics were first held in Paris in 1924 by the Comité International des Sports des Sourds (CISS; also referred to as the International Committee of Sports for the Deaf) (Hums & MacLean, 2008). The games, which are sanctioned by the International Olympic Committee, are held every four years in the year after the Olympic Games (i.e., 2013, 2015) (DePauw & Gavron, 2005). Winter Deaflympics were added in 1949 (CISS, 2013b). The Deaflympics, like the Paralympics, has grown immensely since its inception. The 1924 games hosted 145 athletes from nine nations participating in athletics, cycling road, diving, football, shooting, swimming, and tennis (CISS, 2013c). In 2013 Sofia, Bulgaria, hosted over 2,500 athletes from 90 nations who par-

ticipated in 16 sports (athletics, badminton, basketball, beach volleyball, bowling, cycling road, football, handball, judo, karate, mountain biking, orien-
teering, shooting, swimming, table tennis, taekwondo, tennis, volleyball,
wrestling freestyle and wrestling Greco-Roman) (Sofia, 2013). In addition to
competition, the Deaflympics also provides a medium for sharing cultural information (Stewart, 1990).

Special Olympics

Founded in 1968 by Eunice Kennedy Shriver, the Special Olympics provide
athletic opportunities to almost three million people with intellectual disabilities in more than 180 countries (Special Olympics, 2013a). Events are held at
local, regional and national levels (Hums & MacLean, 2008). The World Games,
which are separated into summer and winter games, are held every four years
for all levels of athletes with cognitive and developmental disabilities (Hums
& MacLean, 2008). The first World Summer Games were held in Chicago, Illinois, and hosted 1,000 athletes from the United States and Canada; Ireland
hosted over 5,500 athletes at the 2003 World Summer Games, the first time
the Games were held outside the United States (Special Olympics, 2013a). The
2011 World Summer Games in Athens, Greece, hosted more than 6,000 athletes from 170 countries (Special Olympics, 2013a). The 2013 World Winter
Games were held in PyeongChang, Republic of Korea (Special Olympics, 2014).
The World Games also act as instruments of change. After hosting events, Ireland and China both made legislative change that positively impacted policies
towards including people with intellectual disabilities in all aspects of society
(Special Olympics, 2013b).

In addition to sports only for people with intellectual disabilities, Special
Olympics offers a Healthy Athletes program which provides free health care
for athletes at their events (Special Olympics, 2013c), and conducts research
which it uses to impact policy and programs across the globe (Special Olympics,
2013d). Finally, Special Olympics attempts to create change by building communities through its Young Athletes and Project UNIFY programs (Special
Olympics, 2013e, 2013f).

International Wheelchair Athletics

The International Wheelchair and Amputee Sports Federation (IWAS) was
founded by Sir Ludwig Guttmann in 1952 and provides sporting opportunities from recreational to elite for people with disabilities (IWAS, 2009a). The
IWAS represents the merging of two organizations, the International Stoke

Mandeville Wheelchair Sports Federation (ISMWSF, previously ISMGF) and the International Sports Organisation for the Disabled (ISOD) (IWAS, 2013a). The IWAS's mission is "To create and maintain conditions world-wide which will foster and encourage the development and self-determination of athletes with a physical disability internationally through sport from grass roots to elite level in a spirit of 'friendship, unity and sportsmanship'" (IWAS, 2013b, para. 11). IWAS hosts World Games every two years, in the post-Paralympic years, development games, and in the pre-Paralympic years, elite games (IWAS, 2013c). Moreover, IWAS World Junior Games take place each year. These games provide an opportunity for young athletes to gain international experience in their sport (IWAS, 2013c)

Adapted Athletics in the United States

Adapted athletic opportunities in the United States are numerous. Participants can engage in a variety of activities from horseback riding, water skiing, snow skiing, cycling, basketball, track, boccia, swimming, and more. For those looking to get involved, one of the easiest ways is to conduct a search on the U.S. Paralympics website sport club directory (U.S. Paralympics, 2014). This lists the Paralympic Sport Clubs (PSC) by state; PSC are community organizations that are part of the larger U.S. Paralympics structure. For organizations that are not affiliated with U.S. Paralympics, a website search by disability and/or sport is usually helpful (i.e., blind sports, rowing, sit skiing). One of the largest organized team sports in the United States is wheelchair basketball.

Wheelchair Basketball

1946 was the start of wheelchair basketball in the United States (Owen, 1982), and it was the "first nationally organized sport for individuals with lower-extremity impairments" (Hedrick, Byrnes, and Shaver, 1994, p. ix). In February 1947, the first competitive wheelchair basketball game in which all players had some type of physical disability was played between the Birmingham, California, Veteran's Administration hospital team and the Corona, California, Naval hospital team (Owen, 1982). In 1949, the National Wheelchair Basketball Association (NWBA) was formed with six teams (Owen, 1982). The first women's wheelchair basketball team was started in 1970 at the University of Illinois (Owen, 1982).

The NWBA has 190 basketball teams across seven divisions as of 2014 (NWBA, 2014a). The NWBA provides opportunities for qualified people with physical disabilities to participate on men's, women's, intercollegiate, or youth teams throughout the United States and Canada (NWBA, 2014a). Championships for each division are held each year (NWBA, 2014b).

Collegiate Wheelchair Athletics

The first collegiate wheelchair basketball team was formed at the University of Illinois at Urbana-Champaign in 1949 (Hedrick et al., 1994). The first intercollegiate wheelchair basketball game was played December 3, 1970. In 1977, the first National Intercollegiate Wheelchair Basketball Tournament was held, and the Central Intercollegiate Wheelchair Basketball Conference was founded in 1978 (Hedrick et al., 1994).

Exhibit 9.1 reflects the current competitive wheelchair athletic programs offered at universities in the United States (Alabama Adapted, 2013; Edinboro University, 2013; SMSU, 2013; UA, 2013; UIUC, 2013; UTA, 2013; UWW, 2013).

In addition, many other higher education institutions across the United States have developed programs offering recreational opportunities for students with disabilities.

Case Study 1: The University of Alabama Wheelchair Basketball Teams

Started in 2003 by Dr. Brent Hardin and Dr. Margaret Stran, the University of Alabama Adapted Athletics program has become a powerful force in collegiate wheelchair athletics in a short time. The program began with women's wheelchair basketball; the men's team was started in 2006. Adaptive rowing, golf and tennis were added in 2012 and track in 2014. The tennis team won college nationals in 2013. The university community, including former President Robert Witt, has been very supportive of the program and its teams.

Alabama, with men's and women's wheelchair basketball teams, is one of only five programs in the United States that sponsors both. The Crimson Tide women compete in the intercollegiate division of the National Wheelchair Basketball Association (NWBA). While one of the newest teams in the division, they have been a consistent national championship contender, winning national titles in 2009, 2010, and 2011. The Alabama men play in the NWBA intercollegiate division and won the championship in 2012 (Alabama Adapted, 2013).

Exhibit 9.1: Competitive Wheelchair Athletic Programs Offered at Universities in the United States

College	Men's Basketball	Women's Basketball	Track/Cycling	Swimming	Quad Rugby	Power Lifting	Tennis	Rowing	Golf
Edinboro University of Pennsylvania	X	X				X			
Southwest Minnesota State University	X								
University of Alabama	X	X					X	X	X
University of Arizona	X	X	X		X		X		
University of Illinois at Urbana-Champaign	X	X	X						
University of Missouri	X								
University of Texas-Arlington	X	X	X	X			X		
University of Wisconsin-Whitewater	X	X							

Technology and Equipment in Disability Sports

Disability is not simply a medical or functional classification; it is also dependent upon the environment. For example, it does not matter that a person uses a wheelchair if everything is accessible—houses, businesses, and sidewalks. The wheelchair becomes a factor if there are no curb cuts, ramps, or elevators. The same can be said for a person who is deaf and uses American Sign Language. Around others who sign she is fine; when she encounters those who cannot sign her deafness because a problem because she cannot communicate. Recognizing this, the World Health Organization (WHO) developed the International Classification of Functioning, Disability, and Health (ICF) (WHO, 2013). This checklist evaluates disability based on body functions and structures, activity and participation, and environmental factors (WHO, 2013).

Adapted equipment is available to assist people with disabilities in all aspects of life: daily living, leisure, and sports/recreation (Quickie Wheelchairs, 2013). People missing legs or arms often use prosthetic limbs; wheelchairs, walkers, and canes are used by people with paralysis, limited mobility, joint problems, and so on to allow them to move about more easily. Other equipment is available that assists people for specific purposes (Quickie Wheelchairs, 2013). For example, a long handled grabber allows people who cannot reach the floor to easily pick things up or to reach things that are high; a shower chair permits someone to sit in the shower rather than having to stand or, if not able to stand, to transfer easily in and out of the tub and not have to sit on the tub floor; a rolling, padded bench gives someone who cannot get on and off the ground easily a way to sit and move while gardening, weeding or engaging in other outdoor work. Hand controls can be installed in automatic vehicles to allow people who are paralyzed or missing legs to drive a car. Finally, there is specific adapted equipment that provides people with disabilities opportunities to compete in sport. There are legs that amputees can use that are specifically designed for jogging, sprinting, and other sports (Ossur, 2013). There are wheelchairs designed for basketball, tennis, rugby, cycling, racing, water and snow skiing and many other sports (Colours In Motion, 2013; EagleSportschairs, 2013). For individuals who are blind or visually impaired, there are balls with bells or beeps that can be used for goalball or baseball (NBBA, 2013; USA Goalball, 2013).

Access to adapted equipment is limited to what people are willing and able to pay for it. For many people, insurance covers equipment for daily living (i.e.. everyday wheelchairs and prosthetics). Sport equipment is not generally covered by insurance. Thus, many athletes end up applying for grants through an organization like the Challenged Athletes Foundation (CAF, 2013), getting used equipment, securing a sponsor (for top athletes in the field; Per4Max, 2013), or paying out of their own pocket.

It should be noted that with technological advances comes certain areas of concern regarding the potential for an uneven playing field. For example, certain athletes may have resources available to have the best equipment money can buy or access to superior technological resources. Other athletes, due to geographic location, financial wherewithal, or other factors may be precluded from the same advantages. In as such, there may be considerations and provisions as to what may or may not be allowed.

In addition to concerns about playing advantages due to equipment, concern also exists in regards to the use of performance enhancements such as drug use. Concerns such as this led to initiatives such as the International Paralympic Committee's Anti-Doping Code, which is aimed at preserving fair competition (Hums & MacLean, 2008). This development was made in congruence with the standards enacted by the World-Anti-Doping Association (WADA). An interesting point of consideration in the policing of performance enhancing drugs in aspects of disability sport is the potential for athletes to receive medications for conditions which might be viewed as illegal or banned substances. In such instances, administrative decisions and policy initiatives should take into account what is responsible and appropriate (Hums & MacLean, 2008).

Athletes with Disabilities in Non-Disabled Settings

While most people with disabilities engage in sport in segregated settings, there are some instances when people have pushed to be included with people without disabilities. For example, golfer Casey Martin, who is ambulatory but has Klippel Trenaunay Weber syndrome in his right leg which limits his ability to walk long distances, won the right to use a cart to play golf with his peers without disabilities in the Professional Golfers Association (PGA) Tour (Stevens, 2000). The Supreme Court decided that the use of the golf cart did not fundamentally alter the nature of the game and that the use of the cart was a reasonable accommodation (Stevens, 2000).

Tatyana McFadden is a Paralympic wheelchair racer. She has won 10 Paralympic medals: bronze and silver in the 2004 Games, a bronze and three silver medals in the 2008 Beijing Games, and a bronze and 3 gold medals in the 2012 London Games (IPC, 2013f). McFadden hails from Maryland and as a high school student wanted to participate on her track team. The high school would not allow this so she, with her parents, filed suit. She won the right to race in her wheelchair on the track with her able-bodied peers (Dahlberg, 2006). What she fought for was not winning races—having participated in the Paralympics at 15 she already had medals—but the right to be a part of the team which included sitting on the infield with her friends, starting the race with everyone else, and riding the bus to and from the meets (Dahlberg, 2006).

Case Study 2: Oscar Pistorius

Sprinter Oscar Pistorius is a highly successful Paralympic athlete, winning two gold medals and one silver in the 2012 London games, three gold medals in the 2008 Beijing games and a gold and bronze in the 2004 Paralympics (IPC, 2013f). In 2007, he attempted to qualify for the 2008 Beijing Olympics. During 2007 he was running against his able-bodied peers on two carbon fiber prosthetic running legs, called Cheetahs (IAAF, 2008). In December 2007, after investigation into the prosthetic legs, the International Amateur Athletic Federation (IAAF) concluded that Pistorius' prosthetics gave him an unfair advantage over able-bodied sprinters (IAAF, 2008) and banned him from further competition, essentially stopping his bid to qualify for the Olympics. Moreover, IAAF amended its rules to ban the "use of any technical device that incorporates springs, wheels or any other element that provides the user with an advantage over another athlete not using such a device" (IAAF Competition Rules, 2009, p. 119). After Pistorius appealed the decision to the Court of Arbitration for Sport (CAS) it was decided in May 2008 that the scientific evidence supporting this exclusion was not sufficient and Pistorius was again allowed to compete against his able-bodied peers (IAAF, 2008). He attempted to qualify for the 2008 Beijing Olympics but did not make the qualifying time (Ledsom, 2008). Pistorius ran in the IAAF 2011 World championships against his able-bodied peers and qualified for the 2012 London Olympic Games. In London he made it to the semi-finals, a pool of 24 runners down from 51 (IOC, 2013).

(Note: In 2013 Pistorius was embroiled in a controversy where he was arrested in the shooting death of his girlfriend Reeva Steenkamp. In 2014, he was found guilty of culpable homicide. This has halted his racing career and greatly harmed his public image.)

Current Challenges in Disability Sport

Youth Sport Development

In wheelchair sports, the growth of youth leagues during the past 20 years has been enormous. When the NWBA junior division started it hosted a handful of teams in one division. Currently, the junior division has 60 teams in two divisions: 10' division and prep (children under 14) (NWBA, 2013a). Wheelchair and Ambulatory Sports USA's junior division, started in 1984, has grown to encompass 30% of its total activities (WASUSA, 2013). Despite the growth in junior sports, the pace of competitive collegiate programs, in all sports, has lagged. As of 2014, there are only eight collegiate wheelchair programs, only six of which offer basketball for men and women, and only two colleges that offer track and field. There are only a few college programs that offer other sports such as tennis, rowing, power lifting or quad rugby; individuals interested in other sports do not have collegiate opportunities. As a result, youths who want to compete collegiately or internationally in these sports have to do it on their own without benefit of teammates and coaches on campus.

Resources and Opportunities

In the United States, there are many opportunities for youth and adults to participate in sports on an elite or recreational level, but these opportunities are not available at every parks and recreation or after school sports program like they are for people without disabilities. As a result, location and information often determine whether or not people are aware of and involved in recreation activities in their area or state.

In most junior programs, parents pay for everything: transportation, housing, meals, and equipment (D. Murray, personal communication, March 12, 2008). The team sponsor may provide uniforms or used equipment, but this varies from city to city (American Association of Adapted Sports, 2013a; BlazeSports, 2013). As a result, parents who can afford trips and events are more likely to involve their children in adapted sports. In addition, because many sponsors are rehabilitation hospitals located in larger cities, those who live outside of the cities have to travel many hours to attend activities. The Lakeshore Foundation in Birmingham, Alabama, offers many activities for youth and adults with disabilities, but they are the only programs in the state that offers these programs (Lakeshore Foundation, 2013).

An exciting development in youth sport is school/county-sponsored leagues. In Georgia the American Association of Adapted Sport Programs (AAASP) supports, in conjunction with schools and with support from the Georgia Department of Education, school based athletics for youth with disabilities (AAASP, 2013a). Children practice and compete weekly, similar to their peers without disabilities and compete in games such as wheelchair basketball, wheelchair football, track and field, and wheelchair handball (AAASP, 2013b). Part of AAASP's mission is spreading this model across the nation (AAASP, 2013a).

Additional opportunity considerations include providing opportunities for female participation. As initiatives are enacted to promote further development of female programs, it should be noted that females can be confronted with what Cody (2002) referred to as a *duality of discrimination*. Essentially, this notion states that females often find that they have to contend with barriers based on gender as well as disability. Hums and MacLean (2008) identified this as a "double barrier" (p. 296) to participation. For example, in the junior division of the NWBA, there are no girls' teams. Young women play on boys' teams and many teams have no girls playing. Another example within the collegiate division is of the eight summer wheelchair basketball camps typically offered, only one, the University of Alabama, hosts a camp just for young women.

Media Representation

Across the world, to varying degrees, there are sports and activities for people with disabilities at various levels (i.e., recreational, collegiate, elite). Yet in many countries, media representation of these athletes is non-existent. This may be because "Disability sport has not been viewed as legitimate sport, but rather as something less ... opportunities, rewards, public recognition and the like have not been afforded athletes with disabilities" (DePauw & Gavron, 2005, p. 12).

The media coverage that is undertaken tends to fall into to two categories: traditional and progressive. Traditional coverage places people with disabilities outside mainstream society and regards them as dysfunctional while the progressive model looks at people with disabilities as part of pluralist society (Schantz & Gilbert, 2001). In looking at disability sport, the "supercrip" model is most useful (Shapiro, 1994). In this model, the media view people with disabilities as having no value until they are able to "overcome" their disabilities and do something amazing and inspiring, such as fish with no arms or play wheelchair rugby (Iwakuma, 1997; Schell & Rodriguez, 2001; Shapiro, 1994). In contrast, progressive media coverage recognizes the social construction of disability. They include a minority/civil rights model, which recognizes people with disabilities as a distinct group with legitimate social grievances. Another model is the cultural pluralism model, which recognizes individuals with disabilities as multifaceted and not defined by their disabilities (Hardin & Hardin, 2003, p. 249).

Disability Litigation and Legislation

The Disability Rights Movement can trace its roots to the 1954 United States Supreme Court decision in *Brown v. Board of Education*. The 14th amendment of the United States Constitution guarantees equal protection of the laws for all citizens. *Brown v. Board of Education* challenged the application of this Constitutional amendment—allowing for "separate but equal" educational opportunities. The United States Supreme Court's unanimous decision in favor of Brown struck down laws and policies based on discrimination against people according to their race/ethnicity, religion, culture, and physical abilities. This pivotal decision became a catalyst for the civil rights movement and laid the foundation for future policies concerning the disability rights movement.

In 1959, the President's Committee on Employment of the Physically Handicapped and the National Society for Crippled Children co-sponsored the development of American National Standards Institute (ANSI) A117.1, a voluntary national standard for building, facility, and site accessibility and the first of its kind (Sherrill, 2004).

In June 1963, President John F. Kennedy urged the nation to end racial discrimination. Kennedy encouraged Congress to consider legislation that would address issues such as voting rights, school desegregation, public accommodations, and more. President Lyndon Johnson, who succeeded to the presidency after Kennedy's assassination in November 1963, signed Kennedy's proposal—the Civil Rights Act of 1964—into law on July 2, 1964. Although the Civil Rights Act of 1964 targeted racial discrimination, it set the precedent for demanding equality by other minority groups. The disability rights movement took its cue from the foundation laid by the civil rights movement and sought to bring an end to discrimination of people with disabilities.

While Washington encouraged voluntary compliance with ANSI building standards and was hesitant to pass legislation mandating compliance, many states moved to adopt the ANSI accessibility standards and required state-funded facilities to comply with the legislation. By 1966, thirty states had legislation concerning accessibility and by 1973, every state except Kentucky had enacted access legislation. Enforcement, however, continued to be a problem at all levels (Yell, 2006).

In 1965, Congress passed the Vocational Rehabilitation Amendment Act to encourage public facilities to comply with ANSI A117.1. The Act established the National Commission on Architectural Barriers to Rehabilitation of the Handicapped to study architectural barriers and to determine what was being done to eliminate barriers. The Commission concluded that the public was largely unaware of disability access problems and that little was being done to provide access. Recognizing the ineffectiveness of voluntary compliance, Congress passed the Architectural Barriers Act (ABA) in 1968. The ABA was the first measure passed by Congress to ensure accessibility to buildings, government or non-government facilities, designed, built, or remodelled with Federal funds or leased by Federal agencies. Facilities built before the law was passed are exempt, but alterations or leases undertaken after the law was enacted can trigger coverage (Yell, 2006).

A significant shift in disability public policy occurred in 1973, with the passage of Section 504 of the Rehabilitation Act (PL93-112). Section 504 bans discrimination on the basis of disability and applies to employers and organizations that receive federal funds. This law is significant because, for the first time, people with disabilities were viewed as a minority group.

In 1975, Congress passed Public Law 94-142 (Education of All Handicapped Children Act), now known as IDEA (Individuals with Disabilities Education Act). IDEA is considered by many to be the most important civil rights legislation ever passed in the United States concerning students with disabilities. This legislation guarantees students with disabilities free, appropriate public education (FAPE) in the least restrictive environment (LRE) and, when feasible, in the same learning environment as children without disabilities. In addition, students with disabilities are ensured the right to nondiscriminatory testing, evaluation, and placement procedures and the right to procedural due process of law. IDEA is the primary federal law governing Individualized Education Programs (IEPs) and the special education process. The Individuals with Disabilities Education Act was last authorized December 2004, as PL108-446 (U.S. Department of Education, 2004).

IDEA is the primary federal legislation that impacts physical education. For students with disabilities, physical education includes the development of motor skills, physical fitness, and skills in various domains such as aquatics, dance, and individual and group games and sports. IEPs must address physical education, and the IEP Committee is responsible for determining if evaluation for adapted physical education services is required (U.S. Department of Education, 2004).

The Amateur Sports Act of 1978 (PL95-606) set up the governing structure for amateur sports in the United States and required the United States Olympic Committee (USOC) "to encourage and provide assistance to amateur athletic programs and competition for handicapped individuals, including, where feasible, the expansion of meaningful participation by handicapped individuals in programs of athletic competition for able-bodied individuals" (Sherrill, 2004).

In the 1980s, the disability movement continued to actively support disability rights and legislation and was successful in thwarting attempts to deregulate Section 504 and the Architectural Barriers Act. The Civil Rights Restoration Act of 1987 re-established the broad scope of coverage and clarified the application of the Civil Rights Act of 1964 (e.g., when any program, department, branch, or activity of an organization or institution receives federal funding, the entire organization or institution must comply with laws prohibiting discriminatory practices based upon race, color, national origin, religion, gender, age, or disability) (Sherrill, 2004).

The first version of the Americans with Disabilities Act was crafted by President Ronald Reagan's appointees to the National Council on Disability and was modelled after earlier laws concerning discrimination based on race and gender. In just two years, Congress passed the Americans with Disabilities Act of 1990 (ADA). The ADA prohibits private employers, governmental entities, employment agencies, and labor unions from discriminating against qualified individuals with disabilities in job application procedures, employment, compensation, job training, and other terms and conditions of employment. In addition, the ADA prohibits discrimination in state and local government services, transportation, and telecommunication relay services. ADA impacts adapted physical education and disability sport in prohibiting discrimination in access to leisure and recreational services and facilities. It was an historic moment for all people with disabilities when President George Bush signed the ADA into law thereby ensuring civil rights for all Americans (Sherrill, 2004).

In 1998, at the urging of Senator Ted Stevens of Alaska, the Amateur Sports Act of 1978 (PL95-606) was amended to become the Olympic and Amateur Sports Act (OASA). Due to his efforts to direct this law through Congress, the amendments are often referred to as the "Stevens Amendments." The amendments place responsibility on the USOC and its constituent organizations to serve athletes with a disability, particularly Paralympic athletes (constituent disability sports organizations include Disabled Sports USA, Dwarf Athletics Association of America, National Disability Sports Alliance, Special Olympics International, USA Deaf Sports Federation, U.S. Association of Blind Athletes, and Wheelchair Sports USA). Also in 1998, Congress reauthorized the Rehabilitation Act of 1973.

On December 15, 2000, the United States Congress approved a massive spending bill, which included a $5 million appropriation for the Physical Education for Progress Act (PEP) for fiscal year 2001. Grants were established to help start, expand and improve physical education programs for kindergarten through grade 12 students. The funds can be used to purchase equipment, develop curriculum, hire and/or train physical education staff, and support other initiatives designed to enable students to participate in physical education activities. Since Congress passed the PEP bill in 2001, more than 1,000 PEP grants have been awarded across the country. In its first year, the PEP bill was approved for $5 million. In Fiscal Year (FY) 2002, Congress allotted $50 million; $60 million in FY 2003; $70 million in FY 2004; $73.4 million in FY 2005; $72.7 million in FY 2006; $72.7 million in FY 2007; and $75.7 million in FY 2008 (DePauw & Gavron, 2005).

The Improving Education Results for Children with Disabilities Act of 2003 called for reforms to strengthen accountability and results for students, reduce IDEA paperwork for teachers, provide greater flexibility for local school districts to develop early intervention strategies, decrease the number of children wrongly placed in special education classes, reduce litigation and restore trust between parents and school districts, and align IDEA with the No Child Left Behind (NCLB) Act signed by President George W. Bush in January 2002. NCLB requires federally funded schools to be accountable for providing a quality education for all students, including students with special needs (DePauw & Gavron, 2005).

On December 13, 2006, the United Nations adopted the first comprehensive international human rights treaty of the 21st century, the Convention on the Rights of Persons with Disabilities. The Convention reaffirms that individuals with all types of disabilities must enjoy all human rights and fundamental freedoms. It includes the right to play and to participate in sports, because that right is directly linked to other human rights, such as the rights to personal mobility and the right to participate in cultural life. The Convention was the fastest negotiated human rights treaty to date, having been negotiated during only eight sessions of an Ad Hoc Committee of the General Assembly (2002–2006). The Convention was opened for signature on March 30, 2007. There were 82 signatories to the Convention, 44 signatories to the Optional Protocol, and 1 ratification of the Convention. This is the highest number of signatories to a UN Convention on its opening day.

In January 2013, the United States Government Accountability Office published a report that reflected the health benefits of participation in physical activity for persons with disabilities (USGAO, 2013). It also indicated that students with disabilities are not being offered the same access to extracurricular sport as their peers without disabilities (USGAO, 2013). In response to this report, the United States Department of Education offered guidance on how to include students with disabilities in extracurricular sport (USDOE, 2013). The letter concludes "OCR is committed to working with schools, students, families, community and advocacy organizations, athletic associations, and other interested parties to ensure that students with disabilities are provided an equal opportunity to participate in extracurricular athletics" (USDOE, 2013, p. 12). It is hoped that, based on these directives, recreational and competitive opportunities for students with disabilities will increase at all levels, including post-secondary institutions.

Exhibit 9.2 shows a timeline indicating important milestones in litigation and legislation important to adapted physical education and sport.

Exhibit 9.2: Important Events in Disability Sport

1944	Sir Ludwig Guttmann established the Stoke-Mandeville Hospital for treatment of spinal cord injuries and introduced sport as rehabilitation.
1945	Formation of the American Athletic Association for the Deaf (AAAD).
1949	Formation of the National Wheelchair Basketball Association (NWBA).
1956	Formation of National Wheelchair Athletic Association. Name changed to Wheelchair Sports, USA in 1994, and to Wheelchair and Ambulatory Sports, USA in 2010.
1960	First Paralympic Games held in Rome.
1967	National Therapeutic Recreation Society created.
1968	Congress passed the Architectural Barriers Act (ABA). Special Olympics founded by Eunice Kennedy Shriver.
1975	Public Law 94-142 enacted. Called the "Education for All Handicapped Children Act." It stated that children with disabilities shall be provided instruction in physical education.
1976	Formation for U.S. Association for Blind Athletes.
1977	First Annual National Wheelchair Marathon held in conjunction with the Boston Marathon.
1988	Paralympics held in Korea. This was the first time all athletes with physical disabilities competed at same venue as Olympic athletes.
1990	Americans With Disabilities Act (PL 101-336) Enacted.
1993	First International Special Olympics meet held outside of USA in Salzburg, Austria.
1996	Formation of Intercollegiate Wheelchair Basketball Conference.

Case Study 3: Eli Wolff

Eli Wolff works at the Center for Human Centered Design in Boston and is director of the Inclusive Sports Initiative. In addition, he directs the Sport and Development Project at Brown University in Providence, Rhode Island, and manages the SportsCorps program for the Fitzgerald Youth Sports Institute.

From 2001–2011, Wolff worked at the Center for the Study of Sport in Society at Northeastern University. Wolff managed research and advocacy and coordinated the Research Fellows Program. Wolff's work also allowed him to organize initiatives that combine sport and social change education, research, and advocacy. To create social change in and through sport, he applies the scholar-educator-activist methodology.

Wolff helped found and continues to work with three research groups: Rhythm & Flow, Sport in Society's Disability in Sport, and Athletes for Human Rights. From 2002 to 2006, Wolff was part of the International Olympic Academy where he was a coordinator and lecturer; his current involvement is an ambassador of Olympism and Olympic education. Wolff is actively involved in sport and human rights through talks, workshops and consultations.

Wolff is a former Paralympic athlete who participated in the 1996 and 2004 games in soccer. In 2001, Wolff received the first Nike Casey Martin Award, which is given to a person with a disability who has made a difference in sport. In 2009, he received the Heroes Among Us recognition from the Boston Celtics. Wolff was instrumental in helping draft the sport and recreation section of the United Nations Convention on the Rights of Persons with Disabilities. He believes sport is for all people (Institute for Human Centered Design, 2013).

References

AAASP. (2013a). About. Retrieved from http://www.adaptedsports.org/adapted sports/about/about.html.

AAASP. (2013b). Adapted Sports. Retrieved from http://www.adaptedsports.org/ adaptedsports/athletics/overview.html.

Alabama Adapted. (2013). Alabama Adapted Athletics. Retrieved from http:// alabamaadapted.com/.

BlazeSports. (2013). BlazeSports programs. Retrieved from http://blaze sports.org/.

CAF. (2013). Programs. Retrieved from http://www.challengedathletes.org/ programs/access_for_athletes.htm.

CGF. (2013). 2002 Commonwealth Games. Retrieved from http://thecgf.com/ games/intro.asp.

CISS. (2013a). Deaflympics. http://www.deaflympics.com/.

CISS. (2013b). Games. http://www.deaflympics.com/games.asp.

CISS. (2013c). Paris 1924. Retrieved from http://www.deaflympics.com/games.asp?1924-s.

CISS. (2013d). Taipei 2009. Retrieved from http://www.deaflympics.com/games.asp?2009-s.

Cody, A. (2007). Sport for people with disabilities. In M.A. Hums, G.G. Bower, and H. Grappendorf (Eds.), *Women as leaders in sport: Impact and influence* (pp. 261–268). Reston, VA: National Association for Girls and Women in Sport.

Colours In Motion. (2013). Products. Retrieved from http://colourswheelchair.com/idx_products.htm.

Dahlberg, T. (2006, April 29). Teen wins races, hearts and right to belong. Retrieved from http://nbcsports.msnbc.com/id/12536669/.

DePauw, K. P. & Gavron, S. J. (2005). *Disability sport*. Champaign, IL: Human Kinetics Publishing.

Eagle Sportschairs. (2013). Home. Retrieved from http://eaglesportschairs.com.

Edinboro University. (2013). Fighting Scots, Wheelchair Basketball. Retrieved from http://www.gofightingscots.com/index.aspx?path=wcbball.

EXG (2013). Extremity Games. Retrieved from http://www.extremitygames.com/.

Hardin, B., & Hardin, M. (2003). Conformity and conflict: Wheelchair athletes discuss sport media. *Adapted Physical Activity Quarterly, 20*, 246–259.

Hedrick, B., Byrnes, D., & Shaver, L. (1994). *Wheelchair basketball* (2nd Ed.). Washington, D.C.: Paralyzed Veterans of America.

Hums, M. A., & MacLean, J. C. (2008). *Governance and policy in sport organizations* (2nd ed.). Scottsdale, AZ: Holcomb Hathaway Publishers.

IAAF. (2008, May 16). Pistorius is eligible for IAAF competition. Retrieved from http://www.iaaf.org/aboutiaaf/news/newsid=44917.html.

IAAF. (2009). Competition rules 2009. Retrieved from http://www.iaaf.org/mm/Document/Competitions/TechnicalArea/04/95/59/20090303014358_httppostedfile_CompetitionRules2009_printed_8986.pdf.

INAS. (2013) Our Vision. Retrieved from http://www.inas.org/about-us/who-we-are/.

Institute for Human Centered Design (2013). Eli Wolff. Retrieved from http://www.adaptenv.org/about-us/people/eli-wolff.

IOC. (2013). London 2012. Retrieved from http://www.olympic.org/olympic-results/london-2012/athletics/400m-m.

IPC. (2013a). The IPC-Who we are. Retrieved from http://www.paralympic.org/TheIPC/HWA/HistoryoftheMovement.

IPC. (2013b). Paralympic Games, Italy. Retrieved from http://www.paralympic.org/paralympic-games/rome-1960.

IPC. (2013c) Paralympic Games. Retrieved from http://www.paralympic.org/paralympic-games/london-2012.

IPC. (2013d). Paralympic Games, Sweden. http://www.paralympic.org/paralympic-games/ornskoldsvik-1976.

IPC. (2013e) Paralympic Games. Retrieved from http://www.paralympic.org/
news/sport-classification-project-strikes-gold-podium-awards.

IPC. (2013f) Athlete Search Results. Retrieved from http://www.paralympic.org/
Athletes/Results.

Iwakuma, M. (1997). *From pity to pride: People with disabilities, the media, and
an emerging disability culture.* Paper presented to the Association of Journalism and Mass Communication Conference, New Orleans, LA.

IWAS. (2013a). History. Retrieved from http://www.iwasf.com/iwasf/index.cfm/
about-iwas/history/.

IWAS. (2013b). ISMWSF History. Retrieved from http://www.iwasf.com/iwasf/
index.cfm/about-iwas/history/ismwsf-history/.

IWAS. (2013c). IWAS Games Programme. Retrieved from http://www.iwasf.com/
iwasf/index.cfm/games/iwas-games-programmes/.

Kelly, L. E. (2011). Spinal cord disabilities, in: J. P. Winnick (Ed) *Adapted
Physical Education and Sport, 5th Ed.*(Champaign, IL, Human Kinetics),
311–345.

Lakeshore Foundation. (2013). Lakeshore. Retrieved from http://www.lake
shore.org.

Ledsom, M. (2008, July 16). "Blade-runner" Pistorius fails in Olympic bid.
Retrieved June 28, 2009 from http://uk.reuters.com/article/idUKL16
50429520080716.

NBBA. (2013). Beep Baseball Equipment. Retrieved from http://www.nbba.org/
equipment.htm.

NWBA. (2013a). NWBA Team Resources. Retrieved from http://nwba.org/
index.php?option=com_docman&task=cat_view&gid=39&Itemid=330.

NWBA (2013b). 2014 Nationals. Retrieved from http://nwba.org/
index.php?option=com_content&view=article&id=256&Itemid=374.

Ossur. (2013). Sprint feet. Retrieved from http://www.ossur.com/?PageID=13462.

Owen, E. (1982). *Playing and coaching wheelchair basketball.* Urbana, IL: University of Illinois Press.

Per4Max (2013). Athletes. Retrieved from http://per4max.com/athletes/.

Quickie Wheelchairs. (2013). Quickie Wheelchairs Home. Retrieved from
http://www.quickie-wheelchairs.com/.

Schantz, O. & Golbert, K. (2001). An ideal misconstrued: Newspaper coverage of the Atlanta Paralympic Games in France and Germany. *Sociology
of Sport Journal, 18,* 69–94.

Schell, B., & Rodrigues, S. (2001). Subverting bodies/ambivalent representa-
tions: Media analysis of Paralympian Hope Lewellen. *Sociology of Sport
Journal, 18,* 127–135.

Shapiro, J. P. (1994). *No pity: People with disabilities forging a new civil rights
movement.* New York: Three Rivers Press.

Sherrill, C. (2004). *Adapted Physical Activity, Recreation and Sport: Crossdisci-
plinary and Lifespan* (6th Ed.) Boston, MA: WCB McGraw-Hill.

SMSU. (2013). Southwest Minnesota State Athletics. Retrieved from http://sm sumustangs.com/index.aspx?tab=wheelchairbasketball&path=wheelbball.

Sofia. (2013). Games. Retrieved from http://sofia2013.com/games/country.

Special Olympics. (2013a). History of Special Olympics. Retrieved from http://www.specialolympics.org/history.aspx.

Special Olympics. (2013b). A world stage to build awareness. Retrieved from http://www.specialolympics.org/world_games.aspx.

Special Olympics. (2013c). Providing Health Services World Wide for the Most Underserved. http://www.specialolympics.org/healthy_athletes.aspx.

Special Olympics. (2013d). Leading research and influencing policy. Retrieved from http://www.specialolympics.org/leading_research.aspx.

Special Olympics. (2013e). Young athletes. Retrieved from http://www.special olympics.org/young_athletes.aspx.

Special Olympics. (2013f). Project UNIFY. Retrieved from http://www.special olympics.org/Sections/What_We_Do/Project_Unify/Project_Unify.aspx.

Special Olympics. (2014). World Winter Games. Retrieved from http://special olympics.org/Games/2013_World_Winter_Games.aspx.

Stevens, J. (2000). Supreme Court of the United States, Syllabus, PGA Tour Inc v Martin. Retrieved from http://www.law.cornell.edu/supct/pdf/00-24P.ZS.

Stewart, D. A. (1990). Global dimensions of World Games for the Deaf. *Palaestra, 6*(2), 32–35, 43.

UA. (2013). Athletics. Retrieved from http://drc.arizona.edu/athletics.

UIUC. (2013). Adapted athletics. Retrieved from http://www.disability.uiuc.edu/athletics/.

United States Department of Education, Office of Civil Rights (2013). Retrieved from http://www2.ed.gov/about/offices/list/ocr/letters/colleague-201301-504.pdf.

United States Department of Education. (2004). Twenty-fifth annual report to Congress on the implementation of the Individuals with Disabilities Education Act. Washington, DC.

United States Government Accountability Office, *Students with Disabilities: More Information and Guidance Could Improve Opportunities in Physical Education and Athletics*, No. GAO-10-519, at 1, 31 (June 2010), *available at* http://www.gao.gov/assets/310/305770.pdf.

U.S. Paralympics. (2014). Current Paralympic Sport Clubs. Retrieved from http://www.teamusa.org/US-Paralympics/Community/Paralympic-Sport-Clubs/Current-Clubs.

USA Goalball. (2013). How to start playing goalball. Retrieved from http://www.angelfire.com/hi5/usa-goalball/start_playing.html.

UTA. (2013). Movin' Mavs. Retrieved from http://www.uta.edu/movinmavs/athletics/basketball/index.php.

UWW. (2013). Wheelchair Athletics. Retrieved from http://www.uww.edu/recsports/wcathletics/.

WASUSA. (2013). About Us. Retrieved from http://www.wasusa.org/aboutus.htm.

WHO. (2013). International Classification of Functioning, Disability and Health (ICF). Retrieved from http://www.who.int/classifications/icf/en/.

Yell, M. L. (2006). The law and special education. (2nd). Upper Saddle River, NJ: Prentice Hall.

Chapter 10

Human Rights, Fairness, and Personal Freedoms in Sport: Further Perspectives

Jason W. Lee, University of North Florida
Fritz G. Polite, Shenandoah University
Steven N. Waller, University of Tennessee
B. David Ridpath, Ohio University

This chapter examines the concepts of human rights and personal freedoms while addressing various representative contemporary sport considerations. Sport administrators, participants, and other stakeholders should be aware of the issues associated with personal freedoms and human rights. This chapter will take a deeper view into a wide assortment of issues impacting the world of sport.

Sport has been identified as being a microcosm of society. Sport is a lens that views the governance of sport, including the same values and general norms, as any civil society (Eitzen, 2012). In this sense, inequalities, injustices, and improprieties found in greater society can be and are reflected in the world of sport and thus laws regulating human behavior in greater society can also be applicable to those participating in sport.

This chapter aims to provide coverage of several contemporary issues regarding human rights in sport. They are:

1. Player Conduct and Restrictions
2. Freedoms of Speech and Expression
3. Freedom of Religion
4. Privacy and Confidentiality
5. Liberty and Property Interest (Right to Participate in Athletics)

What Are Human Rights?

Human rights can be manifest in a holistic manner or viewed more specifically across cross-sections of society, such as women's rights, children's rights, or worker's rights. "The teaching of human rights is not a new idea ... [though] [n]one of the ideologies that dominated this century is so pervasive and persuasive as that of human rights, which extol the dignity and the worth of the human person" (Bhuvandendra, 1999, p. 18).

The *American Heritage Dictionary* (2000) defines human rights as the basic rights and freedoms to which all people are entitled including the right to life and liberty, freedom of thought and expression, and equality before the law. According to the United Nations (UN), human rights compose rights that are:

> Inherent to all human beings, whatever our nationality, place of residence, sex, national or ethnic origin, colour [sic], religion, language, or any other status. We are all equally entitled to our human rights without discrimination. These rights are all interrelated, interdependent and indivisible (United Nations Human Rights, n.d.).

The UN expands on this by explaining that:

> [U]niversal human rights are often expressed and guaranteed by law, in the forms of treaties, customary international law, general principles and other sources of international law. International human rights law lays down obligations of Governments to act in certain ways or to refrain from certain acts, in order to promote and protect human rights and fundamental freedoms of individuals or groups (United Nations Human Rights, n.d.).

Human rights is an obligation not only national, but also international (Bhuvandendra, 1999). Countries such as the United States and Canada, for example, have been at the forefront of issues such as personal freedoms and rights. Such freedoms and rights have been protected through legislative initiatives such as the U.S. Constitution and the Canadian Charter of Rights and Freedoms. The United Nations has been a forerunner in championing human rights throughout the globe. Such efforts are evidenced by United Nations Freedom Charter, The United Nations Convention on the Rights of the Child, and the Universal Declaration on Human Rights ("Human Rights," n.d.).

Examples of such rights are the rights to life, freedom, protection, etc. Bhuvandendra (1999) identified sport as a human right. Bhuvandendra expounds on this by addressing the Olympic Charter by stating:

Incidentally, the Olympic Charter clearly defines sport as an aspect of human rights. In its Fundamental Principle number 8, the Olympic Charter provides that "The practice of sport is a human right. Every individual must have the possibility of practicing sport in accordance with his or her needs." Furthermore, Article 6 of the Charter observes that "The goal of the Olympic Movement is to contribute to building a peaceful and better world by educating youth through sport practiced without discrimination of any kind and in the Olympic Spirit, which requires mutual understanding with a spirit of friendship, solidarity and fair play" (pp. 19–20).

In the United States, human rights have been defined and protected by initiatives such as the Constitution, legislative acts, and other forms of public policy. However, it would be remise to say that people and organizations do not always comply with these values and ideals. In American sport, there have been many instances where administrators and participants have digressed from the spirit of human rights and denied one or more groups or individuals their rights (examples of these could be the rights of children, the rights of people with disabilities, or the rights of girls and women to participate in sport, etc.).

Player Conduct and Restrictions

Sport stakeholders do not relinquish their human rights when engaging in sport. For example, coaches and administrators are not to act as though they are absolute dictators who remove personal freedoms and legal provisions. Whether it is through policy initiative, court legislative initiatives, or other endeavors individual rights and considerations of broad authority control have presented much fodder for governance considerations in sport.

The notion of human rights provides fertile ground for various points of discourse. When addressing issues such as personal freedoms and organizational control (i.e., team, league, or athletic department) many controversies and concerns may arise—especially when issues occur which may infringe upon an athlete's rights (e.g., constitutional or legal).

Various issues associated with restriction placed on athletes can be identified. Among such issues are restrictions placed on playing eligibility (i.e., NFL or NBA requirements age requirements), dress codes (such as that imposed by the NBA), transfer eligibility issues, and the debate over collegiate student-athlete compensation (in general or special circumstances issues such as the Jeremy Bloom situation addressed in this chapter).

Liberty and Property Interest in Athletic Participation

Although governing bodies should recognize that athletes generally have the same rights as the general public when participating in sport, it is not always the case when considering certain areas of sport governance. Many times participants will give up some rights by signing a professional contract, albeit restrictions that are usually agreed upon. Many times the athlete simply does not have access to accepted due process and standard rights afforded most citizens in the United States. Specifically, in American intercollegiate and scholastic athletics it is long held that it is a privilege to participate and not a right, therefore some basic rights can be limited (*Due Process and the NCAAb*, 2004). In other words, to receive due process, or in essence pursue individual right claims, the activity must have a substantive liberty or property interest, participation in intercollegiate athletics, or any athletics simply, does not rise to that level unless there is a contract present.

The term liberty interest according to the *Merriam Webster Dictionary of Law* means an interest in freedom from governmental deprivation of liberty especially without due process. Even though many schools and higher education institutions would be considered arms of the government, participation in sports is considered extracurricular and therefore many rights are likely limited. The conundrum of American collegiate sports is the participants are the ones who have the least amount of rights with regard to control of their sporting endeavors while in enrolled in college and participating in intercollegiate athletics. Scholars have called this a "plantation" system, where the administration and universities get rich but the labor (athletes) who generate the revenue are not getting a reasonable return for the work and revenue they provide (Rhoden, 2009; Splitt, 2004). There are many arguments in for and against compensating student-athletes but that is beyond the scope of this discussion.

For many years in professional and collegiate sports, the athletes simply did as directed and played by the rules set forth, so they could compete regardless if it was violating their rights. However, like the Civil Rights movement of the 1960s and anti-war protests of the 1970s. Several "athlete's rights" movements began to take center stage, such as Curt Flood challenging the reserve clause, which led to greater freedom of movement and free agency in professional sports (Snyder, 2006). The same happened in amateur and intercollegiate athletics with regard to payment for services and better working conditions, and while many changes have been made for the better, there is still a groundswell of athlete activism, such as the development of the National Collegiate Players Association, to insure more individual rights and protections.

Other notable challenges to the status quo of athlete control and limiting basic worker rights include the sagas of Maurice Clarett and Mike Williams, and that of Jeremy Bloom. Maurice Clarett and Mike Williams challenged the NFL's Collective Bargaining Agreement (CBA) to gain entrance to the NFL Draft. The NFL and NBA arguably contribute to many of the issues in intercollegiate athletics by instituting collective bargaining agreements that do not allow prospective professionals to choose their time of entrance, they are often restricted by collective bargaining rules that literally force athletes to go to college to a system where many argue they do not have basic rights (*Due Process and the NCAA, 2004a*).

One of the more notable challenges to the NCAA's system of athlete control and a right to participate was by former University of Colorado wide receiver Jeremy Bloom, who simultaneously was a world champion moguls skier and Olympic medalist needed to be able to procure commercial endorsements to finance his skiing career. The NCAA balked at Bloom doing this stating that doing so would endanger his amateur status because these commercial endorsements could be interpreted as endorsing Bloom the football player. Bloom was later ruled ineligible to compete by the NCAA for accepting these endorsements after he self financed his skiing career for two years enabling him to play for the Buffaloes (*Due Process and the NCAA, 2004a*).

This scenario details many of the inconsistencies in application of NCAA rules with regard to student-athlete rights. The NCAA has long recognized that a student-athlete can be a professional in one sport and amateur in another. The history of college athletics is filled with examples of many stellar athletes who have accomplished this feat (Danny Ainge played professional baseball with the Toronto Blue Jays while he was a student at Brigham Young University playing college basketball; Kirk Gibson, Ricky Williams, John Elway, and Trajan Langdon are just a few of many who played professional baseball while remaining amateur in other sports). The example more closely related to Bloom is that of Tim Dwight, who played professional football with the Atlanta Falcons and maintained his amateur status in track and field at the University of Iowa. Dwight received income from endorsements as a member of the Falcons, but simply did not ask the NCAA for permission to do it until after the fact. The NCAA forgave Dwight and did not saddle him with any eligibility consequences. However when the NCAA gets caught seemingly unprepared, they have at times reacted in harsh fashion, and Bloom had the misfortune of being the next one with the ability to gain significant endorsement income by competing professionally in another sport. Even after allowing Dwight to do the exact same thing, the NCAA refused to give Bloom, a stellar student and role model, the chance to participate in intercollegiate athletics (*Due process and the NCAAa, NCAAb*).

Freedoms of Speech and Expression

Administrators and coaches need to be mindful of the athletes' rights to freedom of speech and expression. In the United States, the freedoms of free speech and free expression are protected by the First Amendment to the US Constitution.

Exhibit 10.1

Protections for free expression and free speech provide defenses for verbal as well as non-verbal communications. While verbal communication may be more self explanatory, expressive conduct may need further explanation. Examples of expressive communications can include:

- The Mexico City Games political statement by Tommie Smith and John Carlos (see Appendix C)
- Former NBA point-guard Mahmoud Abdul-Rauf (formerly Chris Jackson) and the controversy associated with his refusal to stand for the "Star-Spangled Banner" prior to NBA games
- Former NFL quarterback Jake Plummer not being allowed to wear a decal representative of his friend Pat Tillman's number
- Or another former NFL quarterback, Jim McMahon, and the headband that said "Rozelle"

Exhibit 10.2

Furthermore, expressive conduct may incorporate a large variety of gestures, some of which may be tolerated, and some, which may not. For instance:

- An NFL wide receive trying out his latest celebratory post-touchdown performance
- A soccer forward running with his hands above his heads and running towards the fans before celebrating further

> • An athlete (e.g., Tim Tebow) pointing heavenward after a score or extraordinary play (or any number of religious displays; i.e., athletes thanking God after a win before the media)

Exhibit 10.3

Beyond the aforementioned example, there are various other issues associated with expression and personal freedom. Consider the following examples:

- A high school senior being "highly encouraged" to cover his tattoos by his coach
- A high school football player is told to cut his hair to comply with coach's orders (is there a safety consideration or does the coach not want his players to look like "hippies"?)
- A high school baseball player wishes to wear his uniform akin to the style worn by Major Leaguer Prince Fielder—however, the player's high school coach says that players may not wear baggy uniforms (would it make a difference if the player had body consciousness issues and felt more comfortable wearing less form-fitting attire?)
- The NBA establishing dress codes for players

Specific sports have their own rules in regards to safety, etiquette, and fair play. Athletes, officials, and other stakeholders have rules that they are to abide by and specific behaviors for which they are to comply. Technology again has provided new opportunities for player codes of conduct. Social networking sites such as Facebook and Twitter have made athletes and others very accessible for the fans. While on the surface this can be a new exciting way to market individuals and teams, it can also come with pitfalls, such as a player revealing too much about his/her private life that could be detrimental to the team. The numerous contemporary example of athletes "tweeting" leading up to (if not during say the halftime of) a sporting event can show that the athlete is not focused on the task at hand, or commenting publically on trades, draft picks, or relationships with team members can backfire into a full-fledged scandal. In such instances many teams and universities have taken the conservative approach and restricted use of these sites by athletes and coaches, even going as far as putting it in a contractual clause.

Freedom of Religion

Freedom of religion can include the right to expression of individual faith and spirituality. Putnam (1999) identified the interface of sport and religion by explaining how the connection of these two aspects of life "can be found in nearly every part of the sports world, from the energized boxing rings of Las Vegas and Atlantic City to the sprawling stock car tracks of the South, from the boisterous stadiums of football to the lush, green fairways of professional golf" (p. 103).

The role of religion, as it pertains to sport, has generated debate and controversy in regards to implementation in workplaces, classrooms, and playing fields throughout the United States (Alexander & Alexander, 2000). Whether it is questions pertaining to the right to participate in religious services provided by the athletic department or aligned organizations, the presence of prayer in public sport settings, or a variety of other occurrences, the differing views on appropriateness of sport and religion's interface, the prevalence of these relationships abounds.

Issues of freedom of religion and separation of church and state have been greeted with differing views about what is acceptable and what is appropriate, as well as what is ethical and/or legal (Lee, 2005). In regards to personal freedoms, individual rights come into play when addressing religious freedom (the right to freely exercise one's religious beliefs (e.g., the Free Exercise Clause) and the right not to have religious forced upon another (e.g., the Establishment Clause)).

Sport administrators need to be mindful of how they will address issues that may arise dealing with constitutionally protected rights. In terms of religious beliefs and practices, various considerations may arise such as prayer and worship matters, as well dietary, time and date considerations/restrictions (i.e., observance of religious holidays), and various other matters that need to be addressed.

Various connections of sport and religion, particularly the implementation of prayer within public educational (and other public settings) provide ethical and even legal considerations on the part of players, coaches, sport managers, and other stakeholders.

Exhibit 10.4

Consider the following examples of sport intertwining with religion:

- Coaches who expect their teams to pray before a match should be mindful of religious differences and practices.

- The debate over the appropriateness of religious freedoms are aspects such as wearing of religious garments or symbols.
- Practices such as that of Shawn Green, former NY Mets right fielder/ first baseman, who sat out playoff games in the 2001 and 2004 MLB due to games falling on Yom Kippur.
- The utilization of team chaplains in collegiate athletic programs. It is not uncommon to find sport chaplains aligned with the athletic departments of major public colleges and universities across nation. Many are employed by organizations such as the Fellowship of Christian Athletes and Athletes in Action while others serve in a volunteer capacity (Waller, Hardin, & Dzikus, 2008).
- Religious pluralism among athletes. As the number of athletes playing in college athletics becomes more racially/ethnically diverse, religious diversity is a by-product. While the majority of athletes playing in collegiate athletic programs may embrace Christianity (e.g., Tim Tebow), the number of athletes that openly embrace Islam, Judaism, and other faith traditions must be reckoned with (Woods, 2011). Of particular concern is how athletic departments at public institutions, through sport chaplains, equitably provide opportunities for the spiritual growth and development of athletes across faith traditions.
- In West Virginia in response to a ban on pregame prayer for the fans in attendance over the public address system, local radio stations began conducting the pregame prayer and the fans would just turn up the volume. An interesting twist on separation of church and state.

"The issue of the legality and appropriateness of issues such as prayer within public school settings and the upholding of a 'wall of separation' between religion and public education institutions have been engulfed in a variety of legal battles in our country" (Lee, 2004, p. 26). These legal battles have predominantly focused on individual rights, personal freedoms, and constitutionality of the religious-based actions. Issues such as public prayer over public address systems, team prayer, and other forms of religious activity associated with sport, and these expressions and freedoms in generate legal concerns pertaining to constitutional law, "as the constitutionality of prayer implementation within school athletic competitions is at the heart of this matter" (Lee, 2005, p. 23). "Administrators have commonly shied away from the issue of prayer as it relates with sport activity. Concerns about the violation of Constitutional rights, issues of team disunity and other areas of concern have caused problems for administrators in the past" (Lee, 2005, p. 23). Furthermore, these associations between sport and religion can result in litigation. Numerous legal actions have been brought based on the implementation of religious components with public setting. "In the United States, many of the battles to establish the boundaries of religious influence on civil government have been fought on the playing fields and in the classrooms of public education" (Alexander & Alexander, 2000, p. 130).

Privacy and Confidentiality

Considerations of individual's privacy and confidentiality arise as athletes and other individuals involved with the sport process are to have the right to have the privacy of their bodies and belongings or effects respected. This can have implications for sport administrators, coaches, and other involved parties. This can include issues such as locker or bag searches, access to private records, or considerations of drug testing.

Athletes, particularly those who are young, quite often confide in their coaches. Athletes' health or medical screening records should also be regarded as confidential and only used for "official" sports reasons and only by those authorized to do so. They should be filed in such a way that non-authorized personnel do not have access to them. Coaches or medical personnel who maintain such confidential records in electronic format should take special precautions to protect privacy if they work on a network or they share their files with other personnel.

However, it is important to note that many of these rights are "forfeited" by simply agreeing to participate on a team. Still, sensitive and specific information should only be disseminated on a need to know basis. In intercollegiate athletics, the Family Educational Rights and Privacy Act (FERPA) and Health Insurance Portability and Accountability Act (HIPPA) are also the rules to follow, but many times there is widespread misunderstanding of exactly what information constitutes private educational and medical records. Many times colleges and universities will stretch the limits of these laws to prevent notifying the media of alleged criminal activity and other non-medical issues, however FERPA, as written, is intended to keep individual educational records and information private, and HIPPA is the same for medical records and information (Splitt, 2004). These statutes can be stretched to keep an athlete's name confidential to hide something a team or institution does not want public, but if the actual names are not identifiable, it can be a public record if from a public institution (Splitt, 2004).

In a case that could clarify once and for all what is private and public information regarding student records and specifically intercollegiate athlete records, Florida State University won a court ruling against the NCAA to have documents concerning an NCAA investigation into its football program made public. The state of Florida says that records are public if they are received by a state agency. The NCAA countered that many of the records had identifiable student information that was protected from disclosure under FERPA. Circuit Judge John Cooper disagreed stating that records were fine to be viewed by the public since the names of the students were, or could be blacked out ("Judge Rules," 2009).

It is still a best practice to guard confidential records and be proactive rather than reactive when information is requested. Always seek legal counsel when dealing with the educational and medical records of individuals in all area of sports.

Furthermore, in regards to international consideration, entities such as National Governing Bodies and International Federations should pay careful attention to changes in social customs and cultural changes and the sport-related laws of those specific countries or regions.

References

Alexander, F. K., & Alexander, R. H. (2000). From the gridiron to the United States Supreme Court: defining the boundaries of the First Amendment's Establishment Clause. *Journal of Legal Aspects of Sport, 10*(3), 129–137.

American Heritage Dictionary (2000). (4th ed.). Retrieved from http://www.bartleby.com/61/95/H0319500.html.

Bhuvandendra, T. (1999). Human rights in the realm of sport, Olympic Review, XXVI(24), 15–25.

Due process and the NCAAa: Hearing before the Subcommittee on the Constitution, of the House Committee on the Judiciary, 108th Cong., (2004) (testimony of Jeremy Bloom).

Due process and the NCAAb: Hearing before the Subcommittee on the Constitution, of the House Committee on the Judiciary, 108th Cong., (2004) (testimony of Josephine Potuto).

Eitzen, D.S. (2012). *Fair and foul: Beyond the myths and paradoxes of sport* (5th ed.). Lanham, MD: Rowman & Littlefield Publishing Group.

Human Rights (n.d.). United Nations. Retrieved from http://www.un.org/en/globalissues/humanrights/.

Judge rules but records still sealed. (2009, August 20). *Associated Press.* Retrieved from http://sports.espn.go.com/ncf/news/story?id=4411868.

Lee, J.W. (2004). An Overview of the reciprocating relationship between sport and religion, SMART (Sport Management and Related Topics) Online Journal, 1(1), 26–30. Retrieved from http://www.thesmartjournal.com/SMART-religion.pdf.

Lee, J.W. (2005). Prayer and athletics: A legal profile, SMART (Sport Management and Related Topics) Online Journal (now known at the SMART Journal), 1(2), 23–27. Retrieved from http://www.thesmartjournal.com/prayer.pdf.

Putnam, D.T. (1999). *Controversies of the sports world*. Westport, CT: Greenwood Press.

Reipenhoff, J. & Jones, T. (2009, June 27). Colleges hiding behind federal law. *The Columbus Dispatch*. Retrieved from http://www.dispatch.com/live/content/local_news/stories/2009/<d>05/31/FERPA_MAIN.ART_ART_05-31-09_A1_VFE0G7F.html?sid=101.

Rhoden, W. C. (2009, July 22). Sports of the times: A lasting image: Standing up to the NCAA. *New York Times*. Retrieved from http://www.nytimes.com/2009/07/23/sports/ncaabasketball/23rhoden.html.

Snyder, B. (2006). *A well-paid slave: Curt Flood's fight for free agency in professional sports*. New York: Viking: The Penguin Group.

Splitt, F. (2004, July 13). *The faculty driven movement to reform big time college sports*. Chicago: IEC Publications.

Waller, S., Dzikus, L., & Hardin, R. (2008). Collegiate sport chaplaincy: Problems and promise. *Journal of Issues in Intercollegiate Athletics*, 1, 107–123.

Woods, R. B. (2011). *Social issues in sport* (2nd ed.). Champaign: Human Kinetics.

Appendix A

Tennessee Secondary School Athletic Association: An Overview

Robin Hardin, University of Tennessee
Joshua R. Pate, James Madison University

The Tennessee Secondary School Athletic Association (TSSAA) is the non-profit organization managed by school personnel, which oversees scholastic sports in Tennessee. Funding for the organization is derived from membership dues and championship revenue, including ticket sales and sponsorships. The budget is approximately $3 million per year. It is one of 51 similar organizations in the United States with each state and Washington, D.C., having its own governance structure that conducts and manages scholastic sports in the state or district.

TSSAA was first organized in 1925, and a permanent office was established in 1946 at Peabody High School in Trenton, Tennessee. This was also the time a full-time employee was hired by the organization. The role of the executive secretary was to oversee the day-to-day operations of the organization. The office moved to its present location in Hermitage, which is in the Nashville area in 1970.

The chief administrator is also known as the executive director. This position evolved from the executive secretary position established in 1946. The office staff has since grown to approximately 20 fulltime employees, which includes the executive director and three assistant directors. Other management positions are in the areas of technology, student services, and marketing. Two positions act as assistants to the executive director, and there are other administrative positions.

Member institutions of the TSSAA numbered nearly 400 for the 2013–2014 academic year with approximately 110,000 student-athletes. Nearly 5,500 teams competed for 80 team championships offered by the organization as well as the numerous individual champions in specific events such as track and field events, golf, tennis, and wrestling by weight class. An estimated 6,000 coaches and 5,000 officials are also involved in the management and operation of the TSSAA.

The Constitution, Bylaws and Handbook outline the structure and governance of the organization. It addresses the organization at the state level and the composition of administrative bodies, and it also covers general issues associated with scholastic sports. The Constitution and Bylaws do not cover the rules of play or competition but apply to issues and questions outside the actual competition itself. It outlines, among other things, criteria for being a coach in the state, academic rules, transfer regulations, recruiting and amateurism, and it establishes the sports calendar and conducts championship events. National Federation of State High School Associations (NFHS) publishes official rulebooks for most sports. The rules of the United States Golf Association (USGA), United States Tennis Association (USTA), and United States Bowling Council (USBC) are used in their respective sports under TSSAA governance.

State-Level Administrative Structure

Board of Control

Scholastic sports in Tennessee are governed by the Tennessee Secondary School Athletic Association. The administrative authority of the TSSAA is the Board of Control which is comprised of nine members. Those nine members represent the nine athletic districts in the state. The districts are comprised of counties and are grouped geographically. The term of service on the Board of Control is three years with a member being elected from each of three Grand Divisions (East, Middle, and West) each year. Three districts are in each Grand Division so each Board of Control is comprised of a member from each Grand Division who is in his or her first year, second year, and third year of service.

Members of the Board of Control hold academic administration positions within the scholastic level and are typically principals or superintendents. Assistant principals are eligible to serve if their service to the school is totally administratively based. Superintendents can only serve if they have only one four-year high school in his or her system. The Board of Control has a president and vice-president who also serve as the president and vice-president of the TSSAA.

The powers of the Board of Control are broad, and it basically governs all aspects of scholastic sports in Tennessee. The Board of Control (1) appoints the executive director who manages the day-to-day operations of the association; (2) oversees the budget; (3) determines qualifications for officials; (4) hears appeals from decisions of the executive director; and (5) rules on any issue not covered in the bylaws and constitution of the association.

Legislative Council

The composition of the Legislative Council is just that of the Board of Control: nine members (three from each Grand Division) with a term being three years. A member from each Grand Division will be in the first, second and third year of the term. Grand Divisions are subsequently divided into three districts. A representative from each district within the Grand Division has membership on the Legislative Council. Only members from that particular district have a vote for the representative from that district.

Like the Board of Control, Legislative Council members hold academic administration positions and are usually principals or superintendents. Assistant principals are eligible to serve if their service to the school is totally administratively based. Superintendents can only serve if they have only one four-year high school in his or her system. The Legislative Council will also have a president and vice-president. The president will attend all meetings of the Board of Control just as the president of the Board of Control will attend all meeting of the Legislative Council.

The basic duty of the Legislative Council is to make amendments to the Constitution and Bylaws of the TSSAA. The Council also acts upon suggestions and ideas when submitted by a minimum of 25 member institutions of the association. Proposals for adjustments to the governance of the association are derived from regional meetings, any committee established by the Board of Control or Legislative Council, and the TSSAA staff. Proposals may also come via the Executive Director who has a proposal submitted by a member institution.

Executive Director

The association's Executive Director is the chief administration official of the organization. Primarily responsibilities include accounting for all financial matters, maintaining records, and ensuring the Constitution and Bylaws are upheld by the association members. In regards to the final duty, the Executive Director initiates investigations and leads the investigation into possible violations. The Executive Director determines if violations occur and penalties associated with the violations.

In addition, the Executive Director serves as the Secretary to the Board of Control and Legislative Council and is an ex-officio member of all committees of the two groups. He or she also oversees all rules and regulations regarding the certification of officials as determined by the Board of Control.

Membership

Secondary schools in Tennessee serving grades 9 or higher are eligible for membership. Schools must be meet criteria set forth by the State Department of Education or approved agencies of it or the Southern Association of Colleges and Schools (SACS). This includes both public and private schools. However, schools compete in separate divisions based upon whether student-athletes receive need-based financial aid or scholarships. Division I consists of schools where student-athletes do not receive financial aid which includes all public schools and some private schools. Division II is comprised of schools in which financial aid is awarded to student-athletes.

The responsible stakeholder within each member institution is the chief administrator, in most cases the principal, of the school. The principal oversees all budget matters, revenues and expenses, scheduling and all other issues associated with the conduct of sports within the school. This would include things such as eligibility and practice guidelines, and ensuring coaches and players adhere to all other bylaws of the organization.

Member Institutions

Members are classified into their completion level based upon enrollment and status as to awarding of financial aid. The basic system is three classifications for public schools with those being Division I-A, Division I-AA, and Division I-AAA. Private schools that do not award financial aid based on athletic ability also compete in Division I. Schools that award financial aid based on athletic ability are classified in Division II with two divisions: A and AA. Classification within the divisions is based upon enrollment (see Exhibit A.1).

Districts and regions are also a part of the organizational process and is a determinant in who plays whom in postseason play. There are 16 districts based on geographical location. Two districts comprise a region, which means there are eight regions in the state.

Member institutions may compete against other members of the TSSAA or members of other state associations. They may also compete against a collaborative team of home-schooled student-athletes. A collaborate team of home-schooled student-athletes however is not eligible to compete for TSSAA championships. Home-schooled student-athletes may also compete in individual sports such as golf, track, and tennis but again cannot compete for TSSAA championships. For example, if an area golf association held a tournament for high school students, a home-schooled student may participate in that tournament. A home-schooled student may also participate in a track meet hosted by a track club. A change for the 2011–12 school year did change home-schooled student-athletes ability to compete in team sports and TSSSA championships. A home-schooled student-athlete may compete for a school's sports team in which he or she is currently zoned to attend. This is also true for individual sports. Certain administration and eligibility requirements must be met but the student-athlete can participate if those are satisfied.

Sponsored Sports

The TSSAA sponsors 13 sports: (1) baseball, (2) girls' softball, (3) basketball, (4) bowling, (5) cross country, (6) football, (7) golf, (8) tennis, (9) track and field, (10) girls' volleyball, (11) soccer, (12) girls' soccer and (13) wrestling. Membership in the TSSAA gives institutions to right to compete for championships. The organization pays the expenses of teams competing in the state championship events for all sports in which a championship is contested, not just for football and basketball. Institutions are responsible for post-season expenses at the district and region level though.

Championships are sponsored in each of the 13 sports that are offered by TSSAA. Championships are awarded based on classification, but not every classification has a championship in a sport. Class A and Class AA are collapsed into one for the championships in track, wrestling, cross country, golf, soccer and tennis in Division I. But conversely, football is expanded from three to six classifications in Division I for championship purposes. Schools also have the option of moving up in classification if they so desire. So, a school may not have the enrollment numbers that classify them into Division I-AAA but it can chose to "play up" in classification.

Reclassification occurs every five years based on enrollment. The number of students required for each classification changes with each reclassification period to ensure equal distribution of schools in each classification. For example, a school with 550 students may be classified as Division I-AA but during reclassification it may move to Division I-A even though enrollment did not change because the enrollment at other high schools increased. So, it is being moved to a lower classification to have equal number of schools in each classification. The same can be true for schools moving up in classification. So, the number of schools in each classification is fluid from one classification period to another. Enrollment is the factor for classification but the TSSAA wants to ensure equal distribution among the classifications. Basically, the schools are divided equally into three categories for standard classification and then the enrollment numbers for classification are based on these categories.

Eligibility

The basic tenant of eligibility is the student-athlete must be enrolled, taking at least five classes, and actually attending a member institution. The student-athlete must also earn five credits toward graduation the previous year if less than 24 credits is required to graduate or six credits if 24 or more credits are required to graduate. Credits earned in the summer can be applied to meet these requirements. High school graduates are ineligible for competition as are students who are age 19 or older on August 1 of the upcoming school year. Student-athletes have eight semesters to compete once they begin the ninth grade. Eighth graders are eligible to participate if they are enrolled in the school but they still only have eight semesters to compete once they begin the ninth grade.

Agents of Change

The TSSAA was a trailblazer in terms of providing opportunities for girls and for blacks. Girls' high school sports date to the 1920s in Tennessee with the first girls' basketball championship awarded in 1926. Blacks were also more quickly integrated into scholastic sports at the state level in Tennessee than in other states. Many states were forced to integrate sports programs under Federal Court order but Tennessee began integration as early as 1966 with boys' basketball.

[*Note: Information in this appendix is based on the 2013–14 TSSAA Constitution and Bylaws. Additional information was derived from e-mail correspondence and phone conversations with TSSAA staff members.*]

Exhibit A.1: TSSAA Classification 2009–2013

Standard Classification	Enrollment*
Division I-A	Less than 520**
Division I-AA	531–1,065
Division I-AAA	1,066 and higher
Division II-A	Less than 1,065
Division II-AA	1,066 and higher

Football Classification	
Division I-A	Less than 389
Division I-2A	390–520**
Division I-3A	531–802**
Division I-4A	805–1,065**
Division I-5A	1,067–1,464
Division I-6A	1,465 and higher
Division II-A	Less than 1,065
Division II-AA	1,066 and higher

* Classification enrollment is adjusted during reclassification to ensure equal representation across divisions.

** Gaps appear between classifications because no schools were identified with those enrollments during the reclassification period.

Exhibit A.2: TSSAA Staff and Responsibilities

Title	Responsible Areas
Executive Director	Catastrophic insurance, coaches' education, cross country, financial aid, Middle School Association, softball, sportsmanship, eligibility, Bylaws, Constitution
Assistant to Executive Director	Cheerleading, merchandising, sanctions and tournament approval, tennis, tickets, Athletic Donors Conference, volleyball, hotels/motels, eligibility, Bylaws, Constitution
Assistant to Executive Director	Transfer forms, board and council agendas and minutes, eligibility, Bylaws, Constitution
Assistant Director	Middle School Association, non-faculty coaching, track
Assistant Director	Football, soccer, wrestling

Assistant Director	Baseball, basketball, reporting of unsportsmanlike conduct, sportsmanship, officials, eligibility, Bylaws, Constitution
Assistant Director	Bowling, media relations, Mr./Miss Basketball, Mr. Football, TSSAA News, legislature, football playoffs, printing, tickets
Technology Director	Web site development, office networking, special projects, statistical analysis, e-mail, development technology
Director of Student Services	Student services
Student Services	Student services
Director of Marketing	Marketing
Administrative Assistant	Registration of officials, updating of officials files
Administrative Assistant	Fines, receptionist, online eligibility, membership, rules meeting attendance
Administrative Assistant	Hall of Champions, Hall of Fame
Administrative Assistant	Awards, TMSAA membership, programs, Website information
Administrative Assistant	Academic achievement awards, rule book orders, back-up receptionist, office machines, video tapes
Administrative Assistant	Accounts payable, accounts receivable, payroll, finances of organization
Receptionist	Telephone

Appendix B

Motorsport Governance: NASCAR

Jim Hand, Catawba College
Travis Teague, Wingate University

History of NASCAR

The mega-sport of stock car racing in the United States has an interesting history with regards to sport governance. The major governing body of stock car racing in the United States is the National Association of Stock Car Automobile Racing, better recognized as NASCAR. Multi-million dollar tracks and numerous Fortune 500 companies participating as sponsors have transformed the sport of stock car racing from its humble beginning.

The earliest form of governance with regards to managing the fast cars of the 1930s and 1940s was the responsibility not of sport sanctioning bodies, but rather the state and federal authorities of the time. The reason for this was that the earliest racers were actually drivers moving illegal alcohol to consumers. Moonshiners, as they were called, produced and delivered their wares both during Prohibition and after legislation was introduced that ended it (Hagstrom, 1998).

As the cat-and-mouse game of eluding the authorities continued, more and more drivers began to make modifications to their cars to make them faster, all the while developing a specific skill set for driving on the curvy roads of the southeastern United States. This continued until eventually the inevitable conflict arose as to who had the fastest car and who was the better driver. These discussions turned into modest competitions at first, and then eventually drew the attention of a few bystanders. The few bystanders grew into larger and larger crowds and more cars being included in the races. Eventually the popularity grew throughout the region and tracks, usually dirt, began to appear to celebrate this new found sport of stock car racing.

One name that must be mentioned when discussing the evolution of governing stock car racing is Bill France, Sr. France had moved his family from the Washington, D.C., area and had settled in the growing tourist destination of Daytona Beach, Florida. In 1935, France was taken in by the land speed record attempts that had taken place on the beach (Hagstrom, 1998). The American Automobile Association (AAA) sanctioned the first land speed record course that ran from Ormond Beach to Daytona Beach. The course was nine miles long allowing four miles on either end of a one-mile length called the "measured mile" (Lazarus, 2004). Unfortunately for the Daytona Beach economy, the land speed drivers decided to move their attempts to Utah's salt flats the following year (Hagstrom, 1998). This left a vacancy at the track that was soon utilized by France for stock car racing.

Prior to NASCAR, the primary governing body in all of racing in the United States was the AAA. The AAA sanctioned the pinnacle of American motorsport, the Indianapolis 500, and most other forms or divisions of racing as well. The organization was very strict in its policies and ruled in an autocratic fashion in its dealings with all things motorsport. Bill France, Sr. and others helped organize the AAA sanctioned first beach race in 1936 on the road and beach course. The track was a 1.6 mile trip up Florida's highway A1A and the same distance on the beach. The purse for that event was $5,000 and there were four divisions for the 1935–36 model "strictly stock cars" that ran that day. The divisions were based upon the sticker price of the car (Lazarus, 2004). Some specific governing rules that day for the cars included only one spare tire; no bumpers; upright windshields; doors anchored; and hoods strapped down (Lazarus, 2004).

Eventually due to some critical factors, including the deaths of more than 80 spectators at the tragic incident at the 1955 24 Hours of LeMans race, the AAA got out of the sanctioning business. Initially, the United States Auto Club (USAC) managed what AAA had relinquished, but still ended up sharing the sanctioning responsibilities with NASCAR. Eventually no one could argue that the primary governing body in all of stock car racing had one name, NASCAR (Yates, 2004).

Stock car racing took a leave of absence when the United States entered World War II, but with the aid of France and others, the sport came back with a vengeance soon after the troops came home. After the war's end and numerous complaints and economic growth near the beach course, France became involved in helping other tracks draw the same kind of large crowds to their venues and in 1947, he created the National Champion Stock Car Circuit (NCSCC) that included 10 events (Lazarus, 2004).

In December of that same year, a meeting of the NCSCC occurred in the lounge of the Streamline Hotel in Daytona Beach. Out of that meeting came the realization that a sanctioning body needed to be formed, one that among other things, would properly award prize money and develop a national championship points system. So with the motion and a then a vote and re-vote, a new name was approved. It would be called NASCAR (Lazarus, 2004). In 1948, NASCAR sanctioned 85 races, in 1949, 394 and by 1951, more than 1,000. (Lazarus, 2004). As of 2012, NASCAR sanctions nine racing series in the United States, one in Mexico, and one in Canada. A series is similar to a league in other sports—a group of teams or individuals who compete in a set number of events and follows rules established by a sanctioning body. Three of these series (Sprint Cup, Nationwide, and Camping World Truck) are considered to be "professional" with the top level being the Sprint (title sponsor) Cup Series. The Cup Series is the No. 1 spectator sport in the United States with 17 of the 20 highest attended live sporting events. It is the second most watched sport on television in the U.S. and is televised in more than 150 countries in 20 languages (NASCAR 2010 Prize Money & Decal Program, 2009). The Nationwide Series and the Camping World Truck Series are the No. 2 and No. 3 rated motorsports series on television respectively (NASCAR 2010 Prize Money and Decal Program, 2009). The local series, Whelen (title sponsor) All-American Series, sanctions 1,200 races in the United States, Mexico, and Canada with more than 10,000 men and women competing each weekend. In addition to sanctioning series, NASCAR sanctions 76 tracks in the U.S., Mexico and Canada (NASCAR in Your Neighborhood '10, 2009).

NASCAR defines itself as the sole and final authority for the: development, maintenance, and distribution of championship point funds; the awarding of championship points; the naming of car manufacturer, series-sponsored and other NASCAR champions; control over all aspects of competition during NASCAR-sanctioned events; and the governance, interpretation, and implementation of NASCAR rules including but not limited to NASCAR membership and licenses, entries, disciplinary action, the substance abuse policy, and the determination of driver eligibility, in the manner set forth in NASCAR rules. If a particular NASCAR sanctioned event counts towards another sanctioning body's (or track) championship, NASCAR reserves sole authority to settle any dispute that may arise during such NASCAR event (NASCAR Sprint Cup Series Rule Book, 2009). NASCAR also imposes sanctions to those members and competitors that break the rules set forth in the NASCAR rule book. Such sanctions include, but are not limited to, monetary fines, deduction of championship points, probation, and expulsion from NASCAR.

Rules Enforcement

Any person that is served with a penalty has the right to appeal the decision to the National Stock Car Racing Commission within 10 days. There are 32 commission members that are selected based on their knowledge and experience. They include men and women from a variety of motorsport backgrounds, either active in the sport or retired. They include promoters, industry leaders, and even dignitaries from other forms of professional motorsport. To file an appeal, a written request, along with a $200 non-refundable hearing fee, must be hand-delivered (may use approved courier service) to the chairman of the commission. A date is set and the case is heard by the commission and any pertinent parties involved. The chairman and at least two other commission members constitute a quorum (NASCAR Sprint Cup Series Rule Book, 2009). The three-person panel has the right to leave the penalty as is, reverse the penalty in its entirety, or modify the penalty (Aumann, 2008). The appellant may either accept the decision or appeal to the NASCAR Commissioner.

The National Stock Car Racing Commissioner is appointed by the president of NASCAR. A written appeal accompanied with a non-refundable $200 fee must be made within ten days of the National Stock Car Racing Commission's decision. The Commissioner may summon any NASCAR member to testify at the hearing. Any member who is summoned to testify and either refuses or fails to appear and testify, may be subject to indefinite suspension or other disciplinary action as deemed appropriate. NASCAR has the right to publish the decisions of the commission or commissioner and the names of the parties involved. The results most often become public information the same day the decision has been made (NASCAR Sprint Cup Series Rule Book, 2009).

Sprint Cup Organization

The Sprint Cup season is divided into two sections, a 26-race segment, followed by a 10-race playoff to determine the season champion. For each race, 43 cars make up the field of competitors. The first segment includes 26 races in which each driver earns points based upon their on-track performance. The winner of each race earns 43 points and the 43rd, or last place car, earns one point (see Exhibit B.1). A driver also earns three bonus points for a win and one bonus point for leading a lap in the race. A bonus point is also awarded to the driver who leads the most laps of each event. (NASCAR Sprint Cup Series Rule Book, 2012). Therefore, a race winner can actually earn a maximum of 48 points (43 points for finishing in first position, three for the win, one for leading a lap, and one point for leading the most laps).

Changes expected for the 2014 NASCAR Sprint Cup Series season include qualifying procedures and the Chase for the Cup (NASCAR Sprint Cup Series Rule Book, 2014).

At tracks measuring less than 1.25 miles in length and Road Courses, qualifying will consist of two (2) rounds:

1) The first qualifying round is 30 minutes in duration, unless otherwise authorized by the NASCAR Sprint Cup Series Director.
2) All cars must compete in the first qualifying round. Upon the completion of the first qualifying round, the 43 eligible cars for starting positions 1–43 will be determined.
3) The twelve (12) eligible cars that post the fastest single lap time from the first qualifying round will advance to the final qualifying round.
4) The remaining cars will be sorted based on their times posted in the first round of qualifying in descending order. There will be a ten minute break after the completion of the first round and the twelve (12) eligible cars that advance to the final round will have their times reset. The final qualifying round will be 10 minutes in duration, and the fastest single lap time posted in the final round will determine positions 1st through 12th in descending order.

At tracks measuring 1.25 miles in length or larger, qualifying will consist of three (3) rounds:

1) The first qualifying round is 25 minutes in duration, unless otherwise authorized by the NASCAR Sprint Cup Series Director.
2) All cars must compete in the first qualifying round. Upon the completion of the first qualifying round, the 43 eligible cars for starting positions 1–43 will be determined.
3) The twenty-four (24) eligible cars that post the fastest single lap time from the first qualifying round will advance to the second round.
4) The remaining cars will be sorted based on their times posted in the first round of qualifying in descending order.
5) There will be a five minute break after the completion of the first round and the twenty-four (24) eligible cars that advance to the second round will have their times reset.
6) The second qualifying round is 10 minutes in duration and the twelve (12) eligible cars that post the fastest single lap time will advance to the final round.
7) The fastest remaining cars will earn positions 13th through 24th based on their times posted in qualifying in descending order.

8) There will be a five-minute break after the completion of the second round and the twelve (12) eligible cars that advance to the final round will have their times reset.

9) The final qualifying round is 5 minutes in duration and the fastest single lap time will determine positions 1st through 12th in descending order.

Qualifying for the 2014 Chase for the Cup will consist of the following change in procedures:

The field will expand from 12 to 16 teams, with three shootout-style rounds resulting in a championship round with the final four remaining competitors. The 16 available qualifying positions for the Chase will be awarded to those drivers that have at least one victory through the first 26 races, as long as he or she is in the top 30 in points and has attempted to qualify for each of the season's previous points races. If more than 16 drivers earn at least one win, only those highest in the standings following the 26th race would advance. If fewer than 16 drivers have at least one win, all remaining positions to fill the grid would be determined based on points standings. Drivers not in the Chase will continue to earn points under the current non-Chase points format.

The Challenger Round—Opens the Chase and twelve of the 16 drivers will advance from this round. A win in any of the three races automatically advances the driver to the next round, with remaining positions to be determined based on points earned during the round.

The Contender Round—Consists of 3 races and eight of the 12 drivers will advance from this round in a similar way as the Challenger round.

The Eliminator Round—Consists of 3 races and four of the eight drivers will advance from this round to earn a berth in the season-ending Sprint Cup Championship (final) round.

Sprint Cup Championship—The highest finisher of the four remaining drivers at the final race will win the Sprint Cup championship (NASCAR Sprint Cup Series Rule Book, 2014).

Governance Issues

Issues within motorsport governance, particularly NASCAR, are many and varied. From the latest safety initiatives to ensuring a level playing field for the hundreds of competitors, the task is monumental. Two current governance is-

Exhibit B.1: NASCAR Points Based on Finish Position, 2012

Finish	Finish Points	Finish	Finish Points
Win	43	23rd	21
2nd	42	24th	20
3rd	41	25th	19
4th	40	26th	18
5th	39	27th	17
6th	38	28th	16
7th	37	29th	15
8th	36	30th	14
9th	35	31st	13
10th	34	32nd	12
11th	33	33rd	11
12th	32	34th	10
13th	31	35th	9
14th	30	36th	8
15th	29	37th	7
16th	28	38th	6
17th	27	39th	5
18th	26	40th	4
19th	25	41st	3
20th	24	42nd	2
21st	23	43rd	1
22nd	22		

Source: http://www.jayski.com/teams/chase2012.htm
NOTE: The driver that leads a lap (under green or yellow flag) gets one bonus point. The driver who leads the most laps gets one bonus point. As of 2011, the winning driver gets three bonus points. The driver who starts the race gets the points and the finishing position credit.

sues within the sport that deserve special mention include the policies, procedures and legalities of developing and implementing a prudent substance abuse policy. The other topic spanning across not only NASCAR, but all forms of racing, is the critical issue of implementing necessary "green" initiatives with regards to environmental impacts of the sport.

NASCAR has updated its substance abuse policy to fall in line with other professional sports. In fact, NASCAR consulted with "other professional leagues and a lot of industry experts" and re-wrote their substance abuse policy in 2008 (Rodman, 2008). This policy mandated that every NASCAR driver, official, and pit crew member be tested prior to the start of the 2009 season. For the first time ever, random drug tests occurred weekly at all three national series events. Twelve to 14 people were randomly tested each week by an outside agency; two drivers from each series, and six to eight NASCAR officials and crew members. The last update includes the inclusion of testing for steroids (Rodman, 2008). An often criticized aspect of NASCAR's Substance Abuse Policy has been the lack of "banned substances" distributed to the competitors. In 2010, NASCAR published a list of banned substances in the rulebook for the first time.

Another issue that is especially important to NASCAR is their comprehensive approach to making the sport "greener" and environmentally responsible. NASCAR Chairman and CEO Brian France met with environmentalist Al Gore and as a result, hired a director for Green Innovation. NASCAR is currently developing a comprehensive strategic plan that will include all of NASCAR's departments, drivers, teams, and tracks. This increased effort should significantly enhance the environmentally sound practices currently being made by NASCAR and industry partners Goodyear, Safety Kleen, and Waste Management (France, 2009).

With technology and safety innovations continuing to develop, so does the responsibility of governing the sport. NASCAR judiciously adjusts to these changes by adding, deleting, or adjusting its rules and policies. While valuing its history, NASCAR has always been forward thinking when dealing with the issues of tomorrow. NASCAR continues to lead the sport of stock car racing by facing and meeting the challenges of today and the future.

References

Aumann, Mark. (2008). The Commission: Inside NASCAR's Appeals System. Retrieved from http://www.nascar.com/2008/news/features/03/21/maumann.national.stock.car.racing.commission/index.html.

France: NASCAR focused on Economy, Going Green. (2009) Transcript from speech given on January 22, 2009. Retrieved from http://www.nascar.com/2009/news/headlines/official/01/22/bfrance.transcript.media.tour/index.html.

Hagstrom, Robert. G. (1998). *The NASCAR way: The business that drives the sport.* John Wiley and Sons, Inc.: New York.

Lazarus, B. (2004). *Sands of Time: A Century of Racing in Daytona Beach.* Sports Publishing LLC.

NASCAR 2010 Prize Money & Decal Program. (2009) National Association for Stock Car Auto Racing. Daytona, FL.

NASCAR in Your Neighborhood '10. (2009). National Association for Stock Car Auto Racing. Daytona, FL.

NASCAR Points. (2012). Retrieved from http://www.jayski.com/teams/chase 2012.htm.

NASCAR Sprint Cup Series Rule Book 2009. (2009) National Association for Stock Car Auto Racing. Daytona, FL.

NASCAR Sprint Cup Series Rule Book 2012. (2012) National Association for Stock Car Auto Racing. Daytona, FL.

NASCAR Sprint Cup Series Rule Book 2014. (2014) National Association for Stock Car Auto Racing. Daytona, FL.

Rodman, D. (2008). Random Testing Now Part of NASCAR's Drug Policy. Retrieved from http://www.nascar.com/2008/news/headlines/cup/09/20/nascar.updates.drug.policy/index.html.

Yates, B. (2004). *NASCAR off the record.* MBI Publishing Company. St. Paul, MN.

Appendix C

International Politics in Sport

Elizabeth A. Gregg, University of North Florida

Throughout the course of modern history, sport has been used as a political tool. In some cases sport serves as a vehicle through which countries exhibit to their global neighbors the superiority of a nation or a particular ideology. For example, Fidel Castro organized a sporting culture in Cuba based on the principles of amateurism and patriotism. The system is designed to benefit the masses; a reflection of their socialist government. In other instances, sporting festivals such as the Olympics can be used as a political tool to lobby for power and social change. Hitler's Nazi Berlin games and the Olympic boycotts are a few such examples. In other cases, individual athletes can become a symbol highlighting political principles. Specific examples of how sport is used as a political tool follow.

Hitler's Germany and the 1936 Olympic Games

In 1931, with their country suffering under the climate of a great depression, two German members of the International Olympic Committee (IOC) successfully convinced the IOC after many years of attempts that Berlin, Germany would be an ideal site for the 1936 Olympic Games. Dr. Karl Ritter von Halt and Dr. Theodor Lewald were longstanding members of the IOC, and had dreamed of hosting the Olympic Games in their native Germany for years. The two men won the right to host the 1936 games in Berlin, which increased the morale of the nation (Walters, 2006).

Adolph Hitler is unquestionably one of the most villainous political figures in contemporary history. The German leader convinced the global society that his persecution of Jewish persons and people of color was acceptable. While a comprehensive overview of his dictatorship is beyond the scope of this text, his use of sport as a means to convince the world of Nazi Germany's fascist approach is notable. Hitler's political party, The Third Reich, was born on January 30, 1933, just three years from the Berlin Olympic Games. The timing of the upcoming Games could not have been better for Hitler and the Nazi party. The Olympics represented an opportunity to develop athletic skills among Germany's youth and more importantly, presented Hitler with a grand stage for Germany to demonstrate to the world the superiority of the nation and nazism in general. For Hitler "the games had little to do with athletics. Instead, they would prove that his fascist regime was an example other nations would have to follow" (Shirer, p. 22, 1990).

In an attempt to woo the global society, the physical facilities in Berlin were enhanced in magnificent fashion. Further, Berlin was temporarily transformed to create the illusion that the country and all of its citizens were thriving under Hitler's rule. Nearly all signs of religious persecution and most Nazi symbols were eliminated from storefronts and hotels. This is particularly remarkable because the IOC committee and the global public were intent that Jewish citizens would be granted equal access to earn spots on Olympic teams; a promise Hitler would later violate. Conceivably the most impressive feature of the transformation in preparation for the games was the manner in which the German people rallied around Hitler. The entire nation embraced their leader's vision and behaved hospitably and enthusiastically to their guests (Walters, 2006).

There was of course the issue of religious persecution to address. To appease the IOC, Germany agreed to allow its Jewish citizens an equal opportunity to try out for its Olympic team. After securing the bid to host the games, Hitler and Olympic coaches found cause to eliminate even the most talented Jewish German athletes from teams for obscure reasons unrelated to their athletic prowess. It was one of many successful efforts to manipulate the global society. Despite attempts to diminish the prevalence of religious persecution in Germany during the 1930s, Olympic athletes, IOC officials, and national governments learned of Hitler's transgressions. Primarily through letter writing and word of mouth, German citizens relayed information regarding the horrific treatment of Jewish persons to external entities (Kruger & Murray, 2003).

While there was widespread discussion regarding a boycott of the 1936 games, the majority of athletes elected to take part in the Olympics. For Jewish athletes, earning a medal would present the opportunity to speak to the media regarding Hitler's concentration camps and widespread murdering in Germany. For Avery Brundage, president of the United States Olympic Committee, partaking in the games represented an opportunity to take a stand against communism, which he believed was the underlying impetus of Hitler's regime.

It is also believed that Brundage underestimated the severity of the anti-Semitism under Hitler's control (Walters, 2006).

When the Games began, it was clear that Hitler had accomplished his goal of projecting Berlin and the Nazi regime in an immensely positive light. During the opening ceremony alone, more than 100,000 spectators rose to their feet and saluted the tyrant, chanting "Heil Hitler!" It was clear that the enthusiasm the German citizens felt for their leader was infectious. While Hitler was unmistakably the star of the opening of the Games, it would be an American who would win the hearts of almost all of the attendees over the course of the Olympic festival.

Jesse Owens, an African American track and field athlete, performed magnificently at the 1936 Games, claiming four Gold Medals. To the racist Hitler, Owens success was disgraceful. It is widely presumed that after claiming his first Gold Medal, Hitler intentionally affronted the athlete by leaving the stadium before congratulating Owens. Regardless, the outstanding performance of Owens successfully dented Hitler's myth of Aryan superiority (Senn, 1999).

The overall success of African American athletes at the 1936 games was a black eye on the otherwise spotless face of Hitler's Games. In order to explain the disproportionate achievement of non-white athletes, the German press released a series of stories that propagated the superiority of African Americans came from abnormally large bones, which were "animal like" and provided the athletes with an athletic advantage. According to Walters (2006) "as the blacks were in fact animals and not humans, the Americans had cheated—they might as well have entered racehorses" (p. 300). This statement is indicative of Aryan thought in general. Any action or behavior which did not coincide with the belief system of the people was manipulated in a way that allowed the Nazi party to maintain its aura of supremacy (Walters, 2006; Kruger & Murray, 2003).

Despite the success of non-whites at the Games, the Germans felt that they had achieved their overall goal of demonstrating to the world their superiority both athletically, and as a fascist society. Not surprisingly, almost immediately after the Olympics concluded, Hitler returned his attention to the war and persecution. Jewish citizens were sent to concentration camps at an alarming pace. Many of the Jewish German officers and other individuals that had helped the Berlin Games to be a success were among the first to be arrested after the Olympics. Nazi symbolism returned to the streets, and Hitler prepared for the impending war (Hargreaves, 1992; Walters, 2006).

The Cold War and the Olympic Movement

The IOC has historically been composed of some of the world's most influential individuals from elite social classes. The leaders of the IOC have maintained a keen awareness of world politics since the organizations inception. The Cold War was essentially a fierce debate between America and the Russian Federation over ideals and governance structures. The global tensions that arose during the period had a significant impact on the international sporting culture and the Olympic Games. In 1948, Germany did not receive a bid to attend the Olympic Games because of Hitler's actions during the Second World War. After the war ended, the IOC and its member countries had to carefully determine how to handle the membership of communist nations like Germany. This task was complicated because the IOC has prided itself as being an apolitical organization with the preservation of a strong sporting culture as its highest objective. Following the successful petition of the Soviet Union to join the IOC in 1951, the proverbial door was reopened for other communist countries to unite with the Olympic movement (Woods, 2007).

The president of the IOC during the Cold War, Avery Brundage, was intent on having the Germans rejoin the organization and force the then divided country to compete on a unified team. With this goal in mind, it became impossible for the IOC to ignore the additional communist countries, such as China and North and South Korea, which also sought membership with the IOC. According to Sarantakes (2009) "The People's Republic of China made the participation issue easy for the IOC in the 1950s and 1960s when it initiated a policy of self-imposed isolation in world affairs" (p. 137). The nation competed under the auspices of Taiwan in 1960. America remained somewhat neutral in the politically charged communist selection bedlam, at least until Richard Nixon became president of the United States in 1969.

Nixon was a diehard sports fan. Although baseball and American football were his favorite pastimes, the Olympics eventually captivated Nixon. The same year Nixon assumed the presidency, a powerful group of businessmen were lobbying with the United States Olympic Committee (USOC) to host the summer Games in Los Angeles in 1976. Their primary competition for the bid was the Soviet Union. Recognizing that the outcome of the IOC bidding war had broader social implications, Nixon and his administration began supporting the efforts of Los Angeles to win the right to host the games. Nixon was likely persuaded by the USOC's fear that with the support of the Russian government the IOC might be swayed in favor of Moscow as the host city. Nixon also took it upon himself to write letters to each member of the IOC supporting Los Angeles as the host city. He explained in his writings that the climate, both meteorologically and politically, was ideal in the American metropolis. The Nixon administration also sent gifts to the IOC members in an attempt to win their favor. Despite the finagling of the United States federal government, the IOC chose Montreal as the host of the 1976 Summer Olympics. In doing so, the IOC temporarily maintained its neutrality among the polar opposite world powers. The IOC was unable to avoid taking sides in the Olympic bidding war indefinitely however. This was directly attributable to the fact that only Canada, the Soviet Union, and the United States submitted bids during the 1970s. Since Montreal was awarded the summer games of 1976, the IOC came to the decision to award the Soviet Union the 1980 games, and Los Angeles the 1984 summer games (Sarantakes, 2009).

Olympic politicking grew more heated when countries began to use boycotts to strengthen their stance on critical social issues. Twenty-eight nations withdrew from the 1976 Montreal summer games after the Supreme Council for Sport in Africa recommended withdraw from the Olympics. The United States followed suit in 1980 by refusing to participate in the Moscow games in response to the Soviet Union's invasion of Afghanistan in 1979 (Young, 2008). President Jimmy Carter maintained that the boycott was necessary to defend international law and human rights. While the USOC maintained that using the Olympics as a political tool was unwise, they were at the mercy of the White House. American athletes would be unable to afford training for and competing on the world stage without federal financial support. Sixty-one countries followed the lead of America and boycotted the Moscow games. The Soviet Union's boycott of the Los Angeles summer Olympics was likely a reaction to the shunning four years prior. The IOC lobbied to reduce the number of countries refusing to participate in the 1984 Olympics. As a result of many phone calls and visits to foreign nations, only 17 nations refused to participate in Los Angeles (Hill, 1998).

Sport in Fidel Castro's Cuba

All professional sports were banned soon after Castro gained power in 1959. Gambling and gate receipts associated with sporting events were also eliminated. The prevailing ideology was to make sport available to all Cuban citizens. The Instituto Nacional de Deportes, Educacion Fisica y Recreacion (INDER) was formed to develop, organize, and govern amateur athletics in Cuba in February of 1961. The scope of INDER ranges from physical education for children to the development of world-class Olympic athletes. One of the first tasks assigned to INDER in the 1960s was to enhance the sport related infrastructure in Cuba's major metropolitan centers. More than 10,000 venues have been constructed (Pye, 1986).

A primary purpose of INDER centers is to develop young Cubans into elite athletes and to indoctrinate them into the socialist society. Values such as sacrifice, nationalism, dedication, and a strong sense of volunteerism are paramount. Further, INDER centers effectively identify talented athletes at a young age, which allows the organization to cultivate and develop athletic talent at an exceptional rate. Products of INDER go on to represent Cuba at world-class sporting events such as the Pan-Am Games and the Olympics. These athletes are in essence used to demonstrate the strength of the Cuban national and Castro's socialist regime. Amateur athletics are essentially the only option for Cuban athletes. Under the socialist regime, lucrative salaries evident in America would be contradictory to the philosophy of the government (Carter, 2008).

The sports program in Cuba was thriving throughout the 1970s. During the 1980s however, the economy took a turn for the worse. Sugar and oil prices tumbled globally, and there was a decrease in Cuban tobacco and coffee production. Those events, coupled with a strict United States embargo, resulted in an extremely weak economy in Cuba. To compensate for losses, Castro turned to tourism to enhance economic productivity. Then during the 1990s new trading partnerships with Asia and Latin America were created in an attempt to help the feeble economy. The efforts were in vain however; the economy continued to decline. Cuban citizens replaced cars with bicycles as gas grew scarce. Even the military resulted to using horses and bicycles to propel their equipment (Pettavino & Pye, 1994).

Despite the failing Cuban economy, sports programs have remained competitive. This fact is attributable to the intrinsic dedication to their nation developed in Cuban athletes at a young age and the high priority Castro and INDER have placed on athletic success. In the 1990s, Cuba entered into partnerships with foreign entities to create profitability in marquee sports. One strategy was to allow members of the Cuban National Baseball team to compete in professional leagues and funnel their salaries back into amateur athletic programs in their homeland. This strategy was somewhat effective, but it also created problems. Athletes sometimes defected once out of the grips of poverty in Cuba. Those that remained allegiant often grew bitter when their salaries were siphoned for the greater good (Price, 2000).

As conditions grew worse in Cuba, defections became more prevalent. Baseball has been the most noteworthy sport to witness the mass defection of talented athletes. For many, making the short but dangerous trip to reach America can result in multi-million dollar salaries. More than 36 Cuban baseball players have signed Major League Baseball contracts since Castro took control

(Solomon, 2011). Notable stars such as Orlando "El Duque" Hernandez and Rey Ordonez are just a few athletes to risk their lives for a better life playing baseball in the United States. For other would-be defectors, the risk does not pay off. Some athletes get stranded in foreign lands unable to pass through customs to reach the United States. Others lose their lives at sea. Regardless of the outcome, many young Cuban stars are faced with making the choice of remaining loyal to their country living in poverty, or leaving their families and the land that they love to chase the dream of a better life (Weir, 2005).

Sport in South Africa

In apartheid South Africa, sanctioned sports were controlled exclusively by a select few elite sport associations composed entirely of white men. While these sporting clubs were independent of the national government, the South African regime recommended in 1956 that white and non-white sporting competitions be organized separately. Any governing body of sport that practiced integration was threatened with a loss of government financial support. Moreover, the faction that encouraged the intermingling of white and non-white athletes would lose their passport and forfeit any international recognition for sporting success. These policies made it nearly impossible for talented athletes of color to rise to any global prominence (Booth, 1997).

While South Africa's discriminatory practices during the 1950s and 1960s were not a violation of international law, their actions did spark broad political controversy. The United States condemned the practice of apartheid as a threat to international security in 1960. The public condemnation led to serious ramifications for South African sport. The Federation Internationale de Football Association banned the South African Soccer association in 1961. Soon thereafter, South Africa was expelled from the Commonwealth Games in 1961, and IOC barred South Africa from competing in the 1964 and 1968 Olympic Games. The IOC doled out a permanent South African suspension after the country foolishly hosted an all-white Olympic themed ceremony in 1969. All of the above boycotts were implemented for the purpose of overthrowing apartheid, an official policy of the Republic of South Africa that segregated nonwhites and discriminated against them with legal policies and procedures (Krotee, 1988).

During the late 1970s, there were minor victories in the movement to integrate South Africa. A policy passed in 1979 officially desegregated nearly all sports in South Africa. The Hawks basketball team of Soweto was a non-racial team, meaning individuals of color were permitted to participate with whites. Additionally, Peter Lamb was appointed to the South African Davis Cup team, the first non-white to achieve such status. In the 1980s and 1990s when South Africa began to explore integrating its society, "sport moved ahead of negotiations between political parties, creating unity and eliminated the vestiges of apartheid" (Nauright, 1997, p. 2).

Under the leadership of Frederick Willem de Klerk, South Africa made major strides towards equality. The former Prime Minister of Sports and Recreation assumed the role of President in 1989. One of his first actions as president was to call for an end to apartheid. He lifted the ban on the African National Congress and released Nelson Mandela from prison ("de Klerk Calls for Change," 1989). South Africa had their first democratic election in 1994. Nelson Mandela was elected to lead the unified, albeit fractured nation. Recognizing that amalgamation was necessary, Mandela used sport as a means to heal the deep wounds caused by apartheid in his country. Mandela once stated that "Sport has the power to change the world. It has the power to inspire. It has the power to unite people in a way that little else does" (Hughes, 2010). As highlighted in the popular 2009 film *Invictus*, Mandela and the South African Springboks Rugby squad helped unite the nation through athletic success. After the Springboks defeated New Zealand in the 1995 Rugby World Cup, it appeared that anything was possible in South Africa (Höglund & Sundberg, 2008).

Despite a history of racial discrimination, South Africa made tremendous progress towards equality under the leadership of Nelson Mandela. A visionary, Mandela wisely recognized that sport was a vehicle through which the fractured nation could begin to become a unified nation.

References

Booth, D. (1997). The South African council on sports and the political antinomies of the sports boycott. *Journal of African Studies, 23*(1), 51–67.

Carter, T. F. (2008). New rules to the old game: Cuban sport and state legitimacy in the post-Soviet era. *Identities: Global Studies in Culture and Power, 15*(94), 194–215.

Hargreaves, J. (1992). Olympism and nationalism: Some preliminary consideration. *International Review for the Sociology of Sport, 27*(2), 119–135.

Hill, C. R. (1998). The Cold War and the Olympic movement. *History Today, 49*(1), 19.

Höglund, K., & Sundberg, R. (2008). Reconciliation through sports? The case of South Africa. *Third World Quarterly, 29*(4), 805–818.

Hughes, R. (2010, July 11). In Host's Success, Change Triumphs. *The New York Times*. Retrieved from http://www.nytimes.com/2010/07/12/sports/soccer/12iht-wcsoccer.html?pagewanted=all&_r=0.

Krotee, M. L. (1988). Apartheid and Sport: South Africa Revisited. *Sociology of Sport Journal, 5*, 125–135.

Kruger, A. & Murray, M. J. (2003). *The Nazi Olympics: Sports, politics, and appeasement in the 1930s*. Champaign, IL: University of Illinois Press.

Nauright, J. (1997). Sport, cultures, and identities in South Africa. Strand, London: Leicester University Press.

Pettavino, P., & Pye, G. (1994). Sport in Cuba: Castro's last stand. *Studies in Latin American Popular Culture, 11*, 165–185.

Price, S. L. (2000). *Pitching Around Fidel: A journey into the heart of Cuban sports*. New York: NY. Harper Collins Publishers.

Pye, G. (1986). The ideology of Cuban sport. *The Journal of Sport History, 13*(2), 119–127.

Sarantakes, N. E. (2009). The Olympics and the Cold War: Moscow versus Los Angeles: The Nixon White House wages Cold War in the Olympic selection process. *Cold War History, 9*(1), 135–157.

Senn, A. E. (1999). *Power, Politics, and the Olympic Games*. Champaign: IL. Human Kinetics.

Shirer, W. L. (1990). *The rise and fall of The Third Reich: A history of Nazi Germany*. New York: NY. Simon and Shuster.

Solomon, R. D. (2011). Cuban baseball players, they unlucky ones: United States-Cuban professional baseball relations should be an integral part of the United States-Cuba Relationship. *The Journal of International Business and Law, 10*(1), 153–190.

Walters, G. (2006). *Berlin Games: How the Nazis stole the Olympic dream*. New York: NY. Harper Collins Publishers.

Weir, T. (2005, July 5). Cuban defectors having a tough time adjusting. *USA Today*. Retrieved from http://www.usatoday.com/sports/baseball/2005-07-05-cover-defectors_x.htm.

Woods, R. B. (2011). *Social issues in sport* (2nd ed.). Champaign, IL: Human Kinetics.

Wren, C.S. (1989, September 21). De Klerk calls for gradual change. *New York Times*. Retrieved from http://select.nytimes.com/gst/abstract.html?res=FA0713FD355F0C728EDDA00894D1484D81.

Young, C. (2008). Olympic Boycotts: Always tricky. *Dissent, 55*(3), 67–72.

Index